THE GENOCIDAL GAZE

Elizabeth R. Baer

THE GENOCIDAL GAZE

*From German Southwest Africa
to the Third Reich*

Wayne State University Press | Detroit

© 2017 by Wayne State University Press, Detroit, Michigan 48201.
All rights reserved. No part of this book may be reproduced without formal permission.
Manufactured in the United States of America.

ISBN 978-0-8143-4438-5 (hardcover) | ISBN 978-0-8143-4385-2 (paper)
ISBN 978-0-8143-4386-9 (e-book)
Library of Congress Control Number: 2017950993

Wayne State University Press
Leonard N. Simons Building
4809 Woodward Avenue
Detroit, Michigan 48201-1309

Visit us online at wsupress.wayne.edu

FOR CLINT | again and always

Contents

List of Illustrations ix

Acknowledgments xi

Introduction 1

ONE The African Gaze of Resistance in
Hendrik Witbooi and Others 17

TWO The Genocidal Gaze in Gustav Frenssen's
Peter Moor's Journey to Southwest Africa 45

THREE Uwe Timm's Critique of the Genocidal Gaze
in *Morenga* and *In My Brother's Shadow* 63

FOUR William Kentridge's *Black Box/Chambre Noire*:
The Gaze on/in the Herero Genocide,
the Holocaust, and Apartheid 99

FIVE Ama Ata Aidoo's *Our Sister Killjoy*:
The African Gaze of Resistance Today 115

Afterword 131

Notes 137

Bibliography 155

Index 167

Illustrations

Illustrations follow page 82

FIGURE 1. "Map of Deutsch Südwestafrika, 1904" (German Southwest Africa)

FIGURE 2. "Der Nama-Führer Hendrik Witbooi, um 1900" (The Nama Leader Hendrik Witbooi, around 1900)

FIGURE 3. "Surviving Herero after the escape through the arid desert of Omaheke, c. 1907"

FIGURE 4. "Herero chained during the 1904 rebellion"

FIGURE 5. "Samuel Maharero (1856–1923), son of Maharero"

FIGURE 6. "Gustav Frenssen, Schriftsteller, Pastor, Deutschland"

FIGURE 7. Cover design for 1943 edition of Gustav Frenssen's *Peter Moors Fahrt Nach Südwest*

FIGURE 8. Edition of Frenssen's *Peter Moor* created for the Wehrmacht

FIGURE 9. "Le major Leutwein lors de son mandat dans le sud-ouest africain (1894–1904)" (Major Leutwein during his Mandate in Southwest Africa)

FIGURE 10. "Portrait of General Lothar von Trotha, ca. 1905"

FIGURE 11. "Photo of the Death Camp at Shark Island, German South West Africa (now Namibia)," circa 1903

FIGURE 12. "Photo of Lieutenant von Durling at the death camp at Shark Island, German South West Africa (now Namibia)," December 1904

FIGURE 13. "German Soldiers Packing the Skulls of Executed Namibian Aborigines at Shark Island Concentration Camp, circa 1903"

FIGURE 14. "Kamelreiterpatrouille" (Camel rider patrol)

FIGURE 15. "Deutsch-Südwestafrika, Herero-Aufstand" (German Southwest Africa Herero Uprising)

FIGURE 16. "Jacob Morenga, leader of African partisans in the insurrection against German rule"

FIGURES 17–19. William Kentridge's *Black Box*

FIGURE 20. Mohrenköpfe

Acknowledgments

I often turn to the acknowledgments as I open a new book, curious to know what the author reveals about her/himself, and who the author's influences have been. Did the author get financial support for the project? Do archival research? Rely on other scholars for critiques? Who brought coffee?

As I think back over a long career and the work on this, my fifth scholarly book, I have many debts to acknowledge and much gratitude to express. I want to begin with profound thanks to the people who have been important teachers, many of whom are no longer living. These include my parents, who so highly valued education; Sister Emma, a Dominican nun who taught me the joy of research in seventh and eighth grade; and Terry Plunkett, a professor of American literature at Manhattanville College, who pushed his students to think critically and theoretically. In graduate school, at Indiana University, I had the enormous good fortune to study with Susan Gubar, whose pioneering work in women's studies literally opened new worlds for me and gave voice to what I was dimly beginning to grasp. Vladka and Ben Meed, of blessed memory, survivors of the Warsaw Ghetto, took me to Poland and Israel with the Jewish Labor Committee, teaching me at every step about the Holocaust in a visceral and unforgettable way.

More recently, I have had the pleasure of being taught by those far younger than I. These include my children, Hester Baer, Chair of German Studies at the University of Maryland, with whom I have traveled to Germany many times and whose regular consultations considerably enriched this book, and my son, Nathaniel Baer, Energy Program Director at the Iowa Environmental Council, who inspires me daily with his dedication to addressing climate change. My sister Mary Louise Roberts, who is the Distinguished Lucie Aubrac Professor in the Department of History at the University of Wisconsin, gave me invaluable advice on the book at every stage—proposal, drafts, final manuscript, dealing with academic presses. She read chapters and encouraged me to think historically.

She told me, "You are not writing everything you know," which somehow gave me permission to do so. My sister Pamela Bonina is an exemplar of generosity and caring, of which I have been the frequent beneficiary. My students over the years at Gustavus, the University of Minnesota, and Stockton University made many contributions to my understanding of the Holocaust, postcolonial literature, and theory.

During the five years in which I was writing the book, many other people offered support, financial and otherwise, providing me the opportunity to make *The Genocidal Gaze* the best book possible. These include Phyllis Lassner, Professor of Jewish Studies, Gender Studies and Writing at Northwestern University, who mentored me through the final year of writing in a most candid and sage manner; Alejandro Baer, Stephen Feinstein Chair and Director of the Center for Holocaust and Genocide Studies at the University of Minnesota, who provided me the opportunity to teach portions of the manuscript, always a clarifying experience; and the African Studies Association, whose stellar conferences taught me a lot and gave me a venue to try out ideas over the past four years. Because my career during the writing of *The Genocidal Gaze* was at a small, liberal arts college in a rural location, the daily assistance of Interlibrary Loan was essential; no scholar could ask for or find a finer ILL librarian than Sonja Timmerman at Gustavus Adolphus College. No request was too small or too obscure for Sonja. Similarly, the archivists Dr. Hartmut Bergenthum and Christina Sokol in the Lesesaal Afrika at Universitätsbibliothek Johann Christian Senckenberg in Frankfurt, Germany, were an unrivaled source of help and support, both electronically and in person. The thirty or more books I had requested to review during my visit there were neatly collected on a dolly when I arrived and further requests were handled promptly. I owe a great deal to Gustavus Adolphus College: the college partially funded three trips I made to Africa to do research, awarded me a sabbatical for writing, and recognized my work with the Faculty Scholarship Achievement Award. The Faculty Shop Talk provided a venue for sharing my ideas with colleagues as the book neared completion. Kathryn Wildfong, editor in chief at Wayne State University Press, demonstrated great enthusiasm for the book in the abstract and in its final iterations and accepted the manuscript expeditiously. Her staff have been terrific to work with. Fast friends Carolyn O'Grady, Michele Rusinko, Lois Peterson, Pat Conn, and Cathy Ahern commiserated and celebrated with me along the way.

Granddaughters Della and Flora brought joy to my life as I wrote about a dark topic.

In addition to thanking those who taught me and those who supported my work in various ways, I want to thank those who have saved me. Zoe Barta, a healer and friend extraordinaire, has taken me through many crises during the past twenty-plus years. Dr. Todd Brandt literally saved me, resolving an unexpected and severe health problem. And, finally, and most significantly, my husband of almost fifty years, Clint Baer, to whom this book is dedicated. He nourishes me in so many ways, most importantly when the work has made me cranky.

THE GENOCIDAL GAZE

Introduction

> Here . . . are black men standing, black men who examine us; and I want you to feel, as I, the sensation of being seen. For the white man has enjoyed for three thousand years the privilege of seeing without being seen. . . . Today, these black men have fixed their gaze upon us and our gaze is thrown back in our eyes. . . . By this steady and corrosive gaze, we are picked to the bone.
> JEAN-PAUL SARTRE | *Black Orpheus*

> There is a certain sense in which vision amounts to colonization.
> JOHN NOYES

After the genocide of the Herero and Nama people in the German colony of Southwest Africa between 1904 and 1907, the surviving indigenous men, women, and children were subjected to forced labor. Some of these forced laborers worked in the confines of a concentration camp; others built railroads or worked as miners; and many were farm laborers for the German settlers. Such laborers, in all locations, were frequently subjected to brutal floggings with a *sjambok*, a kind of whip made of heavy rhinoceros hide. Floggings had been commonplace prior to the genocide and were one of the atrocities, in addition to rape of indigenous women, land and cattle theft, and murder, cited by Herero as causes for their rebellion.[1] Photographs of these beatings were taken by the military and sent home as postcards.

Farm laborers were particularly vulnerable to unwarranted punishment, which was often administered by the local police at the direction of the farmer; those doing the flogging were sometimes themselves Herero.[2] Just as often, the farmer took it upon himself to administer the flogging without pretext; the law required that such floggings be limited to no more than twenty-five lashes at any one time and that women be spared such beatings; both of these regulations were routinely flouted. The custom of such floggings came to be called *Väterliche Züchtigung*, or "paternal chastisement" (Silvester and Gewald, 204), a shocking euphemism when one learns about the damage inflicted on the victims. "Flogging . . . came to our people more regularly than their meals," stated a Herero headman (Silvester and Gewald, 135).

One Ludwig Cramer, a farmer with a large number of forced laborers, offers a particularly gruesome and infamous example of cruelty and murder under the auspices of such "paternal chastisement."[3] He almost always selected women as his targets. In 1912, he flogged two pregnant women with impunity, both of whom miscarried. Using as an excuse his desire to learn more about supposed poisons hidden by his laborers, Cramer, with the assistance of his daughter Hildegard, beat a woman named Maria all evening until she fell unconscious; the beating was resumed the following day. Brought to the hospital a week later, she had wounds infested with maggots on her back, on her face, and on her breasts. A photograph of her back that appeared in the 1918 Blue Book reveals the horrifying extent of these wounds. She never recovered and died six months later. A similar fate was suffered by a woman named Auma, in her late fifties, who was sent to the Cramer farm as a replacement for the women Cramer had killed. She too was flogged unmercifully and died two weeks later.

Because the floggings were made known when the women were brought to hospital, Cramer was accused in court of assault and battery of eight victims, seven of them female. Such a trial was an anomaly; Germans could usually punish their laborers without fear of reprisal. Cramer's initial sentence of imprisonment for a year and nine months was appealed and downgraded to four months plus a fine of 2,700 Marks. The judicial system, such as it was, was rigged against indigenous people: the corroborated evidence of seven indigenous people was required to outweigh that of one white man (Silvester and Gewald, 93). Imperial Commissioner Theodor Leutwein declared, "Beating to death was not regarded as murder; but the natives were unable to understand such legal subtleties" (Silvester and Gewald, 204). And that is the crux of the matter: the perception of the Africans was that they were subhuman, could be treated as ignorant children, or worse, as animals. This attitude and the resulting violence were openly acknowledged by Governor Theodor Seitz in a circular of warning sent to magistrates in 1912, only because Seitz feared another rebellion: "It is, therefore, in the best interests of the whole white population if those who indulge in an orgy of violence against the natives *in the belief that their white skin gives them the right to perpetrate* the most revolting crimes are brought to justice" (Drechsler, emphasis mine, 235). Racist attitudes, passed from generation to generation, that give license to exterminate: that is the *genocidal gaze* which is the subject of this book.

The Study of German Genocides of the Twentieth Century

Since its inception in 1961 with the publication of Raul Hilberg's two-volume *The Destruction of the European Jews*, Holocaust Studies as a field has undergone several shifts, in what one might describe as a widening gyre. The field began, appropriately, with a focus on the victims, particularly the Jewish victims, then expanded to include study of the perpetrators. By the late 1980s, after a period of significant resistance to such an approach, scholars began to incorporate insights about gender difference. Then the field widened again, once more against stiff resistance, this time to make links with the growing field of Genocide Studies. Now scholars are beginning to integrate the concepts and vocabulary of Postcolonial Studies in their efforts to understand the Shoah. Much-needed attention is being given by scholars to the transnational aspects of genocide. This new approach sits at the intersection of Holocaust Studies and Postcolonial Studies; it promises to be richly rewarding by widening yet again the vocabulary and theory with which we talk about the Holocaust, beyond the boundaries of Europe, to include earlier and related genocides committed in Africa.

German colonialism (1884–1919) has come under particular scrutiny as a possible source for grasping how the *racial/racist hierarchies* implicit in imperialism are connected to Nazi ideology. The Germans committed the first genocide of the twentieth century in German Southwest Africa (GSWA: the country we now call Namibia) between 1904 and 1907. Though the word had not yet been invented, genocide, in the terms subsequently defined by the United Nations Convention on Genocide, was clearly intended as the infamous pronouncement of German general Lothar von Trotha reveals: "I finish off the rebellious tribes with *rivers of blood and rivers of money*. Only from these seeds will something new and permanent be able to grow."[4]

Jürgen Zimmerer and Joachim Zeller's pioneering anthology, *Genocide in German South-West Africa: The Colonial War of 1904–1908 and Its Aftermath*, was published in German in 2003 and in English in 2008. Many such studies have followed, creating a new direction in Holocaust and German historiography. Tracing a link between German colonialism and the Holocaust in terms of racial ideology and methods of extermination has come to be called the "continuity thesis." It, too, has been a source of controversy, having been first suggested by Hannah Arendt in 1951. During the 1960s, a young Marxist historian from East Germany, Horst Drechsler, gained access to the colonial archives, recently returned from the USSR where they had been taken at the end of World War II. His resulting account of German imperialism was one of the first critical studies published in Germany; his work implicitly draws connections between imperialism in GSWA and the Third Reich. Other scholars began to use this linkage as the premise for their own work. For example, Mahmood Mamdani noted in the introduction to his history of the Rwandan genocide, "There is a link that connects the genocide of the Herero and the Nazi Holocaust to the Rwandan genocide. That link is *race branding*, whereby it became possible not only to set a group apart as an enemy, but also to exterminate it with an easy conscience."[5]

The marking in Germany of the 100th anniversary of the 1904 genocide brought that genocide out of the shadows. The term "German *Sonderweg*" ("German 'special path,'" a term that has wider application in German history) is used by Zimmerer rather than "continuity thesis," but he leaves no doubt as to his adherence to such a thesis: "The genocide in German South-West Africa is significant as a prelude to the Holocaust . . . it cannot be denied that there are actual structural similarities . . . the common factor is the readiness to exterminate certain groups of human beings. Finally, it is the breaking of the ultimate taboo, not only to talk or write about extermination of entire peoples but to put it into action, which was first carried out in the colonies and then took its most radical form in the Holocaust, which links the genocides."[6] Though some of the essays in the anthology take a less vehement view, the gauntlet had been thrown down.

Yet wholesale acceptance by historians of the continuity thesis has yet to arrive, as evidenced by a 2011 anthology that contains an instructive introduction and essays arguing in nuanced detail for and against the continuity thesis.[7] Prominent among the essays supporting "discontinuity" are those by Birthe Kundrus and Kitty Millet. The former notes the "fleeting" era of German colonialism and the variation in governing policies among its several locations—in Africa, Samoa, and China—as evidence of the lack of a totalizing impact; she also questions the notion that German imperialism was more violent and extreme than that of Great Britain and France.[8] Millet's focus is the necessity of a distinction among victim groups: "The Nazis did not see the Jews as a species unto themselves—a group to be colonized—but rather as an aspect of the environment that had to be removed"; the continuity thesis, she argues, is problematic as "victimization becomes generally interchangeable."[9] In a sense, what Millet argues here is the difference between the imperial gaze and the genocidal gaze: between viewing victims as a subhuman "species" and viewing them as "an aspect of the environment" that simply needs to be removed. Careful study of the language of General Lothar von Trotha and others in GSWA, however, affirms the German focus on annihilation of the Herero and Nama.

Thus, use of the continuity thesis must be grounded in careful definition. In *The Genocidal Gaze*, I follow the threads of shared ideology and methodology in both the genocide of the Herero and Nama, and in the Holocaust. That is, I read the texts of both the colonial era and the post-Holocaust period to demonstrate that such concepts as racial/racist hierarchies, *Lebensraum* (living space), *Rassenschande* (racial shame), and *Endlösung* (final solution) were deployed by German authorities in 1904 and again in the 1940s to justify genocide. Although it is not always noted, the Third Reich was a colonial empire; not only did Hitler colonize eastern Europe but the Nazis savored a hope that their African empire would be returned to them as a result of their imagined victory in World War II. I note the use of shared and systematic means of degradation and killing—concentration camps, death camps, intentional starvation, rape, indiscriminate murder of women and children—in both instances. I demonstrate how texts—letters, memoirs, photographs, postcards, novels, newspapers—conveyed this ideology from Africa to the German public and created an acceptance of the genocidal strategies employed in GSWA, an acceptance that creates a readiness for Hitler. The genocide in GSWA made the Holocaust "imaginable" (Zimmerer, "War, Concentration Camps," 60). But I do not claim the events in GSWA have a direct causality where the Holocaust is concerned. The loss of World War I, the dire economic situation of the Weimar Republic, the centuries-old curse of antisemitism, the "science" of eugenics, and, of course, Hitler himself take precedence as causes of the Holocaust.[10]

Despite the serious attention historians have given to this topic, no full-length monograph in English has been devoted to manifestations of such "continuity" in fiction, memoir, or the visual arts. *The Genocidal Gaze*, then, is an original intervention in the growing body of literature that endeavors to demonstrate the ways in which perception of the "other" ineluctably links the genocide of the Herero and Nama with that of the Nazi Holocaust and thus expands the understanding of this connection into new areas of study: "The debate about 'continuity' and 'discontinuity' between German colonialism and the genocide of Nazi Germany has to reflect on and move beyond existing structures of established historiographic boundaries" (Langbehn and Salama, xiii). It is a truism in Holocaust Studies that the historians have taken the lead in the field; disciplines such as sociology, literary studies, philosophy, psychology, and geography have followed. The complexity of Holocaust and Genocide Studies demands an interdisciplinary and transnational approach.

The Genocidal Gaze

Artistic representation engages its audience through narrative perspective, and a key to many postcolonial texts is the notion of the imperial or colonial gaze as a trope of perspective. The notion of the gaze has been a staple of both feminist theory and postcolonial theory since it was first suggested by Laura Mulvey to analyze how women are objectified by the male gaze in cinema.[11] The colonial, or imperial, gaze, E. Ann Kaplan's phrase, describes the dominating look of the imperialist who assigns an inferior identity to the colonized.[12] The concept of the gaze is always concerned with power, as Foucault has shown.[13] When the imperial gaze, prompted by racist hierarchy or by religious or ideological beliefs that engender a confidence in one's own superiority, evolves into a consideration of the gazed upon as inconvenient, as no longer deserving to live, the gaze can become deadly. How the imperial gaze creates or destroys identity, casts the gazed upon into captivity, and morphs into the genocidal gaze is central to the argument of this monograph. It, too, is a trope of perspective.

Scholars have used the concept of the gaze in various contexts, often to describe a negative gesture occurring in and defining an oppressive relationship. In postcolonial studies, Edward Said's notion of "orientalism" described a gaze, in this case of the colonizer upon the colonized, that resulted in viewing the colonized as an "exotic other" or its opposite, the "demonic other." Said's critics have taken him to task for the lack of gendered analysis and his use, like that of Foucault whom Said admired, of largely Western sources for his work.[14] Another important contributor to the concept of the gaze in a postcolonial context is Mary Louise Pratt, whose book *Imperial Eyes* (1992) traces the ways in which travel writings of various explorers "create" the other.

Here, I introduce the concept of the *genocidal gaze*: the attitude of German imperialists toward the indigenous people of German Southwest Africa that is then perpetuated by the Nazis. While the male gaze and the imperial gaze privilege the gazer and denigrate the gazed upon, the genocidal gaze goes a step further: it provided the German imperialists with a rationale for their depredations on the land and the people of Southwest Africa. Where the imperial gaze has as its aim the control or even enslavement of the colonized, the genocidal gaze has as its aim extermination. Specifically, the genocidal gaze cast the indigenous people in the position of being subhuman, of being *expendable*, a perspective that in turn permitted the Germans to achieve their goal of domination and exclusive possession of the land. Thus, the use of this trope both explains and demonstrates the lethal linkages between imperialism and genocide, between the genocide of the Herero and Nama and that of the victims of the Holocaust, and between German colonialism in Africa and that in eastern Europe.

The genocidal gaze serves as a metaphor for the repellent imperial ideology, founded on a racial/racist hierarchy, that Germans developed. Their perception of the Herero and Nama was conflated with a racialist hierarchy, privileging German imperialists and dehumanizing indigenous people. They were perceived as barbaric, lacking any kind of civilization, history, or meaningful religion; in other words, they were bestial, easily disposed of, a nuisance obstacle to German settlement. A quotation from Gustav Frenssen's colonial novel is useful here. The German commanding officer in Africa tells the main character, Peter Moor, a soldier: "These Blacks have deserved death before God and man . . . because they have built no houses and dug no wells . . . God has let us conquer here because we are the nobler and more advanced people. . . . To the nobler and more vigorous belongs the world. That is the justice of God. . . . For a long time, we must be hard and kill but at the same time as individual men we must strive toward higher thoughts and noble deeds so that we may contribute our part to mankind."[15] The aim of building a "New Germany" in Africa, of providing *Lebensraum*, of maintaining the purity of the German race, of utilizing land that is perceived to have lain fallow "justifies" the move from viewing the Herero and Nama as subhuman to viewing them as expendable.

In the later words of the Nazis who adopted many of these imperial perspectives—racist hierarchies, *Lebensraum*, *Rassenschande*, and *Endlösung*—Africans were *Lebensunwerten Lebens* ("life unworthy of life"). The genocidal gaze is an enabling gaze: it shaped colonial policy and gave German soldiers the moral justification, the "right" to annihilate, to "cleanse" the land and make it available for German appropriation. The texts we will examine in *The Genocidal Gaze* demonstrate the evolution of the imperial gaze into the genocidal gaze; Gustav Frenssen's colonial novel valorizes this deadly gaze as a tool of the German Schutztruppe; a post-Holocaust novel and a memoir by Uwe Timm critique the genocidal gaze and trace the arc of the continuity thesis; an art installation makes a further connection, to Apartheid in South Africa.

But "looking" is, of course, a two-way process and equally important as the gaze of the colonizer is the gaze of the colonized. This act of looking back, the resisting gaze of the colonized, begins to recognize and restore agency to the victims of imperialism, specifically the indigenous people who have been colonized and targeted for extermination. Such a gaze upon the colonizer is a gaze of resistance and self-creation or re-creation: this African gaze is the subject of both the opening and closing chapters of *The Genocidal Gaze*. We look first at the voice of Hendrik Witbooi, a Nama revolutionary whose archive reveals his gradual recognition of the meaning of the genocidal gaze and his response to it. In the concluding chapter, a contemporary African novelist, Ama Ata Aidoo, uses the trope of the genocidal gaze to reveal that Germany is the twentieth-century "heart of darkness." Scrutiny of the African gaze is crucial to this study: African voices have been silenced, lost, ignored, submerged in the discourse of genocides. While Aidoo, as we will see, has received considerable critical attention, very little has been written about Hendrik Witbooi, and what exists does not carefully parse his text, his voice; only after Uwe Timm's *Morenga* was published did the Nama hero Morenga begin to receive long overdue accolades in Namibia. Resurrection of these voices—through archival documents and oral histories or imaginatively in fiction—contradicts stereotypes and misunderstandings and uncovers the suffering, courage, and honor of the Herero and Nama and their distinctive cultures.

Finally, the genocidal gaze *normalized* genocide. Writing and reading about the gaze is an act of mediation, a power dynamic that calls the *genocidaires* to account for their crimes and discloses their malignant convictions. Careful reading of texts and attention to the narrative deployment of the genocidal gaze—or the resistance to it—establishes discursive similarities in books written during colonialism and in the post-Holocaust era.

John Noyes uses the notion of the gaze in a place and time similar to what I explore here. He defines the gaze thus: "I will be arguing that when the colonizer arrives in a new territory the gaze with which he surveys it is an initial appropriation of space . . . the travelling looker and writer develops strategies for rendering the world habitable. This appropriating gaze also tends to establish the ways in which these spaces may be rendered productive."[16] Whereas Noyes focuses on the gaze upon space, my focus here is on the gaze upon the colonized. Yet Noyes's notion that the appropriating gaze concentrates on making the land "habitable and productive" is key: one of the justifications that the Germans broadcast for their domination and eventual genocide of the indigenous people of Southwest Africa was precisely their failure (in German eyes) to use the land for the purpose of creating civilization.[17] Let us turn, then, to a brief history of German colonization of Southwest Africa.

"Colonial Grotesque: German Rule in Southwest Africa"

The Germans came late to imperialism.[18] France, Great Britain, the Netherlands, and Portugal had established colonies in the "Dark Continent" centuries before the Germans entered the "scramble for Africa." King Leopold II of Belgium began gathering treaties with African chiefs in the late 1870s under a smokescreen of philanthropy and through the agency of Henry Stanley. In 1885, Leopold declared the Congo Free State as his personal colony. He began to amass enormous wealth from importing ivory and then, in the 1890s, rubber. Some debate exists among scholars as to whether a genocide occurred there. Though the deaths of the colonized occurred from starvation, beatings, disease, overwork, and lowered birth rates as well as murder, the extermination was less systematic than that found in Germany's colony in Africa. Nonetheless, it is estimated that the population in Congo was reduced by 60 percent and that the manner and magnitude of these deaths do meet the UN Convention on Genocide.[19]

German missionaries from both the Catholic and Protestant churches had been in southern Africa from the mid-1800s, but Chancellor Otto von Bismarck rejected the idea of colonies as too risky a financial investment and thus "had no interest in imperial expansion."[20] A German private citizen, Adolf Lüderitz, set out for southern Africa in 1883 to purchase coastal land, with the purpose of establishing trade. In April 1884, Bismarck agreed to bring this land under the protection of the Reich. The following year, the Treaty of Berlin divided up the African continent; chunks of land were assigned to European countries with little regard for boundaries of ethnic groups or geography. By the 1890s, Germany had colonial holdings in today's Togo, Cameroon, Tanzania, and Rwanda as well as in East Asia, Samoa, New Guinea, and various other Pacific islands. "After those of Britain, France, and the Netherlands, this was the fourth largest colonial empire at the time."[21]

In his monumental study of German colonialism, *The Devil's Handwriting*, George Steinmetz plumbs precolonial documents to arrive at an understanding of the image Germans held of Africans when they established their colonies. Though Germans may still have viewed Africa as the "Dark Continent," many had read the studies of anthropologists, the reports of missionaries, the memoirs of travelers, and plays recounting African adventures (25).[22] In short, the modern colonial state, such as that in German Southwest Africa, was constituted of "state institutions and practices that define, express, and *reinforce a cultural difference and fundamental inferiority of the territorial natives*" and native policies that are "the site at which the colonial state *identifies, produces, and reinforces the alterity that is required by the rule of hierarchical difference*" (emphasis mine, 40–41). Such an existing and constantly reinscribed image of a racist hierarchy as applied to indigenous people in GSWA is the central springboard for the genocidal gaze.

After Chancellor Bismarck agreed to a Protectorate for the African holdings, Heinrich Göring was sent to Southwest Africa as imperial commissioner in April 1885. Göring's son, Hermann, was to be the future *Reichsfeldmarschall* of the Third Reich; he absorbed the racial hierarchies that created the genocidal gaze at his father's feet. Göring began immediately to pressure the chiefs of various ethnic groups to sign so-called Protection Treaties.[23] In fact, these treaties offered no protection and were often negotiated in such a way that the indigenous people were cheated out of their land. As more and more land was wrested from the indigenous people, two of the largest tribal groups—the Herero and the Nama—responded by resistance to these "Protection Treaties."

Armed combat between the indigenous people and the Germans began in a sporadic fashion, continuing for a decade. It is estimated that "by the end of 1903, 3.5 million hectares out of a total of 13 million had been lost" by the Herero to German settler colonialism and railroad construction.[24] As cattle herders, in a land with scarce water supplies, the Herero faced a future that would prevent them from continuing their traditional way of life, which, tragically, did occur as a result of the genocide, the concentration camps, and German appropriation of land and cattle.

In January 1904, the Herero rose in rebellion against the encroaching German military and settlers. They had some early successes in these encounters. But, after considerable planning and importing more soldiers, the Germans staged the Battle of Waterberg on 11 August 1904, a decisive victory over the Herero that intentionally forced those who had survived the battle into the desert, where thousands died of thirst and starvation. A guerilla war with the Nama followed, beginning in October 1904. The three men who served as leaders of their people—Samuel Maherero of the Herero, Hendrik Witbooi and Morenga of the Nama—will be the subjects of chapters in this book. Though the war was protracted until 1907, due to the savvy guerilla warfare waged by the Nama, the Germans eventually prevailed. Large concentration camps and a death camp were established in the aftermath of the wars, where forced labor, inadequate food and shelter, and disease resulted in yet more deaths. A genocide, though the term had not yet been invented, was committed; 80 percent of the Herero people and 50 percent of the Nama perished. While there are some scholars who maintain that the near extinction of these two groups in Namibia does not qualify as a genocide,[25] the general agreement among historians is that "the German massacre of the Ovaherero in 1904 is widely recognized as the first genocide of the twentieth century."[26]

Imperialism and the Third Reich: What Are the Links?

The genocidal gaze, on the part of the Schutztruppe in GSWA and the Nazis during the Third Reich, which translated racist hierarchies into dehumanization and eventual extermination of victims, forged the connection between these two genocides: "It is easy to kill 'subhumans' or 'nonhumans.' Too many German settlers or officials of South West Africa thought of the natives as 'baboons.' . . . There was no moral or ethical penalty to be considered in the treatment of baboons" (Totten and Parsons, 37). We must examine not only the racial paradigms, terminology, and tactics of the military that were brought to GSWA but also trace the ways in which these ideas and ideologies were *transmitted to Germany* during the era of African colonization through language, literature, media, institutional memory, and personal experience. Dozens of compelling and intriguing details have been amassed by historians: German geographer Friedrich Ratzel developed the term *Lebensraum* in 1897 with the settler colonies in GSWA in mind, a concept later adopted by the Nazis to justify taking lands in eastern Europe.[27] "Colonial Namibian literature . . . exposed metropolitan Germans to a new form of racism in which non-Germans had the right to exist only in so far as they served Germans and in which some authors even endorsed extermination" (Madley, 436–37); *Peter Moor's Journey to Southwest Africa*, the subject of chapter 2, is often named as an example of such literature. Several legal concepts, instantiated in law in the colony, then transfer wholesale to the Third Reich: the term *Rassenschande*; the restriction against interracial marriage; and the right under the law for settlers to whip African employees, called "paternal chastisement" as we have seen. "Genocidal rhetoric," invented in the colony, such as *Endlösung* led to a growing acceptance in the Fatherland of the justification of annihilationist wars that clear land of subhumans or enslave them (Madley, 440–41). This goal is echoed in the *Vernichtungsbefehl*, or Annihilation Order, proclaimed by General von Trotha after the decisive Battle of Waterberg, when 80 percent of the Herero were either killed outright or driven into the Omaheke Desert to die of thirst. Copies of the order were published in Germany and publicly debated; eventually the order was rescinded and von Trotha recalled to Germany. But the damage had been done; Herero POWs were systematically killed; such an approach to waging war led to a new term, *Vernichtungskrieg* (war of annihilation), appropriated by the Nazis, which equated victory with the extermination of one's enemies.

Though the British had used concentration camps in the Boer War, the establishment of camps in GSWA represents the first instance of a distinction between concentration camps (of which there were several in the aftermath of the genocide) and a death camp, a distinction reiterated by the Nazis. Shark Island was established near Lüderitzburg, on a windy, rocky island that could in no way sustain life. Here the prisoners were exposed to the raw weather and provided no shelter, were locked behind barbed wire, lacked hospital and toilet facilities, and were systematically and intentionally underfed. Women were raped by soldiers who had no restraints. Prisoners died by the thousands. Concentration camps were established on the coast below Swakopmund, in Windhoek, and in other inland locations. These functioned essentially as slave labor camps, as did Dachau, Ravensbrück, Sachsenhausen, and any number of camps during the Third Reich. As with *Endlösung* and *Rassenschande*, the term *Konzentrationslager* (concentration camp) emerged at this time.[28]

Finally, many personal connections can be found: men who functioned in the genocide apparatus in GSWA who returned to the Fatherland to take up similar roles in Germany. Or, in the case of Heinrich Göring, the first governor in Südwest Africa, the son becomes an early, ardent, and prominent Nazi, having been schooled in imperial ideology by his father (Madley, 450). Other Germans who had participated in the genocide of the Herero subsequently became devoted Nazis, shaping policy under Hitler on future colonization, race, interracial unions, sterilization, and so-called medical experimentation. An early manifestation of eugenics was the decapitation of Herero and Nama in Southwest Africa after the genocides; indigenous women prisoners were forced to scrape the skin from these skulls, which were then sent to Berlin for examination to "prove" that the skulls came from a subhuman species. Images of this atrocity were made into postcards, as were the floggings of laborers, and sent home to the Fatherland. Some of these skulls have subsequently been repatriated to Namibia.[29]

Structure of the Text

The five chapters of *The Genocidal Gaze* provide readings of interdisciplinary texts, both contemporaneous to German colonialism and those appearing post-Holocaust. In studying such representations in letters, fiction, a memoir, and an art installation, the monograph interrogates the transnational perceptions/gaze between Africans and Germans, and traces the ideological and methodological relationship between imperialism and genocide.

The focus of chapter 1 is Nama revolutionary Hendrik Witbooi, a chief of his people who struggled with the growing German presence in GSWA from the arrival of the colonizers in 1884 until his death on the battlefield in October 1905 at the age of seventy-five. Witbooi kept an archive of both his personal papers and the exchange of correspondence with German leaders as well as leaders of the Herero and missionaries. This archive reveals his articulate objection to German aggression, often cannily couched in the language of Christianity; he had been educated by Lutheran missionaries. Witbooi's gaze upon the Germans is unblinking and evolves gradually as he comes to *see* what the German objectives really are. Whereas he initially (and correctly) perceives their plans for the Herero and Nama to be relocation and forced labor—the imperial gaze—his interactions with the Schutztruppe and their treatment of the Herero make it clear to him that the gaze has become genocidal. He then leads his people in a guerilla war against the Germans, which is ultimately futile, and in which he dies. The decision to open this book with Witbooi's voice is an intentional effort to recover African voices, to honor them, and to understand how their gaze of resistance functioned before, during, and after the genocide.

Another African voice in the opening chapter is that of Jan Kubas, also an indigenous African and an eyewitness to the atrocities of the Germans during the war and genocide. He subsequently gave testimony to the British. "Words cannot be found to relate what happened; it was too terrible," he told them. This chapter also analyzes excerpts from a memoir by a former British soldier who prospected for gold and diamonds in Southwest Africa, immediately after the war, from 1907 to 1914; his observations of the Germans as colonizers, their treatment of both the indigenous people and the Boers, and the death camp they established on Shark Island provide yet another lens with which to "look at" German imperialist behavior and ideology, and the links to the Nazi Holocaust.

Gustav Frenssen's fictional memoir, *Peter Moor's Journey to Southwest Africa* (1906, translated into English in 1908), the subject of chapter 2, is often called the quintessential German colonial novel. It is a first-person narrative, written as if by a German soldier participating in the Herero genocide; since Frenssen never traveled to Africa, he relied on accounts by men who had been there for his novel. The text, though unwittingly, reveals much about the genocidal gaze: the narrative is focalized through a fictional soldier, Peter Moor. How he views Africa and the Africans as he arrives on the "Dark Continent" models the racial hierarchies of the imperial gaze; how his attitudes gradually change, to embrace the genocidal gaze in which he is instructed by the army chaplain and his superior officers, forms the substance of the novel. Frenssen applauds the exterminationist approach of the military. He also favors the vision of the German colony that would follow the "cleansing" of the land of "inconvenient" and "uncivilized" indigenous people. This vision ends by World War I, after which the Germans lost control of Southwest Africa, and instead becomes the blueprint for Nazi predations against eastern Europe, the Jews, and others deemed "biologically inferior."

This chapter also reads Frenssen's text to trace transnational links between imperialism and genocide. Examining various editions of the text, created for the general German reading public, for youth as well as Nazi soldiers, and for Namibian readers in the era of Namibian independence (post-1990), reveals the uses to which this profoundly racist text has been put in the service of various political ideologies. As evidence of the "continuity thesis," Frenssen's conversion in later life from Lutheran pastor to avid Nazi Party member is also examined. Colonial photographs, taken largely by German soldiers, that reveal as Frenssen's book does how the genocidal gaze dominated and controlled the colonized are included in the text.

Frenssen's smug approbation of the genocidal gaze is reversed in chapter 3 in which the juxtaposition of two books written by contemporary German writer Uwe Timm presents a searing critique of this deadly gaze. Timm's work is also further demonstration of the usefulness of the "continuity thesis," in this case for understanding late twentieth-century texts. Timm's *Morenga* (1978), an account of the 1904–7 war focalized through the eyes of a German soldier, is an intertextual response to, and correction of, Frenssen's *Peter Moor*. Whereas Moor comes to embrace the genocidal gaze as the "final solution" for the indigenous people of Southwest Africa, *Morenga*'s hero/antihero, Veterinarian Gottschalk, gradually realizes the horror of what the Schutztruppe are doing and his own implication in these crimes.

Timm, son of a Nazi soldier and participant in the student demonstrations of the 1960s and 1970s, wrote this novel when Germany was still silent (or even self-congratulatory) about its colonial history. Timm asks: What is the connection between the violence of colonialism and the violence of genocide? How does silence about genocide, the failure to remember, to mourn, to reconcile, engender other genocides? How is the genocidal gaze of imperialism recapitulated in the Holocaust? Using fiction as well as excerpts from actual military reports, soldiers' diaries, and the diary of Morenga, a leader of Nama guerilla forces in the war, Timm interrogates the ways in which nineteenth-century Germans perceived Africans, how this contributed to the genocide, and how that genocide compared to, and contributed to, the Nazi Holocaust. While the latter has been publicly mourned, the death of the 80,000 Herero, an estimated 80 percent of the group, and 50 percent of the Nama has been called a "forgotten genocide" by Rene Lemarchand, and little exists in Namibia today to memorialize them.[30]

In My Brother's Shadow is a memoir written by Timm twenty-five years later, yet it shares many of the same themes: the German history of violence and genocide, misguided German values. The text is at once an ambivalent tribute to Timm's brother, an SS soldier who died on the Russian front, a portrait of his father's adulation of this brother, and a philosophical interrogation. Tim writes both books in the tradition of *Väterliteratur*, the genre of accusatory novels and memoirs written by the children of the perpetrator generation to call into question the behavior of fathers that contributed to the Holocaust and their subsequent silence. While *Shadow* has been read as a text in this genre, *Morenga* has not, nor have the two texts been read together as protests against genocide. Subsequent to the publication of *Morenga*, Timm published *Deutsche Kolonien* (1986), a book of photos assembled from his archival research for *Morenga*. Like the novel, these photos reveal the genocidal gaze of the Germans through their cameras.

William Kentridge, a white, Jewish South African, created an art installation titled *Black Box/Chambre Noire* that first went on display in Germany in 2005. *Black Box*, the subject of chapter 4, incorporates early twentieth-century German colonial film clips, mechanized figures, music, photographs, newspaper clippings, and animation-like movements. The performance lasts twenty-two minutes and is encompassed within the frame of a small stage with curtains. The subject matter of *Black Box* is the 1904–7 genocide of the Herero people by German colonizers. Kentridge gestures in several directions: the work interrogates the genocidal gaze and German guilt, the silence surrounding this genocide, and *trauerarbeit*, Freud's term for working through grief. Kentridge draws symbolic links between this first genocide of the twentieth century and the Holocaust, initiated less than thirty years later. Kentridge (b. 1955) is also gesturing toward Apartheid; both of his parents were attorneys in the anti-apartheid movement and, it can be argued, the policies and ideology of Apartheid owed much to the Nazis.[31] Much of the analysis of this installation piece focuses on Kentridge's exploitation of animation: *Black Box* moves beyond what Uwe Timm has accomplished in his critique to actually reenact the genocidal gaze through a palimpsest of colonial memorabilia, Nazi images, staged violence, and haunting music.

The final chapter of the book returns the reader to an African voice of resistance, that of Ama Ata Aidoo, a late twentieth-century Ghanaian writer who has spent considerable time in the West. How is Germany perceived by contemporary African novelists? When the gaze is turned back upon the *genocidaires*, what is the impact on Africans? *Our Sister Killjoy, or, Reflections from a Black-eyed Squint* (1977), a title that draws attention to the concept of the gaze, provides responses to these queries. Literary criticism of Aidoo's work has focused on feminist readings whereas my reading occurs at the intersection of Postcolonial and Holocaust Studies. Such an approach unveils the contemporary African perception, and critique, of the genocidal gaze.

Though brief (134 pages), *Our Sister Killjoy, or, Reflections from a Black-eyed Squint* is challenging in that it includes several genres (a frequent feature of Ghanaian literature), unorthodox page formatting, and a shifting narrative voice; analysis of these structural devices focuses on how they suggest both the genocidal gaze of the Germans and the resisting gaze of the Africans. The novel is also highly intertextual, incorporating references to fairy tales, *Jane Eyre*, and historical events, as well as the defiant gesture of "writing back" to Joseph Conrad's *Heart of Darkness*. While a few scholars have noted this link with Conrad, none has made the connection between imperialism and genocide in Africa and the Holocaust in Germany that Aidoo is interrogating. Her novel thus provides a very useful case study with which to conclude the monograph.

ONE

The African Gaze of Resistance in Hendrik Witbooi and Others

> I know enough tribes in Africa. They all have the same mentality insofar as they yield only to force. It was and remains my policy to apply this force by unmitigated terrorism and even cruelty.
> GERMAN GENERAL LOTHAR VON TROTHA

> ... all I see in your peace is the extermination of all of us and our people.
> NAMA REVOLUTIONARY HENDRIK WITBOOI | 1905

> Words cannot be found to relate what happened; it was too terrible.
> JAN KUBAS | witness to the Herero genocide

The Genocidal Gaze: From German Southwest Africa to the Third Reich opens with *African voices*, with the perceptions and reactions of those *gazed upon* by the German colonizers and military, with a description of the gaze they returned upon their colonizers: "African voices [in German Southwest Africa] were forgotten and their witness statements actively erased" (Silvester and Gewald, xiv). It is crucial that these voices, these subjectivities be restored, that we acknowledge the humanity and dignity of the Herero and Nama in the face of the imperial and then genocidal gaze of the Germans. Hendrik Witbooi is one such voice; he was a leader of the Nama people who fought and died in 1905 in the war with the Germans and has been called "a hero" in a recent book on Namibian resistance.[1] Another African voice introduced in this chapter is that of Jan Kubas, an indigenous witness to the German genocide, whose testimony was subsequently published in the British Blue Book of 1918. Affirming these African voices is that of a British prospector who, shortly after the genocide, described what he found in the landscape of GSWA and provided eyewitness information on Shark Island, the death camp the Germans constructed on the coast of their colony. The chapter concludes with excerpts from recent oral histories, conveying stories of German colonization passed down through generations of Namibians.

Hendrik Witbooi comes of age against what George Steinmetz has called the "vast and repugnant repertoire of European, and particularly German, images" of the indigenous people in German Southwest Africa (Steinmetz, *The Devil's Handwriting*, 75). This "repugnant repertoire" initially constituted the German imperial gaze, which destabilized the identities of the colonized while contributing "to any subject's interpellation (in Louis Althusser's sense of a subject being called into being)" (Kaplan, xix).[2] The Germans denied the humanity and cultural identity of the Africans through a sordid ideology that imagined them as subhuman. German missionaries, from the 1840s onward, had referred to the Nama as "Hottentots" (a term now viewed as derogatory and inaccurate),[3] and their reports back to Germany contained the entire panoply of racist stereotypes, resulting in a portrait of "abject and ignoble savagery." These characterizations include: "barbarian," "wild and raw," and "laziness and filthiness," and that "civilization seems to have no attraction at all for them."[4] One German Rhenish missionary opined: "'The Hottentots . . . are nomads, but they are not even competent herdsmen. . . . Their *instability* [*Unbeständigkeit*] . . . is due especially to the fact that the Namaquas don't know how to make anything orderly out of their country'" (Steinmetz, *The Devil's Handwriting*, 116). As we will see in chapter 2, the "failure" of the indigenous people to dig wells and build homes prompted harsh condemnation by the German military and ultimately served as a justification for genocide. These racist characterizations, the perception of these "failures" to create civilization (as the Germans defined it), and the belief that the Herero and Nama lacked history and religion constituted the imperial gaze; in turn, this gaze underwent a transformation into the genocidal gaze that became deadly. With the genocidal gaze, the Herero and Nama are cast into the category of the expendable; their extermination is justified in the eyes of the imperialists who believe they need and deserve the land (*Lebensraum*), which they will put to "good use" after it is cleansed of its original inhabitants.

As to Hendrik Witbooi himself, some missionaries saw him as the "'great exception'" to the Hottentot race's shortcomings, while others deplored his "'ever greater regression into Jewishness, superstition, delusion, fanaticism, and reverie'" (Steinmetz, *The Devil's Handwriting*, 120). The linkage here between indigenous people and Jews is telling in terms of the continuity thesis, described in the introduction, which *The Genocidal Gaze* traces. In 1886, the Cape Colony *Blue-Book* on *Native Affairs* summed up the prevailing attitude toward Hendrik Witbooi as behaving "'in a way which with any other human being but a Hottentot would be a manifestation of complete insanity'" (Steinmetz, *The Devil's Handwriting*, 121). These quotations from German missionaries and others provide a concise definition of aspects of the genocidal gaze.

In the aftermath of the German genocide of the Herero and Nama, the genocidal gaze is also reflected in the views of other Western observers. For example, in 1914, Herman Babson, a professor of German at Purdue University, published an abridged version of Gustav Frenssen's colonial novel *Peter Moors Fahrt nach Südwest*. In his introduction, Babson characterizes Witbooi as "an energetic leader, one destined to make all sorts of trouble for the Germans. With the assuming of power he became an unprincipled robber and plunderer and for many years was a terror to the entire country."[5] Eliminating any mention of the many depredations visited by the Germans upon the Nama people, Babson then declares, "Immediately upon the heels of this revolt of the Herero in the central part of the colony came the uprising of the Hottentots in the south, led by the notorious Hendrik Witbooi. Apparently without any immediate cause, he suddenly declared war against the Germans and with allied Hottentot 'captains' started a new reign of terror in his district" (xxviii). Babson acknowledges neither humanity nor sovereignty on the part of Hendrik Witbooi but rather depicts him as an inconvenient upstart deserving of elimination.

Hendrik Witbooi: "Unrevisable Subalternity" or Nama Revolutionary?

I begin by exploring the astute observations and writings of Hendrik Witbooi, a Nama chief, born circa 1830 into a long line of Nama chiefs and described as "one of the most powerful African leaders at the time when European imperialism began to carve Africa up into colonies."[6] Witbooi's writing (*The Henrik Withooi Papers*, ed. Brigitte Lau) allows us to trace the transition from imperial to genocidal gaze on the part of the German Schutztruppe, to see Witbooi's increasing awareness of this shift, and to recognize his gaze—fiercely resisting German hegemony.

"Unrevisable subalternity" is Steinmetz's term (*The Devil's Handwriting*, 143) for the permanent status to which the Germans relegated the indigenous people of Southwest Africa. The initial goal of the Schutztruppe and settlers was to wrest the land from the Herero, the Nama, and other Southwest African peoples, and to compel them to labor/forced labor/enslavement. Colonial policy to achieve these ends differed with each newly appointed colonial administrator. Theodor Leutwein, the third such administrator in GSWA, "differed from his predecessors by the methods he employed" (Drechsler, 75). Whereas the first administrator, Heinrich Göring (1884–89), had no military troops and tried to proceed by diplomacy, Curt von François (1889–94) readily took up arms. But von François's lack of success at subduing the indigenous people led the chancellor of the Reich to replace von François with Theodor Leutwein in 1894. Leutwein adopted what came to be called the "Leutwein system," which combined diplomacy and military force. "He was a past master of the policy of divide and rule which he readily admitted he had learned from the British" (Drechsler, 75). Leutwein proceeded toward the goal of "unrevisable subalternity" by exacting treaties from individual chiefs. These treaties were presented to the Herero and Nama as "Protection Treaties," that is, the Germans offered to protect one ethnic group from another. Hendrik Witbooi came to be seen by the Germans as the most stubborn obstacle to their successful colonization of Southwest Africa and to their establishment of orderly control over the inhabitants and their land.

Witbooi's Nama name was !Nanseb Gâbemab; he was the third son of Moses and Lena Witbooi. Scholars have proposed various explanations for the designation of "Witbooi." Most agree that the term derives from the white headscarf that the Witbooi (literally, "white boy") troops fashioned on their hats, with a corner creating a peak that may imitate the comb of a fighting cock (Lau, viii, n22). Hendrik Witbooi was educated at missionary schools in Southwest Africa and South Africa. He married !Nanses (Katharina), and the couple had at least a dozen children over two decades, from roughly 1858 to 1879; some of Hendrik's sons subsequently took up arms with him. Witbooi was baptized, with his wife, as a Lutheran in 1868 and remained devoted to his religious beliefs while using them adroitly to both chastise the Germans and explain his motivations. He served as an elder in his congregation, beginning in 1875, and learned various skills from the German missionary Johannes Olpp. Witbooi's early years were occasionally spent in intertribal warfare, primarily against the Herero with the object of the wars being to capture cattle rather than land. Cattle were the primary form of cash and were used as a source of food and drink, as well as to pay off traders for goods, including guns and ammunition.[7] During this period, Witbooi's following increased to the thousands. But Witbooi had the foresight to see that such internal struggles among indigenous people distracted them from the larger struggle, that against encroaching German imperialism.

Witbooi also had the foresight to create an archive, and so we have the enormous benefit of his perceptions about the German invaders. Using a large red leather notebook, Witbooi kept a voluminous archive of his correspondence with missionaries, other African leaders, and the Germans. Both the letters from these correspondents and Witbooi's responses were included in the archive, as well as his journal, minutes of meetings with German officials, and miscellaneous other documents. He wrote in the colonial Cape Dutch language. There is some evidence that he had sustained a battle wound that resulted in the loss of his right thumb; this perhaps explains his frequent use of secretaries to maintain his collected papers (Lau, vi; Hillebrecht, 39).

So valuable is this archive that UNESCO deemed it a Memory of the World object in 2005 and describes it thus: "Witbooi's insights into the nature of colonialism, about the fundamental difference between conflict with African competitors and with European invaders, his attempts at formulating African legal concepts, and the visionary and poetic power of some of his texts are the qualities that set his letters apart and above the bulk of contemporary and earlier African texts of the same genre. The texts include probably the first written formulation of the concept of Pan-Africanism."[8] This red leather notebook was captured in April 1893 by German commissioner Curt von François during an unprovoked German raid on Witbooi's encampment at Hoornkrans; von François carried the leather notebook to Germany but it was subsequently returned to Namibia. Today, Witbooi's personal archive is kept in the National Archives of Namibia in Windhoek. Two other journals belonging to Witbooi, kept between 1893 and 1903, were recently unearthed in a museum in Bremen, Germany.[9]

This extraordinary document, or collection of documents, provides the reader with a clear idea of Nama resistance to the imperial gaze, and finally to the genocidal gaze, in the gaze they returned to the Germans: "The papers of Hendrik Witbooi are the only archival documents to have been published that present an African perspective on the German colonial period" (Silvester and Gewald, xiv). The significance of this archive, both for the history it provides and for its symbolic value, cannot be overestimated. If the genocidal gaze normalizes genocide, making it acceptable for the "civilized races" to visit violence upon those perceived as racially inferior, then the task of the African gaze upon the colonizers is to contradict that very normalization. The African must unsettle or deny racial hierarchies; his/her gaze must be a gaze of resistance to the racist stereotypes with which the imperial gaze and genocidal gaze are imbued. Hendrik Witbooi achieves just such resistance by demonstrating skills Germans denied that Africans could do/have: by the very act of writing, which is an accomplishment of the educated; by speaking in terms of Christian religious beliefs when the genocidal gaze assigns barbarity; and by the act of creating an archive that proves Witbooi has and recognizes a history, understands historical concepts, and values the creation of records for future generations. "White subjectivities . . . can also be destabilized when exposed to the gaze of the Other, since this is a gaze to which such subjects have not been traditionally subjected" (Kaplan, xix). Witbooi's gaze endeavors to do just that.

The first item in the original red notebook, a "Diary entry" dated 18 June 1884, the year the Germans began colonizing Namibia, opens "Yesterday, 17 June, we spotted Herero in Oub. They were spies, and we chased them like game" (quoted in Lau, 1). These two sentences are characteristic of much of the archive: through both letters and such diary entries, Witbooi maintains a running account of his conflicts with both other indigenous people/groups and the Germans. He is also given to poetic language. Here he uses a simile; metaphors are also common in his prose as are frequent references to scriptural verses, traditional Nama stories, and lengthy quotations from the Bible. This first entry, which runs to five pages, recounts a series of skirmishes with the Herero from 17–27 June 1884. The pronouns are variously "we," "he" (referring to Witbooi), and "I," Witbooi's first-person voice. This variation suggests his use of scribes, as mentioned earlier. The entry concludes with a copy of a letter penned by Witbooi on 27 June 1884, addressed to Captain Maharero (Kamaherero, paramount chief of the Herero from 1870s to his death on 7 October 1890). In the letter, Witbooi sets out his conditions for creating a lasting peace between the Nama, who were Witbooi followers, and the Herero. A year elapses before subsequent entries in late 1885: two letters from Witbooi addressed to Kamaherero, the first on 13 October, agreeing to a meeting with Kamaherero to reach a peace agreement, and the second on 19 October, in which Witbooi accuses Kamaherero of deceit because he launched an attack against Witbooi as the latter arrived at the place they had agreed upon to discuss a peace treaty. This second letter contains a warning as well as a powerful metaphor with biblical resonance: "With your talk of truce you had bound my hands; now your treachery has loosened the bonds. As before, I have cast open the gates of war. You shall get war from all sides" (7).

Subsequent early entries include correspondence between Witbooi and Heinrich Göring, the father of the Nazi henchman Hermann Göring. Göring's letters are condescending and reveal his adherence to the racial hierarchies of the imperial gaze; in an effort to get Witbooi to capitulate to a so-called German Protection Treaty, Göring denigrates Witbooi, telling him in a letter dated 21 November 1885: "In *civilized countries* you would be regarded as a rebel and dealt with accordingly." Göring concludes his letter with a threat: "To recapitulate: The

German government cannot permit chieftains who have placed themselves under German protection, to support your enterprise of plunging a protected chiefdom into war for no better reason than its inhabitants belong to another tribe, and that they have at some time in the past perpetrated injustices—which must have happened when you were hated. I trust you will attend to my words" (emphasis mine, quoted in Lau, 11–12). Göring here refers to the fact that Kamaherero had indeed signed a "Protection Treaty" in October 1885 with the Germans. Yet Witbooi and his thousand followers, called a "Namaland Commando Group" by Lau, were feared by the Germans who realized "that no colonization of the country could be effected unless Witbooi was conquered" (Lau, xix). In turn, Witbooi "clearly perceived from the outset [that] the treaties were aimed at creating dependency and subordination to the German empire of independent rulers" (Lau, xviii).

Almost a year later, in September 1886, Witbooi writes a letter to Göring's secretary, Louis Nels, appealing for a supply of ammunition. By this time, the Germans had promulgated a regulation forbidding the importation of ammunition; the regulation was intended to cripple Witbooi's ability to fight. In one of many instances in which he deftly deploys his knowledge of Christianity to achieve his ends, Witbooi says: "You have made noises of peace with your mouth, but that will not bring peace to this country because it does not strike a chord deep in the heart of the people. So let me tell all of you who are in possession of ammunition: supply this freely, for ammunition alone can bring peace to the very heart. Weapons are ordained God's rod of judgement between warring tribes" (quoted in Lau, 15). Witbooi has invoked God's name to persuade Göring's secretary of the counterintuitive claim that supplying bullets will bring about peace! With this move, he alerts Göring to the fact that he is a clever force to be reckoned with, not a subhuman. He shares with Göring Western religious beliefs and has no hesitation in using this knowledge against the German imperialists.

In subsequent letters during 1888–89, Witbooi appeals in an increasingly desperate manner to several individuals for ammunition and guns. In a March 1889 letter to Jan Jonker Afrikaner, the chief of another branch of Nama, Witbooi reveals his keen reliance on the written word: "You ask me why I have sent you copies of my own and your letters. I will tell Your Honour why I did this. I did it to let you judge for yourself how I dealt with Paul [Visser] concerning the [breaking of the] peace. And I sent you your letter so that you may realise that the uprising of the other nations was brought about by you. Because you invited them to crush me. You sowed this seed in their hearts, the fruit of which is that they have risen against me. You touched the spring of the Lord's decree that all men should rise against me" (quoted in Lau, 28). He uses his carefully kept archive to defend himself and, adopting biblical references and metaphors again, to accuse and persuade others. Jan Jonker Afrikaner replies, stating that Witbooi has made false accusations and offering to serve as mediator. Witbooi's reply of 22 March 1889 again reveals his reliance on, and trust of, the written word: "of all the accusations against me you simply state that 'people say.' You cannot bring written proof" (30).[10] Afrikaner is rebuffed. At this time, Witbooi resumes his correspondence with Göring, boasting of his recent exploits and taunting Göring by asking: "I must inform you that at Achenib I captured the [German] flag that you had presented to Manasse [another Nama chief]. It is now in my keeping . . . I should like to know what to do with this flag; I ask because it is an alien thing to me" (33). Witbooi's resisting gaze can be cast in sarcasm as well as terms of Christianity.

In May 1890, Göring resumes his pressure on Witbooi to cease fighting against the Herero; his letter again contains threats. Witbooi astutely replies, deploying biblical language: "I am astonished by this letter in which Your Honour raises great, weighty topics. . . . But you have not left me room and scope to *ponder all in my heart*, so that I might answer you from my own good judgement and free choice. You have not approached me as an impartial peacemaker, but uttered abrupt orders as to what I should do. Consequently, Your Honour cannot expect a satisfactory answer from me now" (emphasis mine, quoted in Lau, 48–49). The following day, Witbooi dispatches a long epistle to Kamaherero, chastising him for renewing his "Protection Treaty" with the Germans: "You will eternally regret that you have given your land and your right to rule into the hands of White men" (51). Using a Nama folktale, Witbooi predicts that surrendering to government by another "will become to you like carrying the sun on your back" (52). Lau's footnote explains: "In the Nama cautionary tale, the jackal accepts the sun as a rider and barely survives with a permanently scorched back" (52). Witbooi continues chastising, appropriating a biblical example: "You are already completely in his [Göring's] power. I am aware that you and Dr. Göring are of different nationalities, and that you have never been good friends, and that you formed this friendship solely in order to crush me. So did Herod and Pilate, in order to get rid of the Lord Jesus, suspend and postpone their hostility and their true interests" (52).

In 1890, Kamaherero dies and Samuel Maherero, his son, assumes the role of chief. This occasions an exchange of several long and thoughtful letters between Maherero and Witbooi. They are warily testing each other in regard to the possibility of pursuing peace between the Herero and Nama. In June 1892, Witbooi takes up his red notebook to write minutes of an important meeting he had with

Curt von François, who has replaced Göring as the imperial German commissioner in the country. Von François urges Witbooi once again to "yield to German Protection" (quoted in Lau, 84) to which the ever alert Witbooi philosophically replies: "What is 'protection'? What are we being protected against? From what danger, or difficulty, or suffering can one chief be protected by another?" (85). After a hypocritical response from von François to the effect that Witbooi's rights will not be abrogated, Witbooi replies that it makes no sense to him that a chief who has surrendered to the Germans will keep his autonomy. He further asserts his hegemony and his pan-African sensibility: "This part of Africa is the realm of us Red chiefs. If danger threatens one of us which he feels he cannot meet on his own, then he can call on a brother or brothers among the Red chiefs, saying, 'Come, brothers, let us together oppose this danger which threatens to invade our Africa, for we are one in colour and custom, and this Africa is ours.' For the fact that we various Red chiefs occupy our various realms and home grounds is but a lesser division of the one Africa" (86). Such a union of the various ethnic groups in GSWA against the Germans is exactly what the imperialists fear. In this one passage, Witbooi has simultaneously issued a threat and signaled his resistance to the German gaze that denigrates him and the other Red chiefs.

Von François replies that he will stop the Herero should they attack again, and anyway, no need to worry: "no one in the territory will be allowed a gun . . . in the past men managed quite well with bows and arrows and assegais" (!) (quoted in Lau, 88). Witbooi promptly rebuts this idea: "We cannot deprive our men of their guns. Those people you mentioned who lived by the bow and arrow and assegai, had no guns in their day: that is why they lived as they did. *We are men of today, and live in the age of the firearm*" (emphasis mine, 88). Witbooi insists that he and the Nama inhabit the present; he will not be cast into a stereotyped primitive past by this German officer.

A few weeks later, Witbooi corresponds with a Nama chief who has already signed a "Protection Treaty" with the Germans. Witbooi scolds him, declaring: "*I see* the Germans *quite differently*. They claim that they want to protect you against other mighty nations, but it seems to me that they themselves are the mighty nation seeking to occupy our country by force . . . *I see* nothing good in the coming of the Germans: they boast of their power and they use it" (emphasis mine, quoted in Lau, 90). Here, Witbooi characterizes the Germans' hypocrisy, and his own gaze of astute perception and defiance, differentiating his gaze from that of some of his countrymen who appear to have deferred to the German vision of the indigenous people. A similar definition of the Germans as cruel and deceitful appears in a letter Witbooi wrote to John Cleverly, a British official, in August 1892. Invoking the terms of the Treaty of Berlin, Witbooi accuses the Germans of being in violation:

> The Germans told [African leaders] that they would protect them against the mighty invaders threatening to take our land by force. . . . But from what I hear and see of the man, it now appears the *German himself is that man who he said was of another nation*, and is doing exactly what he said we would be protected from . . . German officials told my officials how they had beaten the men in a disgraceful and brutal manner, as the *dumb and ignorant creatures they think us*. . . . They stretch people on their backs and hit them across the belly, and even between the legs, be they men or women. (emphasis mine, 98)[11]

Here Witbooi succeeds in *othering* the Germans by calling them out as "that man who he said was of another nation," that is, the German is actually the "other" against whom the Herero and Nama need protection. Witbooi accurately sees the flogging of his people as an indication of the German belief that their victims are subhuman. Again and again in these passages from his archive, Witbooi demonstrates his insightful analysis of the German imperial gaze, their strategy in endeavoring to dominate GSWA, and the increasingly terrifying implications for the indigenous people.

"Go back, get away from me. That is my earnest demand."
HENDRIK WITBOOI | to Theodor Leutwein, 17 August 1894

By 1893, the Germans were beginning to lose patience with the slow progress against the Herero and Nama, who together had reached a peace agreement in November 1892,[12] furthering German frustration. Chancellor Count Leo von Caprivi, in Berlin, declared: "South West Africa is ours . . . and it must remain so." To assure that that happened, he sent 214 soldiers and two officers to GSWA as reinforcements (Drechsler, 69). Witbooi, by this point, was increasingly convinced of the true aim of German imperialism—destruction of the indigenous people—despite the hypocritical appeals made to him by a series of German leaders. His intuition is confirmed when on 12 April 1893 he and his community, lodged at his Hoornkrans stronghold, suffer a surprise nighttime attack by von François and two hundred German troops. The attack was completely unprovoked. "Von François's *new orders were to 'destroy the tribe.'* . . . The ferocity of the attack is suggested by the fact that the German troops, armed with two hundred rifles, used sixteen thousand rounds of ammunition in thirty minutes" (emphasis mine, Steinmetz, *The Devil's Handwriting*, 151). According to Witbooi, ten men and seventy-five women and children were killed; Witbooi escaped (Lau, 129). The Germans proceeded to loot the camp; it is in this attack that the red notebook archive is taken by the soldiers. They also captured one of Witbooi's daughters and his wife, taking them as prisoners along with seventy-nine other women and children (Drechsler, 70). On the following day, the Germans razed the entire village and the surrounding defense walls. This attack was a major turning point in both the colonial policy of the Germans and the understanding of that policy that Hendrik Witbooi confides in his correspondence. The evolution from imperial gaze, with the intent to enslave the indigenous people, to genocidal gaze, with the intent to exterminate them, had begun.

In October 1893, half a year after the Hoornkrans raid, Witbooi writes to a Herero leader, Zacharias Zeraua, urging that they declare peace between their groups and join forces against the Germans. His letter is prescient: "[The recent German raid at Hoornkrans] is a portent of the purpose, hidden behind it, of subjugating the nations of this country and *reducing us to slavery*, and of appropriating our African land . . . the land will be completely occupied by white people, and *whites will govern and develop this land* . . . the Germans are determined to cut me down by force, and *to deport me*. . . . Afterwards, they will turn on you Herero" (emphasis mine, quoted in Lau, 140–41). Here, Witbooi aptly characterizes the German imperial gaze as an apprehension of the indigenous people slated for a condition of slavery. He understands that he may be deported but he has not yet fully grasped the exterminationist colonial policy that was gradually developing in Berlin. How could he imagine such a thing? Even after this genocide, the true aim of the Holocaust to annihilate the Jews and the Roma and Sinti was unimaginable to many.

Hendrik Witbooi's dire predictions are largely realized a decade later, when, after the genocide of the Nama and Herero, the Germans deport Witbooi's followers in three directions: 80 men to Togo in 1905; about 1,600 to the death camp at Shark Island in early 1906; and a tiny remnant of the Witbooi people, about 96, including one of Hendrik Witbooi's sons, to Cameroon in 1910 (Steinmetz, *The Devil's Handwriting*, 172–75). Both Togo and Cameroon were German colonies. All the land and cattle of the Nama and Herero in GSWA were expropriated for German use, and thousands of the best acreage of the country *still* remain in the hands of the settlers' descendants. And both indigenous groups were indeed turned into slaves, or perhaps more appropriately, forced laborers, the distinction being that they were not "owned" by their masters (Drechsler, 231).

By 1894, German presence had increased in GSWA from the initial three officials a decade earlier to hundreds of military troops. Witbooi reveals his powerful ability to use language against the Germans as effectively as they have deployed it against him. In a letter to the recently appointed German commissioner, Theodor Leutwein, he blames the previous German leader von François for his unreasonable behavior: "Von François demanded from me what is mine, and I refused: for I alone have the right to dispose of what is mine. Such conduct by von François I never expected, *because you White people are the most educated and civilized, and you teach us truth and justice*" (emphasis mine, quoted in Lau, 151). Here Witbooi turns the German imperial gaze back upon itself, using it as an accusation thrust in Leutwein's face.

The attack at Hoornkrans was properly understood by Witbooi as an act of war and he moves into action, demonstrating his skills as a guerilla fighter as well as a writer. He and his followers, who grew from 250 at Hoornkrans to 600 within six months, embarked on daring raids to capture German horses, thus unseating the German cavalry, and to successfully block German traders from travel. In August 1893, he "pulled off a great coup," attacking and destroying a train of twenty wagons pulled by oxen and loaded with supplies needed inland; the following month, he seized 2,350 Merino sheep, 125 oxen, and 28 horses from a German farm (Drechsler, 71–73).

The Witbooi troops, having lost their Hoornkrans stronghold, entrenched themselves in the Naukluft Mountains. Correspondence back and forth between Leutwein and Witbooi continues with increasing threats from Leutwein, who is still insisting on a "Protection Treaty"; eventually he presents Witbooi with an ultimatum on 9 May 1894: "I shall give you one more day; and if I still have no answer, launch a final attack" (quoted in Lau, 156). Throughout the summer of 1894, as Leutwein awaits reinforcements, they continue sparring. Witbooi matches Leutwein verbal blow for verbal blow, phrase by phrase, in a frantic exchange of letters, sometimes several in one day; Witbooi cleverly delays the threatened German attack by parsing each letter from Leutwein, calling him to account for his new demands, for new conditions needed for peace, and for the use of German cannons against the Nama during a period of truce. Again and again, Witbooi strategically foils Leutwein's timetable, while he awaits response to his own calls for reinforcements and the always much-needed, scarce ammunition (Lau, 162n198).

On 21 August 1894, Leutwein drops all pretense and starkly makes his final demand: "You *must* subject yourself, or I *must* fight you until you do" (emphasis in the original, quoted in Lau, 177). The Germans attack. Witbooi, outgunned, conducts a guerilla war; eventually, with enormous regret, he agrees to a ceasefire. He addresses Leutwein plaintively: "Now I ask: If I do according to your wish and word, shall my life, my land and all my possessions remain safely mine: and will my chieftaincy be safe?" (quoted in Lau, 180). He succumbs to the so-called Protection Treaty; the prose in his subsequent letters is poignant and dignified. The terms of an 1895 amendment to the treaty required that Witbooi troops fight *with the Germans against other indigenous groups*, and Witbooi, in his upright manner, abiding by the rules of war as he saw them, complies with this requirement. Leutwein described him in a report to Berlin as "the kind of man who . . . has a certain pride in keeping his word" (Steinmetz, *The Devil's Handwriting*, 159). The Witbooi served as trail guides and sharpshooters for the German military; Hendrik Witbooi recognized that he no longer had the power or weaponry to remain independent. For the next decade, from 1894 to 1904, Witbooi and his troops were accorded special privileges in return for his agreement to the "protection" of the Germans; Leutwein created a reservation for the Witbooi in 1898, allowed them to keep their weapons, and began to view them as "noble savages" rather than "barbaric" ones.[13]

But Berlin was again impatient with its leadership in GSWA by the early twentieth century. Rather than regulating the Herero, the Schutztruppe were engaged in a war with them, beginning 11 January 1904. The war dragged on without any significant German successes in the field; the Herero valiantly conducted a guerilla war against the Germans, who had superior weaponry but were less familiar with the geography and climate and had inefficient ox wagons delivering supplies: "The Herero, at first severely underrated by the Germans, turned out to be a formidable adversary" (Drechsler, 150). Leutwein continued his strategy of regular communication with the Herero, under the leadership of Samuel Maherero, in the hopes of a diplomatic settlement of the conflict. Despite his efforts to reassure Berlin, troop reinforcements were sent out from Hamburg.[14]

After five discouraging months, Emperor Wilhelm II appointed Lieutenant General Lothar von Trotha as supreme commander of the military forces in GSWA. Von Trotha was an experienced leader of colonial wars, having ruthlessly suppressed rebellions in German East Africa and China prior to his deployment to Southwest Africa. He had a reputation as a brutal and racist soldier. Arriving in GSWA in June 1904, von Trotha met with Leutwein, who pleaded for a military approach that would spare the Herero to serve as a labor force after the war. Unlike Leutwein, von Trotha had no patience for diplomacy and treaties. He was determined, from the outset, to exterminate the indigenous people in the service of making GSWA a permanent space for German settlement. His gaze upon the Herero and Nama was a genocidal, not an imperial, gaze; "noble savage" was not a concept that he entertained. "I know enough tribes in Africa.

They all have the same mentality insofar as they yield only to force. *It was and remains my policy to apply this force by unmitigated terrorism and even cruelty. I shall destroy the rebellious tribes by shedding rivers of blood and money.* Only thus will it be possible to sow the seeds of something new that will endure," declared von Trotha (emphasis mine, Drechsler, 154).

Because of his treaty with the Germans, Witbooi sends his own men into battle as allies of the Germans in the early days of the 1904 war with the Herero. The decisive Battle of Waterberg took place on 11 August 1904, in which the Germans, under the leadership of Lothar von Trotha, soundly defeat the Herero, killing many and driving the remaining men, women, and children into the Omaheke Desert to die of thirst or starvation. "The decision . . . to continue pushing [the Herero] further into the Omaheke marked a shift toward an explicitly genocidal strategy, since 'death from thirst did not distinguish between men, women and children'" (Steinmetz, *The Devil's Handwriting*, 193). Not satisfied with this "victory," as some heroic Herero managed to survive in the implacable desert and some even began to trickle back to their homelands, von Trotha issues his infamous order of annihilation—*Vernichtungsbefehl*—on 2 October 1904, making it absolutely clear that the Herero were targeted for extinction. "Although von Trotha arrived at this exterminationist policy independently after the Waterberg battle, it was approved at the highest levels" (Steinmetz, *The Devil's Handwriting*, 195). Though von Trotha was forced by the Berlin government to withdraw this order in December 1904, by then it was too late. Thousands of survivors had been imprisoned in camps where the death tolls were enormous—from starvation, forced labor, disease, and murder.

Hendrik Witbooi, just the day before the order of annihilation, writes wrenching letters to Hermanus van Wyk and other Nama chiefs, informing them of his intent to wage war against the Germans. Here is the full text, dated 1 October 1904:

> I send this letter to inform you of the following. As you are aware I have for a long time now been abiding under the law and in the law, following it, as have we all, in obedience—but also in the hope and in the faith that God our Father would in the fullness of time deliver us from the wretchedness of this world. So far I have borne the burden peacefully and meekly; whatever wrenched my heart, I have let pass, trusting in the Lord.
>
> I shall not write at length—merely this. My arms and shoulders have grown weary, and I perceive and believe that the time is now at hand when God the Father shall deliver the world by His grace.

When you read this letter, know that you shall appear as you must appear. I trust you understand this message well.

I tell you that I have given up my position. That is the main point: I have come to the end. I shall also write to the Major [Leutwein], to tell him what I have done; I have also written to all the other chiefs that the time has come. (quoted in Lau, 189–90)

Though his language here is somewhat coded, Witbooi makes it clear that he has chafed under German domination, that he has relied on his religion as a source of comfort, but that his patience has come to an end. He will no longer abide German law but will follow the Herero in rebelling. With the Herero defeated, as he had predicted a decade earlier, Witbooi breaks his treaty with the Germans and initiates a guerilla war against them that lasts until 1907. The eighty Nama men still serving with the German military at the time Witbooi declared war were imprisoned and eventually deported to Togo.

The final letter we have from Witbooi was penned in July 1905, in response to one from a German customs officer well known to him, urging Witbooi to make peace for the sake of his people and warning him that "you simply cannot prevail against the German nation" (quoted in Lau, 194). Ever the shrewd and honorable man, Witbooi responds: "To your remarks on peace I reply, don't lecture me like a schoolchild on your peace. You know very well that I was right there with you many times during your peace, and have come to see in it nothing but the *destruction of all our people*. For you have got to know me, and I have got to know you, through the hard experiences of my life. Here I conclude" (emphasis mine, 95). In this final salvo, he recognizes and refuses the racist trope of infantilization as well as the genocidal gaze that promises destruction of the Nama. With bravado, he declares his intent to fight on, recognizing that the Germans never meant "peace" in the way he and the world understand it. In the end, Witbooi is true to himself and the prerogatives of the Nama people. On 29 October 1905, at the age of seventy-five, he dies on the battlefield from a German bullet to his thigh.[15] "Because I did not create men, nor did you, but God alone. Thus I now sit in your hand, and peace will be at one and the same time my death and the death of my nation. For I know there is no refuge in you," he had written in that final letter. And his predictions, again, were realized: the Germans subjugated the Nama people; those they did not kill in battle were sent to labor camps and Shark Island. The figure often supplied for the number of Nama who perished at the hands of the Germans is 50 percent of the original 20,000. A genocide had destroyed the Witbooi people, who are one ethnicity within the Nama. Steinmetz writes that 1,600 had survived by the time of the signing of the peace treaty with the Germans in November 1905; as a result of imprisonment and exile to Cameroon, by 1912 only 38 Witbooi remained (Steinmetz, *The Devil's Handwriting*, 173–75).

After Witbooi's death, Theodor Leutwein, the German commander who had been at varying times both Witbooi's enemy and ally, wrote a tribute for him. While it is an unabashed statement of admiration, it also contains hints of the genocidal gaze, denigrating Africans, making the genocide seem inevitable:

> I still him see before me, the little Captain, ten years my faithful brother-in-arms.[16] Modest yet self-possessed, loyal yet not without political cunning, never deviating from what he considered his duty or his right, fully understanding the superior culture of the Whites, yet by no means always in love with those who purveyed it—a born leader and ruler: this was Witbooi, who would undoubtedly become an immortal in world history had not the fates decided him to be born to an insignificant African throne. He was the last national hero of a raced [sic] doomed to destruction. (quoted in Lau, 224)

Jan Kubas, Witness to the Genocidal Gaze

Jan Kubas was an indigenous African man of a racially mixed group known as the Griqua. The Griqua are descendants of unions between early Dutch settlers and southern African women, and they have lived for centuries in both South Africa and Namibia. In the nineteenth century, they spoke Dutch, were trained in military tactics, and provided with weapons in order to participate in skirmishes between the Dutch and British colonizers in southern Africa. Such training explains Jan Kubas's presence with German troops in GSWA; he describes here, in an interview done thirteen years later, the aftermath of the 1904 Battle of Hamakari (called Waterberg by the Germans) and the German treatment of Herero fleeing into the Omaheke Desert.

> I went with the German troops to Hamakari and beyond. . . . The Germans took no prisoners. They killed thousands and thousands of women and children along the roadsides. They bayoneted them and hit them to death with the butt ends of their guns. *Words cannot be found* to relate what happened; it was too terrible. They were lying exhausted and harmless along the roads and as the soldiers passed they simply slaughtered them in cold blood. Mothers holding babies at their breasts, little boys and little girls; old people too old to fight and old grandmothers, none received mercy; they were killed, all of them, and left to lie and rot on the veld for the vultures and wild animals to eat. They slaughtered until there were no more

Hereros left to kill. I saw this every day; I was with them. A few Hereros managed to escape in the bush and wandered about, living on roots and wild fruits. Von Trotha was the German General in charge. (emphasis mine, Silvester and Gewald, 117)

"Words cannot be found" calls to mind phrases so often uttered in Holocaust memoirs and histories. The experience of such unimaginable slaughter, whether on roadsides in Namibia or in the Auschwitz gas chambers, was, literally, that: unimaginable, let alone unspeakable. Kubas allows readers today to viscerally see the horrifying results of the genocidal gaze and von Trotha's implementation of it.

Jan Kubas's words were so evocative that they were adopted to serve as the title of a book: *Words Cannot Be Found: German Colonial Rule in Namibia*.[17] The British and the Germans had alternately collaborated in their efforts to suppress indigenous people in southern Africa and sparred with each other over land. In the early years of World War I, the British invaded GSWA and took control of the colony. As the war continued, and an Allied victory became more likely, the British began to take steps to prevent Germany from repossessing its colonies after the war concluded. Toward this end, the Brits put together almost fifty African eyewitness reports, including that of Kubas, as well as other key information condemning German rule in GSWA, and published them as the Blue Book. Some scholars, notably Brigitte Lau, have dismissed these eyewitness reports as "war propaganda," but editors Silvester and Gewald argue that "whilst this [political] context obviously determined the particular selection of evidence and timing of the compilation of a highly critical evaluation of German colonial rule in Namibia, this does not mean nor suggest that the evidence presented in the Blue Book should be judged to be false. The evidence should, instead, be judged on its own merits" (xxii).

Subsequently, due to persistent German complaints about the British depiction of their behavior as imperialists, the Blue Book was suppressed in 1926 and orders issued for all copies within the British Empire to be destroyed. "The dead of the Herero genocide and other atrocities were dismissed and forgotten in the interests of white settler reconciliation" (Silvester and Gewald, xxxii).[18] Its recent republication, in time for the centenary anniversary in 2004 of the Herero genocide, marks a crucial moment when African perspectives on the German colonial endeavor have been once again made available to scholars. As the editors remark in their introduction: "These statements form a rare documentation of African voices describing the encounter of African communities with a colonial power" (Silvester and Gewald, xiii). This text is also an invaluable resource for contemporary scholars seeking to understand the

African perspective/gaze on the German imperialists and *genocidaires* as well as the genocidal gaze itself.

African accounts of treatment after the 1904–7 war are equally shocking. Quoted in the Blue Book of 1918 is this testimony from Edward Fredericks, identified as the "son of the old Chief Joseph Fredericks and at present headman of the Bethany Hottentots," who stated on oath:

> In 1906, the Germans took me a prisoner after we had made peace and sent me with about a thousand other Hottentots to Aus, thence to Lüderitzbucht, and finally to Shark Island [described by historians today as a death camp (rather than a concentration camp) and thus a prototype for Auschwitz]. We were placed on the island, men, women, and children. We were beaten daily by the Germans, who used sjamboks. They were most cruel to us. We lived in tents on the island . . . lashes were given to us in plenty, and the young girls were violated at night by the guards. Six months later we went by boat to Swakopmund, and thence by train to Karibib.
>
> Lots of my people died on Shark Island. I put in a list of those who died. (*Note:* this list comprises 168 males, including the Chief, Cornelius Fredericks, 97 females, 66 children and also 18 Bushwomen and children) . . . but it is not complete. I gave up compiling it, as I was afraid we were all going to die. (Silvester and Gewald, 172, note in the original)

The consistency of German sexual violence against the indigenous people is confirmed by many accounts in the Blue Book as is the high death toll at Shark Island from starvation, the harsh weather conditions, disease, and severe overwork of the prisoners. Fritz Isaac, identified in the Blue Book as "son of the Under-Chief to the Witboois, Samuel Isaac," stated under oath: "After the war, I was sent to Shark Island by the Germans. We remained on the island one year. 3,500 Hottentots and Kaffirs were sent to the island and 193 returned. 3,307 died on the island" (Silvester and Gewald, 173).

The Glamour of Prospecting: A Sidelong Glance at the Genocidal Gaze

The Glamour of Prospecting is clearly meant as a tongue-in-cheek title by its author, Lt. Fred C. Cornell, O. B. E., for there is very little glamour in what he recounts.[19] This memoir, published in 1920, describes Cornell's adventures in German Southwest Africa, as well as in what was then known as the Cape Colony, and the Bechuanaland Protectorate (British territory); a helpful foldout map is tucked in at the back of the book. Cornell was in search of gold, copper, diamonds, and other precious gems. The time frame of his prospecting is 1907–14; the memoir concludes with an account of the opening volleys of World War I. The bulk of his account is devoted to tales of adventure in harsh landscapes—huge sand dunes, deep crevices, steep mountains, the Kalahari Desert—inhabited by a sparse indigenous population as well as leopards, gemshok, and scorpions. Thirst and hunger are frequent companions. Cornell, by his own admission, was largely unsuccessful in his prospecting: "The fruitless searches have been many, and I have often been called upon to make long and arduous trips where the quest of precious stones has proved nothing but a wild-goose chase" (1).

But the book, for twenty-first-century readers, provides brief glimpses[20] of the Germans, their colony, and the treatment of Herero and Nama in the immediate aftermath of the 1904–7 war and the genocide; given the rarity of the text, I have quoted extensively from it in the following pages. Cornell was British and thus a certain national antipathy existed between him and the Germans he encountered. Yet the purpose of his memoir, unlike the British Blue Book, is certainly not political; it is almost completely a wry account of his hardships during challenging and largely unsuccessful treks to find diamonds. Nonetheless, his depictions of Shark Island and of the cruelties and drunkenness of the German military are persuasive and revealing, describing men who embraced racial hierarchies as their worldview and accepted the "necessity" of exterminating those deemed barbaric and useless.

Cornell opens with a four-page summary of early twentieth-century Southwest Africa: "As German South-West Africa, now a Mandate of the Union of South Africa, will figure prominently in these pages, it may be as well to give a brief account of that extensive country" (5). He proceeds to describe the British decision, prior to the Treaty of Berlin, to claim Walfish Bay; the ongoing struggles prior to the arrival of the Germans between "the Damaras (also known as Hereros), a people of Bantu descent who came from the north, and the Namaquas, a Hottentot race who had gradually spread from the south" (6); the arrival of the Rhenish Missionary Society; and the German land grab beginning in 1885. The final three paragraphs of this background information are worth quoting in full for what they indicate about Cornell's attitudes and knowledge, and for their surprising conclusion:

> The Germans . . . set about making the most they could of Damaraland. But red tape, officialism, and their harsh and overbearing methods, hampered them in their attempt at colonization; moreover, much of the land was practically desert and up

to the time of the discovery of diamonds at Lüderitzbucht the country had been run at a loss, and there had been a determined attempt by the Socialists in the Reichstag to force its abandonment.

The Herero and Hottentot rebellion in 1903 [*sic*] dragged on for years, and cost the Germans much blood and treasure, for they found themselves utterly unable to cope with the extraordinary mobility of the native commandos. These, excelling in guerilla warfare, harassed them incessantly, and, although in vastly inferior numbers, gave the raw German troops—fresh to the country—endless trouble before they were subdued or captured.

Towards the end of this costly campaign the warfare was waged with extreme bitterness, and indeed *it ended in the virtual extermination of the Herero race*. (emphasis mine, 8)

Well before the word "genocide" came into existence, Cornell recognized what the Germans had done to the Herero: extermination. Here is a bald statement of the German intent to annihilate, of the genocidal gaze, published just thirteen years after the conclusion of that genocide. It is astonishing that *the Germans themselves would not admit this for almost a century to follow*. Cornell makes a further reference to genocide when describing the enormous German accumulation of weapons and supplies in the latter part of the war with the Herero and the Nama, and observes: "Considering that the two races were practically wiped out at the time peace was declared, it is difficult to understand what all these stores and munitions of war are needed for" (36).

Additional insights can be gleaned from Cornell's memoir regarding the animosity between the Boers and the Germans: "These Germans profess to despise the Boers, and many of the latter who fled into German territory rather than accept British rule after the Boer War had been very glad to return to the protection of the Union Jack" (38). Later, Cornell cites the example of a Boer man he met en route who, "having fought to the last in the Boer War, had refused to live under British rule, and had trekked to German West and there taken up land and settled down. And now, after years of galling and irksome submission to the German régime of red tape and officialism, he had been exasperated beyond all endurance by some sample of German 'justice,' and was trekking back" (81). Further elucidation from Cornell reveals the cause of such German attitudes: "Yet these men [the Boers] are looked down upon as an inferior race by the Germans" (42). Racial hierarchies, specking out not only indigenous Africans but white Africans, informed German minds. These passages are also of significant help when reading Gustav Frenssen's *Peter Moor*, which contains a passage involving Boers that is often misread by scholars. I will revisit this issue in chapter 2.

In his encounters with indigenous people in southern Africa, Cornell saw strong evidence of the memory they held of German treatment during the war. Prospecting in Bechuanaland, Cornell "found a few Hottentots, who made a beeline for the hills the moment they saw us.... They had taken us for Germans, and their actions spoke volumes as to how they fear the white man on the other side of the border. They were all refugees from Damaraland, who had fled after the brave fight put up by Marengo[21] against the Germans had finally ended in their defeat. In this remote spot . . . they had existed unmolested, seeing scarcely a white man a year, yet always in fear lest their old taskmasters should appear on the scene" (194–95). After further trekking in this area, which Cornell describes as "a fastness for the guerilla bands of Hottentots that put up such a game fight against the overwhelming odds of the Germans in the 'Hottentot Rebellion' of 1903–1906" (202), he happens upon a horrific sight:

> On one of the flat-topped mountains well within German territory we came upon the remains of a Hottentot bivouac, evidently dating from the time when Marengo and Simon Cooper fought the Germans here. Scattered about among the bushes were odds and ends of clothing, German ration—tins, etc., and in one heap I found the gilt hilt of a German sword, and a pair of binoculars.... In one of the ravines where a thick bush known as *haak dorn* (hook thorn) abounded we found more gruesome relics in the shape of skeletons, firmly entangled in the thickest part of the bush, where they had apparently been thrown as living men.
>
> The Hottentots claim that in this unhappy war of reprisals the Germans, exasperated by the protracted resistance of the natives, used to treat all wounded men who fell into their hands with horrible severity; breaking their bones, and throwing them bodily into these thorn bushes, from which a sound man could scarcely escape, being a favorite method of disposing of them.
>
> I have had this told me by numbers of Hottentots who fought in this war, and have seen the skeletons in several places where fighting took place. The Germans claim that German wounded were thus treated by the Hottentots, but the rags of clothing clinging to the bones I saw were not part of a German uniform. (203–4)

Here Cornell's witness testimony confirms the increasing German frustration with both the harsh geography and the guerilla style of warfare that combined to prevent a nimble German victory. It is such frustration that contributes to the evolution of the imperial gaze into the genocidal gaze.

Cornell also saw German treatment of the Herero in the aftermath of the war. He visited a German police station on the border of the Orange River and was impressed with the "extremely comfortable" quarters (220), the "queer pets" such as baboons, monkeys, and wildcats, and the "experimental garden" including an apiary created there by the Germans.

> But any admiration I felt for them and their work died a sudden death when I walked through that same garden and found that the work was being done by Herero prisoners working in chains. Not light chains, but heavy manacles on legs and arms, and neck and waist, manacles that were never taken off till they knocked them off when they died. These men, as far as I could gather, were "prisoners of war" only—not criminals in any sense of the word as we understand it. I am no negrophile, but German methods of treating natives are far too heartless for "the likes of me." (220)

German contempt, not reserved for the indigenous Africans and the Boers, extended to a Jewish storekeeper in Ukamas, a German township that Cornell visited. Forced to remain there for several days while his horse underwent medical tests, Cornell observed the behavior of German military in the bar and their unceasing harassment of the Jewish man: "the officers . . . drank to excess in front of their men, and [their] intolerable treatment of the Englishman [the Jewish storekeeper] behind the bar used to compel me to get out. . . . Their crowning witticism would come when he dived down beneath the counter for more beer for them, when at a signal all four of them would bring their riding-whips down on the rickety counter with a crash close to his head . . . in any other army in the world they would have been cashiered, for never a day passed but that they were vilely and blatantly drunk in full sight of their men" (315–16).

The final passage I wish to quote is arguably the most devastating, as it describes Shark Island, the death camp established by the Germans on the coast of their colony after the war. There are very few contemporaneous eyewitness descriptions of the camp,[22] and as it is seen now by many historians as a precursor of Nazi death camps, I quote the passage in full:

> Stuurmann also gave me much interesting detail as to the terrible treatment meted out to the unfortunate natives, both Herero and Hottentot, who were unlucky enough to fall into the hands of the Germans.
>
> I had seen something of this myself, and had heard more from ex-German soldiers themselves, who with extraordinary callousness used to show whole se-

ries of illustrated postcards, depicting wholesale executions and similar gruesome doings to death of these poor natives. One of these, that enjoyed great vogue at the time, showed a line of ten Hottentots dangling from a single gallows, some still standing on the packing cases with a noose round their necks, waiting for the soldiers to kick their last standing place away; some kicking and writhing in the death struggle, for the short drop did not break their necks, but only strangled them slowly, and one having a German soldier hanging on to his legs to finish the work more quickly. And each and every German soldier in the photo was striking an attitude and smirking towards the camera in pleasurable anticipation of the fine figure he would cut when the photo was published. [It might be noted here that very similar photos of Nazi soldiers, pleased with their grisly work, are common in German family albums; see mention of this by German novelist W. G. Sebald as a critical moment in his awareness of the Holocaust.][23] This, I repeat, was only one of the many that enjoyed a big sale in German South-West for the delectation of admiring friends in the Fatherland. Absolutely no mercy was shown to these unfortunate creatures: they were made to dig big graves and were shot down by the hundreds beside them [this is reminiscent of the Nazi Einsatzgruppen squads] whilst the whole remnant of both races who escaped this fate were exterminated in the detention-camps at Lüderitzbucht and Swakopmund. Towards the end of the long, dragging war, the Germans conceived the plan of sending Herero prisoners captured in the north for internment to Lüderitzbucht, where they were strangers to the country and where escape was hopeless, whilst the Hottentots captured in the south were sent north to Swakopmund.

There is a small low-lying promontory in Lüderitz Bay known as Shark Island, and here the Herero prisoners were crowded in thousands, shelterless, with no proper supply of food or water: and here, huddled together like penguins, they died like flies.

Often on a blazing day, such as is common in Lüderitzbucht, they received no water whatever, either having been forgotten, or the supply having failed; the food (?) supplied them was never sufficient for the tithe of them, and they often fought like wild animals and killed each other to obtain it. There were also a large number caged in a wire enclosure on the beach; these were slightly better off, as, although they received no rations from the military in charge of them, a few of their number were let out each morning and went ravenously foraging in the refuse-buckets, bringing what offal they could back to their starving fellow-prisoners. Cold—for the nights are often bitterly cold there—hunger, thirst, exposure, disease, and madness claimed scores of victims every day, and cartloads of their bodies were every day carted over to the back beach, buried in a few inches of sand at low tide, and as the tide came in the bodies went out, for the sharks.

Now Stuurmann and the other men who told me these things were no negrophiles (a Boer as a rule has an excellent idea as to how to keep a native in his place as the white man's inferior), but so terrible had been the treatment of these natives by the Germans that even these case-hardened transport drivers spoke of what they had seen with the utmost horror and abhorrence. Yet these men are looked down upon as an inferior race by the Germans, who themselves, as far as the troops and officials in German South-West are concerned, are utterly devoid of all humanity when dealing with natives. I saw much of the trait myself later; it is unpleasant and distasteful, and bodes but ill for the future relations of white and black in the German colonies.

I was by no means sorry to leave Lüderitzbucht, for during the whole of this brief stay it blew incessantly and the air was a sort of semi-solid mixture of whirling sand, that cut and stung, and choked and blinded, and permeated every orifice and crevice, and generally made life utterly unbearable. When this prevailing wind reaches a certain violence, the whole country practically gets up and walks, big sand-dunes shift along and others come after them, like the waves of a slowly moving sea; wide stretches of hard land are denuded of every grain of sand, and others buried deep in it, and it is a curious fact that these storms actually blow diamonds! (40–43)

Until 2005, no significant account of Shark Island and other German camps had been published; short references such as those I have quoted here were all scholars had. In that year, however, a book with the chilling title *"The Angel of Death Has Descended Violently among Them": Concentration Camps and Prisoners of War in Namibia, 1904–1908* appeared, providing at last a detailed and shocking account of these camps. Casper Erichsen, the author, recounts the origin of the study in his preface: as a student, he had toured Shark Island in 1998 as part of field trip that he and other history students took with Jeremy Silvester and Robert Gordon. Upon his return to Windhoek, he "was still haunted by what I had seen in Lüderitz. I therefore decided to read up on the history of Shark Island, only to find out that there was none" (xv–xvi). He chose the topic for his master's thesis, and this book is the end product of his research, which was conducted largely in the Namibian archives. That was no simple task, as "in 1915, the German Colonial Administration had these files [of the camps] destroyed to avoid them falling in the hands of the rapidly approaching Union troops" (xvi). The Germans took a similar approach with concentration and death camp files during the Third Reich: as the Soviet Army approached Auschwitz, for example, as many files as possible were hastily burned to destroy evidence. Erichsen notes with particular bitterness that "the history of Namibia's concentration camps has long been overlooked and largely forgotten in the existing historiography about the 1904–1908 anti-colonial wars" (3); such "oblivion" has been termed "colonial amnesia" or "colonial aphasia" by scholars.[24]

Erichsen opens his account of the camps by supplying necessary background to the 1904–7 war and evidence for what I have termed "the genocidal gaze" of the Germans. He quotes, for example, the pronouncement of von Trotha that I have used as an epigraph to this chapter, in which the German commander makes clear his intention to exterminate the indigenous people (7). "German sentiments towards their adversaries were characterized by a general belief that the enemy was inhuman and savage" (14). Erichsen delineates the routine killing of noncombatants, that is, women and children, by the Germans, a practice that *precedes* the infamous extermination order of von Trotha of 2 October 1904. This underscores the gaze of the military as genocidal: *all* indigenous people were considered subhuman. Thus, such slaughter was not a military tactic but a belief, an ideology, that these "subhumans" must be cleansed from the land. It should be noted that, in sharp contrast, even after such killing by the Germans, the Nama troops were instructed by Hendrik Witbooi that only the fighting soldiers were to be killed; women and children were to be spared (18). The Herero, too, specifically spared women and children.

Erichsen provides grisly statistics about postconflict deaths of the Herero and Nama. Though von Trotha had his wrist slapped by the German government and was made to rescind the extermination order in December 1904, mortality rates in the camps were so high that, essentially, the order was still in effect (26). With the assistance of many missionaries, von Trotha's troops began a campaign to round up surviving Herero from the bush; this campaign was carried out with brutality (and sometimes with false promises) and succeeded in bringing in and imprisoning in concentration camps in Windhoek, Okahandja, Karibib, Swakopmund, and the death camp at Lüderitz "at least 13,000 Hereros in a period of ten months" in 1905 (27). The two camps in Windhoek held a total of 7,000 prisoners, when the town itself housed only 2,500. Thus, providing sufficient food and facilities presented a serious challenge; indeed, the camps had no sanitation or medical facilities. Sick prisoners, deemed unfit for labor, were simply allowed to die.

Imprisoned women were often forcibly taken to town to serve as laundry women, domestic helpers, and general laborers. There, they were raped by soldiers and settlers. "The casual use of prisoners for purposes of sex was so rife that the official medical report of the war ... described sexually transmitted diseases as a major threat to Windhoek's white population"; of course, the report blamed such diseases on "the natives" (47).

The lasciviousness of German soldiers is indicated by a photograph Erichsen includes of two bare-breasted women and four children. The caption reads: "Children and young women captured by the *Schutztruppe*. The girls' dresses have been ripped off to expose their breasts. In the background is a burning wagon" (62). Another such photo of a bare-breasted woman appears on page 85, with the caption "German hand-colored postcard, satisfying male desires." As evidence that the genocidal gaze objectifies women as sexual objects, to be used and then used up, Erichsen elucidates: "German male fantasies of submissive black women were celebrated in numerous publications including a series of semi-pornographic images of black women in GSWA sent as postcards to Germany and otherwise distributed in the colony. Apart from their sexual purposes, such images were symbols and affirmations of colonial power exerted over African women who would physically have been unable to control their own representation" (86). Further instances of such photos, where it is clearly visible that the women have been forced to pose after having their blouses removed, can be seen on pages 91 and 92. As these images demonstrate, the genocidal gaze is captured *in* (when soldiers are present) *the photograph itself and by the act of the photographer* gazing upon, undressing, and virtually raping his subjects; these women have been granted no humanity. Paradoxically, while their sexuality is hyperemphasized, they have disappeared as women, as people. Rather, they exist in the black-and-white image only to "prove" the power and racial superiority of the photographer who has used his camera to render them painfully conscious of their captivity.[25]

As would be the situation in the Nazi ghettos and *lagers*, the provision of food to the prisoners was intentionally insufficient for them to maintain health and, ultimately, life. The per diem included: ½ kilogram of canned meat (twice a week only) or flour; ½ kilogram of rice or flour (and Erichsen notes that rice was a completely unknown foodstuff to the Africans, who most often had no pot in which to cook it) and .030 kilograms of salt (50). Scurvy, pneumonia, influenza, and sexually transmitted diseases were the most common illnesses. Like prisoners in Nazi camps, Shark Island prisoners who were deemed capable of labor were set to work building a railroad, shoring up an embankment for the tracks, pulling heavy wagons, carrying heavy rail ties, doing laundry. Women, too, were expected to undertake hard labor, for example, carrying sacks of grain weighing 100–160 pounds, despite their debilitated condition (58). Many accounts tell of women staggering and falling under such loads, only to be whipped by the guards. Mortality rates were roughly equivalent for male and female prisoners. Erichsen concludes, "The POWs were not afforded any means of improving their own respective situations and they were therefore totally at the mercy of the Colonial Government, which must subsequently be singled out as the responsible party in the mass dying of African prisoners between 1904–1908" (64).

Erichsen provides a detailed description of Shark Island, its geographic features and the climate conditions there. He includes rare, recently discovered photographs of the camp and its inmates. He delineates the medical experiments that took place there and the fact that heads were taken from dead prisoners to be shipped to Germany for study, the aim of which was to "prove" that Africans were on a lower evolutionary level than whites, a central tenet of the genocidal gaze. In some instances, the skin was scraped from the heads prior to shipping; this agonizing work was done by female prisoners who "were forced to boil the severed heads of concentration camp inmates and then scrape them to the bone with shards of glass" (142–43).[26] Steinmetz concludes that at Shark Island, "there is a systematic pattern of abuse that is suggestive of a desire to kill or cause 'serious bodily or mental harm to members of the group'—criteria for genocide according to the United Nations Convention on the Prevention and Punishment of the Crime of Genocide" (*The Devil's Handwriting*, 174).

The final African voice presented for the reader's consideration is drawn from a book called *Warriors, Leaders, Sages, and Outcasts in the Namibian Past* (1992).[27] A dozen oral histories of the events in precolonial Southwest Africa, as well as in GSWA from 1904 to 1907, were gathered in the 1980s by the Michael Scott Oral Records Project; all of the speakers are indigenous Namibians. They recount the stories that have been passed down from generations, and a good deal of emphasis is placed on the tradition of naming these generations and offering praise of them. In the interstices, African observations of the German Schutztruppe can be gleaned.

One chapter, narrated by Willy Njanekua and Kasisanda Muuondjo in 1986, includes an account of a series of what the Herero viewed as "clever tricks" the Germans played on them (161). These included sending the able-bodied men to Johannesburg and Cape Town to work in the mines; the expectation of the Herero was that these men would return with significant cash. Instead, most of them died. Then the Germans approached "the old men asking for their children to be sent to school. The aim of sending the children to school was to teach them to abandon their national culture and to forsake their customs. . . . They were dressed in European clothes and told not to eat or drink whatever is eaten or drunk by the Hereros at the holy fires" (161). The children never returned to their tribal cultures.

In order to confiscate the guns of the Hereros, the Germans told them that the guns must be immunized, just like the Herero cattle had been against rinderpest. "Do you hear? That was how our land was taken from us. . . . When the Germans saw that all the guns of the Hereros had been confiscated, they began to harass the Hereros. They saw a Herero woman collecting wood and shot her, declaring they had mistaken her for a baboon" (162). Perceiving the Herero as subhuman, as the equivalent of animals to be eradicated, was a central tenet of the genocidal gaze. Also recounted was another German method for acquiring land: "They gave Samuel strong drink and when they saw that he was drunk, they asked for land to live on. . . . They offered him money and boxes of brandy and bags of sugar, mealie meal, rice and coffee" (162). A footnote to this chapter tells the reader: "Interestingly Governor Leutwein himself exposed these manipulative attempts to disarm the Hereros by administrative measures rather than direct force" (172). The footnote includes a lengthy quotation from Leutwein's memoir, *Elf jahre Gouverneur in DSWA*.

The impact of African voices in this chapter provides evidence of both the German imperial and then genocidal gaze in GSWA and the African awareness of, and resistance to, such gazes. Hendrik Witbooi's archive is a rich source for understanding his mind-set, his determination, and his verbal acuity in sparring with German officials. His decision to include various texts from those officials in his archive provides the reader with examples of the demeaning and deceitful language directed toward him and other indigenous people in GSWA. Corroboration of the treatment of the Herero and Nama is supplied by both Fred Cornell's memoir and the later scholarship of Casper Erichsen. As we turn now to a German colonial novel, focalized through a fictional soldier fighting in the 1904 battles against the Herero, the background provided here on the genocidal gaze and African resistance will serve as a counterpoint to Gustav Frenssen's novel.

TWO

The Genocidal Gaze in Gustav Frenssen's *Peter Moor's Journey to Southwest Africa*

> Those literary texts which appear before the First World War, concerning the events of January 1904–1908, end with the annihilation of the Herero.... The murder of the "natives" is seen as a necessary aim of the civilizing colonial mission, and the way this is carried out is even sometimes described as a "work of art."
>
> MEDARDUS BREHL

Gustav Frenssen's *Peter Moor's Journey to Southwest Africa* (1906, translated into English in 1908) is often described as the quintessential German colonial novel by readers and critics. Sander Gilman, in an early (1978) article on German colonial literature, noted that *Peter Moor* is the "most typical of the German colonial historical novels, and the one work cited in all the critical literature on this topic."[1] Identification of *Peter Moor* as a touchstone of German colonial attitudes has continued in the intervening four decades since Gilman's pronouncement. Purporting to be a memoir by a German soldier sent out in 1904 to German Southwest Africa, the novel is based on the memoirs and reminiscences of German men who had done just that; Frenssen himself, never having traveled to Africa, relied on these accounts for his work of imagination. In its review, just after the German release and before the English translation was made available the following year, the *New York Times* described the text as "the depicting of conditions brought about by nature and made worse by *revengeful barbarians* which no *civilized* or highly trained army could be expected to combat" (emphasis mine).[2] While this language is likely to offend readers in the twenty-first century, it is nonetheless an accurate account of the *representation* of indigenous people by Europeans in the nineteenth century. The Germans were no exception: their perception of the Herero and Nama in their colony in Southwest Africa was reductive and unforgiving.

In this chapter, I will be reading *Peter Moor* as a paradigm of the evolution of an imperial gaze into a genocidal gaze. In the last chapter, we explored the resisting gaze of Hendrik Witbooi, a Nama leader and revolutionary against German rule in Southwest Africa. Gustav Frenssen's novel enables us to look in the other direction: to "see" the inhabitants of this rather desolate land as the Germans saw them. The novel is focalized through the eyes of fictional character Peter Moor, who joins the naval corps shortly after finishing high school. When he learns that "in southwest Africa the blacks, like cowards, have treacherously murdered all the farmers and their wives and children," he volunteers to be sent out to GSWA to fight.[3] "I was glad," he tells the reader, "to be revenged on a heathen people for the German blood that had been spilled" (7). In his account of his subsequent travel to Africa, he consistently depicts the Herero and Nama through an imperial lens: as barbaric, as uncivilized, as subhuman. Then, as he engages in battle and listens to the ideology of his officers and chaplain, his gaze becomes genocidal.

Gustav Frenssen's novel reveals much about how the Germans perceived the Herero and Nama whom they slaughtered between 1904 and 1907, as well as how they envisioned the German colony that would follow the "cleansing" of the land of "inconvenient" and "uncivilized" indigenous people. Specifically, they would impose notions of German statehood; those Herero and Nama who survived the genocide, many of whom were incarcerated in camps, would serve as forced laborers to build the new society. This vision of a German community was foreclosed by World War I, during which the Germans lost control of Southwest Africa; the genocidal gaze then becomes the blueprint for Nazi predations against Europe, and against the Jews and others deemed "biologically inferior."

Gustav Frenssen: Lutheran Pastor, Author, Nazi

Gustav Frenssen was born in the small town of Barlt, about fifty miles northwest of Hamburg in Holstein, Germany, on 19 October 1863. While early biographers Wilhelm Alberts (1922) and Numme Numsen (1933 and 1938) described his childhood as happy, even idyllic,[4] more recent accounts point to problematic relationships with both parents. His mother "hovered throughout her life on the psychotic boundary," often contemplating suicide, and his father, a cabinet maker, was "carefree and optimistic, but impractical and economically untalented" (Braun, 456n28). An introverted and highly sensitive child, Frenssen did not thrive in his *Volkschule*, nor when he transferred to the *Lateinschule* in a neighboring town where "he was three years older than his classmates and for eight years he was subjected . . . to the humiliating experience of '*Freitische*'" (Braun, 456).[5]

Between 1886 and 1890, Frenssen studied theology at universities in Tübingen, Berlin, and Kiel, and in 1890, he married Anna Walter, the daughter of a teacher. He devoted twelve years to serving as a Lutheran pastor in rural congregations in Hennstedt and Hemme. During this period (1890–1902), he began to write, publishing both fiction and a collection of "village sermons." His breakthrough as a writer came in 1901 when he published *Jörn Uhl*, an *Entwicklungsroman*, or novel of personal development. Most of his subsequent fiction can be thus categorized; he is also considered to be a writer of *Heimatkunst* or regional literature.[6] By 1911, *Jörn Uhl* had sold a quarter of a million copies.[7] His earnings and fame enabled him to resign from his pastorate and write full-time. "He is now the admired and much loved preacher-poet of Germany," declared Effie Louise Pratt in her 1925 book.[8]

In 1906, Frenssen published *Peter Moors Fahrt nach Südwest*. Like his earlier works such as *Jörn Uhl*, which sold 130,000 copies in its first year (compared with Thomas Mann's *Buddenbrooks*, also published in 1901 and selling fewer than 1,000 copies), this new novel was guaranteed success (Brehl, 104). *Peter Moor* joined a growing number of such books, "portrayals and interpretations of the events of 1904–1908 . . . aimed at a broad middle-class audience. . . . [*Peter Moor*] was the most successful contemporary publication on the Herero uprising and the text can therefore serve as representative" (Brehl, 102). The novel was also published in Sweden, Denmark, and the Netherlands.[9]

A contemporary of Frenssen, Herman Babson, an American professor at Purdue University who edited an abridged version of *Peter Moor* in 1914, had access to a statement Frenssen produced at the request of his publisher, Dr. G. Grote of Berlin. The statement details his motive for writing *Peter Moor* and his manner of accumulating accurate information for the book. I include here Babson's summary, published in his introduction, of Frenssen's document:

> During the Herero Rebellion Frenssen had followed the campaign with the greatest possible interest and sympathy; and aggrieved that his countrymen at home, while looking "with fixed eyes at the happenings in the Far east" (the Russo-Japanese War was then in progress) should be heartlessly indifferent toward the fighting and suffering of soldiers in Southwest Africa, he set himself the task and duty of writing for the German people an account which when read as an artistic whole would arouse patriotism and awaken a feeling of heartfelt thanks for those who

served their country so well. Frenssen had never been to South Africa, consequently it was necessary for him thoroughly to acquaint himself not only with the country, its physical features, its fauna and flora, its native inhabitants etc., but also with the life of the German solider in the field. Complying with the author's request three men willingly offered their services in the way of giving for days at a time exhaustive answers to questions and of permitting him to read journals and letters. The three who aided Frenssen thus were: *Generaloberst* Dr. Schian, *Leutnant* Klinger, and a student named Michaelsen. Each of these men was embodied in the story, the *Generaloberst* exactly as he was in real life, *Leutnant* Klinger as a world-wide rover, who during the campaign fights with the Germans, and the student Michaelsen as *Der Einjärige* Heinrich Gelsen. Two or three non-commissioned officers were also questioned; and the information obtained in this way, coupled with the results of exhaustive reading of reports, newspaper items, and the study of illustrations, gave Frenssen the right to say: "I no longer felt that I was relating things I had not myself seen and experienced." (Babson introduction, xii–xiii)

Frenssen's effort to present an accurate account from the military perspective and to valorize the German soldier in GSWA met with critical acclaim and enormous popular success. "It would therefore be difficult to exaggerate the significance of this text for creating a widely-shared view of the events of 1904 in the conservative middle class and liberal circles" (Brehl, 104). Frenssen's depiction of Peter Moor and his fellow soldiers was thus highly influential on the German population; it suggested an acceptance of racist hierarchies that could ultimately lead to genocide. In 1912, Frenssen was nominated for the Nobel Prize in Literature.

A glance at reviews of *Peter Moor* when it was initially released reveals, however, that praise was not unanimous. That of the *New York Times*, which hails the novel, has already been mentioned. The April 1907 issue of *Journal of the Royal African Society* is also enthusiastic: "It is not often that fiction is reviewed in our pages, but the latest production of the popular Holstein novelist calls for notice on account of its subject." Describing the book as a "plain unvarnished narrative of a young man . . . who volunteered for service in Hereroland" and spent "nine months of privation and suffering in desert marches and typhus camps," the review goes on to declare that "bald simplicity . . . characterises the book all through; there are passages where it becomes epic by sheer force of truth and sincerity."[10] As one might expect, however, the review that appeared in the 1908 issue of the *Advocate of Peace* has a quite different take: "This book might well have been entitled 'The Story of the German Madness in Southwest Africa.'" The anonymous reviewer states that a reading will lead one to question how a supposedly smart and humane nation such as Germany could have "gone into an enterprise so full of insaneness, injustice, cruelty and loathsomeness as this." Reading the text from the perspective of advocating peace, and against the grain of Frenssen's intention, the reviewer concludes: "Whether intended to be so or not, the story is a scathing arraignment of the iniquity and moral loathsomeness of war, and particularly of 'civilized war' against native peoples."[11] Frenssen has failed to convince this reviewer of the justification of German aggression on the basis of racial superiority.

Peter Moors Fahrt nach Südwest

Peter Moor appeared in 1908 in the English translation as *Peter Moor's Journey to Southwest Africa*. The translator, Margaret May Ward, provides a "Translator's Preface" to the text that reads as follows:

> I have always felt that all war stories dwell too much on the glory and glamour of war, and too little on the hardships and horrors and the unnecessary cruelty of it; and so when I read a little German book about the Southwest African war of 1903–04, I wished that every one else might read it. To me it was absorbingly interesting and beautifully told. This summer I have translated it in the hope that it will affect other people as it affected me.
>
> Margaret May Ward
> Temple, New Hampshire, 1907

Also included in the paratextual material of the 1908 translation is this further elucidation of Ward's intention: "This book is dedicated with tender and loving memories to the cause which the translator hoped it might aid, the cause for which she was always ready to give her abounding strength, and to the service of which she brought the wisdom of a loyal nature and a noble mind,—to the cause of PEACE." This dedication is signed A. H. W., presumably the Andrew Henshaw Ward who holds the copyright. His relationship to the translator is unspecified.[12] Despite both Wards' hope that this novel might engender peace in the world, the *Advocate of Peace* review seems a far more accurate prophecy. Ward's dedication supplants the dedication in the original text, which has been eliminated in the translation. That dedication reads: "Der deutschen Jugend, die in Südwestafrika gefallen ist, zu ehrendem Gedächtnis" (To the honorable memory of the German youth who fell in Southwest Africa). One can see why this dedication was quietly excised by Ward, given her focus on peace.

This paratextual material in the translation, which focuses on the hardships endured by German soldiers and the notion of peace, is a telling indicator of reader reception in the early twentieth century and gives twenty-first-century readers a kind of backhanded insight into the text they are about to read. A desire to valorize the genocidal behavior of the Germans is at the heart of Frenssen's novel. He did indeed focus on the challenges facing German soldiers: the lack of water and food, typhoid, dysentery, and the unforgiving geographical features of Southwest Africa, thus *excluding any such sympathy for the suffering of the indigenous people*. The notion of "peace" occurs in the text only to the extent that such a settlement would allow Peter Moor to leave what he viewed as a godforsaken land and return to his beloved *Heimat*. The *New York Times*, too, noted in its review that this is the focus of Frenssen's text: "The chromatic dreams . . . of [Peter Moor] vanish when he reaches the desert coast, to find himself nearly baked alive by day and frozen at night, and to wander about aimlessly without chart or vestige of a road, running the gauntlet constantly between ambushes of natives who stop at no kind of cruel and uncivilized warfare to repel the hated invaders."

A contemporary of Frenssen's declared him to be "a man standing amidst the movements of modern times [who] devotes his life to bettering the life of mankind. In his artistic work he always starts from decisive problems of German life: he recognizes those problems which demand solution, a solution which must be attempted now, in this place, in this very moment, be it an economical, a political, a social or a religious one. Thus his fundaments are the principles of ethics" (E. Pratt, 52). If his focus is ethics, they are an ethics anathema to our twenty-first-century sensibilities. Should the contemporary reader search the text for evidence of ambivalence about the imperial presence and military mission in Southwest Africa, specifically about the genocidal gaze, that search will yield precious few passages. The one such passage, often quoted by critics to demonstrate that there *were* Germans who raised ethical questions, is *not* spoken by the fictional soldier Peter Moor, through whom the narrative is focalized, but rather by the wagoners who accompanied the military. These were a mix of "old Africans," some of whom "had been already ten years or more in the country" (76), and Boers, that is, descendants of Dutch settlers whom the German army had employed to bring provisions to the interior (53).

Sitting around the fire with Peter in the evening, they shared their doubts about the German enterprise and speculated about the causes of the uprising: "They [the indigenous people] were ranchmen and proprietors, and we [early settlers] were there to make them landless working men; and they rose up in revolt. They acted in just the same way that North Germany did in 1813. This is their struggle for independence" (77). Such a comment would have been anathema to the German military, who refused to acknowledge any equation or common humanity between Europeans and indigenous Africans. The discussion continued as another wagoner pointed out the profound contradiction between the message of the German missionaries, "You are our brothers," and the actions of the soldiers in stealing land and cattle: "It is a ridiculous and crazy project. Either it is right to colonize, that is, to deprive others of their rights, to rob and to make slaves, or it is just and right to Christianize, that is, to proclaim and live up to brotherly love" (78). The conversation turned to what would be required to convert the indigenous people to actual "brothers": "They may become that after a century or two. They must first learn what we ourselves have discovered—to stem water and to make wells, to dig and plant corn, to build houses and to weave clothing" (78). This statement reveals the racist hierarchy of the imperial gaze, which often rested on the belief that indigenous people were stuck at an earlier stage of evolution and would need decades to catch up to Europeans. Finally, "one old freight-carrier, who mixed many English and Dutch words in his speech [clearly a Boer], said 'The Germans are probably useful as soldiers and farmers but they understand nothing about the government of colonies. They want this and they want that'" (79).

Thus the conversation concludes. It is significant that these comments, raising doubt about the ethics of German colonization, come *not from the German soldiers* themselves; rather, Frenssen put them in the mouths of the "old Africans" and Boers. The Germans and Boers were often in conflict with one another in Southwest Africa, so by no means can these observations made by the Boers be taken as genuine questioning by the Germans of their imperial goals. Indeed, the Eurocentric Germans placed the Boers in a lower station of the racist hierarchy than themselves. Peter Moor makes no comment about this conversation, no acknowledgment of the validity of these ideas, no expression of ambivalence on his part. Nor does Frenssen interrogate, through other means, the imperial gaze that "justifies" German theft of the land belonging to the various tribal groups in Namibia.

Instead, Moor's narrative is replete with numerous racist and stereotyped depictions of the Herero, the Nama, and the other indigenous people whom he encountered, as well as of Africa itself. Here I can only include a few of the most egregious examples. En route to Africa, Peter worries: "It made us angry to think that the insurrection might perhaps be subdued before we arrived. . . . We wanted at least to land, so that afterwards we could tell at home about the African forests, the herds of monkeys and antelopes, and the straw huts under the palms" (21). As his ship neared Liberia, Peter heard a "stupid shrieking" and discovered "over both sides [of the ship] were climbing like cats and writhing like snakes, the negroes . . . tall, black, and half naked, with large exposed teeth and wild, laughing human eyes" (31). With his imperial gaze, Peter watched them in his free time and noted "how they squatted around the great pots of food, stuffing quantities of rice into their mouths with their fingers, and devouring with their great, beast-like, crunching teeth their meat, bones, and all indiscriminately" (34). Such bestial imagery is a commonplace in the text and in racial hierarchies. Moor concluded: "These blacks are quite, quite different from us, so that there could be at heart no possible understanding or relationship between us. There must always be misunderstandings instead" (34). It is with such an attitude that Peter Moor arrived in Southwest Africa.[13] Regrettably, his encounters with Herero and Nama in the ten months he spends in the German colony do nothing to redeem his rigid attitude. He viewed the Herero and Nama as bestial, as subhuman. Gradually, his gaze turned from imperial to genocidal, of which the reader gets hints in this passage. Peter envisioned no possibility of a "relationship between us" and he developed neither sympathy nor respect for the enemy soldiers. In fact, he mentioned them very little in his narrative, as if they were beneath inclusion in his tale of German valor.

Nor are such attitudes toward Africans unique to Peter Moor and his fellow soldiers. Herman Babson, who as mentioned published an abridged version of *Peter Moor* for college students, included this description of the indigenous people of Namibia in his introduction:

> The original inhabitants are the Nama and the Bushmen. The latter are, culturally speaking, the lowest of all the tribes. The Nama stand much higher in this respect, many of the blacks being clothed like Europeans[!]. Most of the Nama are well-armed, but they are of a changeable disposition, are slothful, and are given to heavy drinking. . . . The Herero . . . are big, sturdy fellows, very muscular, and excellent cattle-raisers and herders. . . . As is true of many of the uncivilized or partly civilized tribes, the Herero are greedy, cruel, and deceitful. (xxi–xxii)[14]

Babson's racist commentary is an apt summary, from a century ago, of the imperial gaze: using the metaphor of hierarchy, he arrays the indigenous people along the lower rungs, assuming, of course, that the Germans always stand at the top.

Peter's initial description of the landscape of Africa revealed his perception of it as forbidding and hostile to civilization. The surf is "surging, leaping . . . heavy, choppy," the sun is "scorching," and the land is "everlastingly deep, hot sand . . . nothing but barren hot sand," with "not a single human being" on the beach to greet them (39–40). As they moved inland by train,[15] they encountered "a monstrous, horribly wild mountain range" and "oppressive heat" (41). Seeing no "shrub or even a spear of grass, and not an animal," Peter's impression was of an "immense, dead wonderwork" (42). Expecting to find the "groves of palms" that are part of Moor's myth of Africa, they instead discovered that the "hot, trembling air" has yielded only mirages (45). As the soldiers neared the capital, Windhoek, the landscape became "more fruitful and attractive" (50), but Moor's companions "didn't like the country; I think it wasn't strange and wonderful enough for them. They wanted Africa to look entirely different in every particular from their native land" (51). The gaze of the newly arrived Germans fell upon a land that failed to present the images of exoticism that they expected. It also bore no resemblance to their *Heimat* and will remain, paradoxically, neither exotic nor familiar enough.

While plying the reader with these racist images and stereotypes, Peter Moor is also describing regularly the physical discomforts of his life as a soldier. These discomforts are undoubtedly real, and they compose the majority of the narrative without any thought being given to the disruption of the lives of the Herero and Nama that the German presence has incurred. Moor's gaze grows increasingly genocidal throughout the text, as if Frenssen is tracing the trajectory that led the Schutztruppe to justify the genocide to come. Moor refused to acknowledge the humanity of the "other," or, indeed, even their presence. Instead, he focused on his own discomforts. The soldiers were undersupplied with water and food, and thus thirst and hunger were constant companions. They marched in the blistering sun toward the site of the pending battle, stopping to rest midday when the sun was at its zenith; they slept on the ground in the cold nights or stayed awake on guard duty. Food was cooked in a hole in the ground and usually consisted of a little rice, meat, flour baked unsuccessfully into pitiful bread, and coffee. As the march continued for weeks, without the opportunity to bathe or change uniforms, these rations thinned out and rice became the main staple. Increasingly, Moor and his comrades long for home; imagining themselves having won the battle, they exulted: "And then . . . we'll travel back to the coast and we'll start for home! What shan't we have to tell about this monkey-land!" (74). Moor looked forward to boasting of his exploits upon his return to Germany: it was just such boasting, in newspapers, journals, and memoirs, in the Reichstag, and in fiction that conveyed the acceptance of racist ideology to his fellow citizens. In turn, this created an acceptance of such attitudes toward the "other" that informs actions during the initial months of the Third Reich. Hitler created Dachau, the first concentration camp, in 1933, almost immediately after he came to power. Initially envisioned as a reeducation camp for communists and other political "subversives," it was ultimately equipped with a gas chamber. As Nazi plans to send those they deemed subhuman and unfit to live with the "Master Race" to Madagascar or eastern Europe failed, Hitler moved inexorably toward embracing genocide as the "Final Solution."

Frenssen's Description of the Herero Genocide

After weeks of such marching, the Germans engaged their enemy in frequent exchange of gunfire, skirmishes that will eventually lead to the decisive Battle of Waterberg on 11 August 1904. A few months earlier, at Easter, Moor provided the reader with several descriptions of the people at whom he was shooting during these skirmishes: "strange men in cord uniform rising *like snakes* out of the grass" (emphasis mine, 97); "a black, half-naked figure *like an ape*, holding his gun in his mouth and climbing with hands and feet into a tree" (emphasis mine, 98). Once again, the use of bestial imagery underscores his imperial gaze. Moor himself was shot in the arm and, as supplies dwindled and he lost comrades to wounds and death, his upbeat mood shifted: "We were getting continually dirtier, hungrier, and sicker" (111). Typhoid fever and dysentery invaded the camp. A situation of gloomy stasis prevailed as the soldiers, outnumbered by the Herero, awaited the arrival of fresh troops from Germany to launch the final siege. Moor and his fellow troops returned to the German military fort in Windhoek to restore their health through rest, better food, and the opportunity to bathe. While there, he was told in passing by another soldier that the "Hottentot women . . . were at our disposal at any time" (130).[16] Such treatment of indigenous women amounted to rape or forced prostitution. Significant consternation arose in Berlin about such interracial coupling and the biracial children that sometimes resulted. Such relationships were outlawed by the German government in 1905; this control of sexuality for "racial" purposes is echoed in the Nazis' 1935 Nuremberg laws.[17]

Moor's four-week respite at the fort came to an end as new German troops arrived and he headed out on expedition again. After an eight-day march, he arrived at a camp where he encountered some of the Nama who have been forced to fight with the Germans against the Herero. As described in chapter 1, Hendrik Witbooi, after years of successfully evading German pressure to sign a hypocritically dubbed "Protection Treaty," succumbed to this demand following severe losses in battle in 1894. Signing the dreaded "treaty" compelled

Witbooi and his troops to fight with the German soldiers against other indigenous people. Moor described them thus: "In one corner was quartered a whole troop of Wittboys, hideous-looking men with wild, yellow faces. They had come from the south of our colony to help us and wore our uniform and were commanded by German officers" (147–48). This is a callous misrepresentation of the truth surrounding the Witbooi presence, which ignores their history and the compulsion they experienced to fight with the Germans against other indigenous people. Such passages reinforced the image of the Nama as subalterns and conveyed a wrongful impression to the German reading public back home. In a subsequent chapter in the novel, titled "The Flight of the Nation," which recounts the beginning of the Battle of Waterberg (though Frenssen does not name it as such), the Witbooi troops are sent ahead of the German soldiers as spies (173).

We know from the accounts of historians that as many as 60,000 Herero men, women, and children were massed near the site of the Battle of Waterberg. The German battle strategy included the formation of their troops in such a manner that the Herero would be forced to flee from the fighting into the Omaheke Desert; indeed, that is what occurred and the German troops pursued them and closed off any escape route. The strategy of forcing the Herero into the desert was intentional on General Lothar von Trotha's part: it would finish the work of the genocide, assuring the death of the Herero from thirst and starvation.

As the Battle of Waterberg wanes (referred to as Hamakari in the novel), Peter Moor and his fellow soldiers "ventured to pursue the enemy" into the desert (189). And beginning with this pursuit, Peter Moor's gaze transitions from an imperial gaze into a genocidal gaze. This shift in the narrative perspective of the novel reflects that of history. Von Trotha's decision to funnel the Herero toward their death "marked a shift toward an explicitly genocidal strategy"; German patrols pursued the Herero for two months (Steinmetz, *The Devil's Handwriting*, 193). While most of this portion of Moor's narrative again focuses on his own discomfort and thirst, the loss of horses and the return of typhoid, he does describe what he saw on the route the Herero took into the desert: "In the path of their flight lay blankets, skins, ostrich feathers, household utensils, women's ornaments, cattle, and men dead and dying and staring blankly. A shocking smell of old manure and of decaying bodies filled the hot, still air oppressively. . . . And there lay the wounded and the old, women and children. A number of babies lay helplessly languishing by mothers whose breasts hung down long and flabby. . . . Somebody sent out our black drivers and I think they helped them to die" (189–90). One day, Moor happens upon a group of six survivors; "I indicated, by signs, [to his fellow soldiers] at which one of them each of us was to shoot" says Moor (192). All six are killed on the spot.

Moor and the soldiers traveled on and learned that a remnant of the Herero have successfully crossed the desert, in which "thousands of them had perished" (199). Von Trotha (never named in the novel but referred to only as "the general") "decided to follow them thither, to attack them and *force them to go northward into thirst and death, so that the colony would be left in peace and quiet for all time*" (emphasis mine, 199). Moor never questioned von Trotha's strategy or the underlying goal. After tracking the Herero for three weeks, two divisions of Schutztruppe met: "Combining our forces, we were now going to attack the enemy . . . and deal them a finishing blow" (219). The general ordered a military parade and religious services for the following day, prior to the planned attack. Moor recounts the words of the army chaplain: "He said that a people savage by nature had rebelled against the authorities that God had set over them and besides had stained themselves with revolting murders. Then the authorities had given the sword, which we were to use on the morrow, into our hands" (221). The genocide they are about to complete is thus deemed morally acceptable. But the expected encounter did not occur; the Herero had fled farther into the desert, indicating they "preferred to die in the desert rather than to fight any more with us" (223). But Moor and two comrades continued the pursuit. They happened upon "a boy with remarkably long, thin legs, as if they had stretched out in death. We hardly turned our horses so that they should not tread on him" (228). Musing to himself, Moor uttered words that evoke the genocidal gaze: "It is strange what a matter of indifference another man's life is to us when he belongs to another race" (228).

Shortly thereafter, Moor and a guardsman, returning to camp after the general called an end to the pursuit, found a "thin Negro dressed in European clothing" in the bush (230). They drag him out and the guardsman began conversing with him. After a while, the guardsman has had enough and sarcastically quoted the words of a missionary: "'Beloved, don't forget that the blacks are our brothers.' Now I will give my brother his reward" (231). The guardsman commanded the black man to run away, "but he had not taken five leaps before the ball hit him and he pitched forward at full length and lay still" (232). This passage is a direct refutation of the conversation, quoted earlier, between Moor and the "old Africans" and the Boers, in which the latter raised ethical questions about colonization. Such "brotherhood" does not exist; the Herero are expendable and can be exterminated at will.

Frenssen delivers the final, ringing endorsement of the ideology that constitutes the genocidal gaze in the closing pages of the novel. He puts these words in the mouth of a lieutenant, who spoke to Moor as they stood by the dark body of the man the guardsman has just shot: "*These blacks have deserved death before God and man*, not because they have murdered two hundred farmers and have revolted against us, but because they have built no houses and dug no wells." Referencing the words of the chaplain two days previous, the lieutenant continued: "God has let us conquer here because we are the nobler and more advanced people. That is not saying much in comparison with this black nation, but we must see to it that we become better and braver before all nations of the earth. To the nobler and more vigorous belongs the world. That is the justice of God" (emphasis mine, 233–34). Then the lieutenant temporarily demurs: "But the missionary was right when he said that all men are brothers" (234).

Peter Moor replies, "Then we have killed our brother." In response, the lieutenant delivers these chilling words, which could well have been spoken by one of Hitler's henchmen: "For a long time *we must be hard and kill*, but at the same time as individual men we must strive toward high thoughts and noble deeds so that we may contribute our part to mankind, our future brothers'" (emphasis mine, 234). The racist hierarchy the Germans established in GSWA becomes the justification for genocide, just as it will in the Holocaust. Those unworthy of being brothers must be vanished from the earth so that the "nobler and more vigorous" can survive and prosper.

A Return to the *Heimat* and an Adventure Narrated: Critical Responses

In the final chapter, "Last Days in Africa," Moor recounts his march back to Windhoek, his growing appreciation for the African landscape, and his fervent desire to return to Germany. A fellow soldier informs him of a further conflict that will require German soldiers: "The Hottentots, who lived in the south, had risen, and that now a second campaign would begin which would probably be as hard as the one which had just ended" (238). This comment refers to the rebellion of the Nama. Hendrik Witbooi and his men turned against the Germans and, following the example of the Herero, engaged the Germans in battle. Their strategy, however, was to use guerilla warfare and thus the war dragged on for three years. But Moor is diagnosed with a weak heart and traveled back to Swakopmund where he boarded a Woerman steamer for home. Arriving in

Hamburg, he encountered a middle-aged man who asked him many questions. "I related to him all that I had seen and experienced, and what I had thought of it all. And he has made this book out of it" (244). And thus the novel ends.

John K. Noyes, in one of the few analytical articles in English about *Peter Moor*, calls this final paragraph of the text "one of the strangest moments in German colonial literature—and it has some very strange moments."[18] Noyes claims that in these closing sentences "the narrative pact we have established with Peter Moor throughout the book is shattered" (88). Essentially, the narrator is outed as Frenssen himself, the middle-aged man on the dock, rather than Peter Moor. Put another way, the concluding sentences of the novel introduce a meta level, calling to the reader's attention the act of writing the novel. "Frenssen's story may be set in Africa, but it is about constructing a place called home and naming it in national terms" (Noyes, 91). Such a deconstruction of the narrative by Frenssen serves the goal of establishing the theme of national identity and creating a justification for the apparent wandering of Moor and other soldiers, which must be defined over against the nomadism of the indigenous Africans. That nomadism, states Noyes, is what enables Moor to call them uncivilized: they have not built houses or dug wells but "wander" across the land, gleaning their sustenance. By contrast, Moor's "wandering" is in the service of Germany: the colonizers intend to settle down, to start families and farms, to build houses and dig wells, to bring "civilization" to the "savages." Noyes's article is useful in naming the nationalist aspects of the genocidal gaze: it is informed by a supposed racial superiority tied to the industry and cultural traditions of Western Europe.

As mentioned earlier, Frenssen is best known for his *Heimatkunst*, his deployment of the genre of regional fiction. Noyes's article places *Peter Moor* in this tradition, despite its African setting: "Well before the Nazis pushed 'degenerate' art aside and elevated *Blut-und-Boden* kitsch to the status of official romance, the regional novel was telling tales of nation and race bonded in idyllic communion by the irrational power of the soil" (90). Noyes further points out: "The term *Heimatkunst* (regional art) had been coined in 1895 by Adolf Bartels, the literary historian whose racist polemics against Judaism would later make him one of the Nazis' authorities on ethnic cleansing in art" (90).

Perhaps, then, it should not come as a surprise that Frenssen made, in the 1930s, what Frank Braun has erroneously called an "apparently sudden shift into the National Socialist camp," though Braun then goes on to delineate what he sees as precursors to this "shift" in Frenssen's earlier work (449). The journey from *Heimatkunst* to Nazi propaganda that Frenssen makes as a writer is yet another indication of the links between the genocide of the Herero and the Nazi Holocaust. As Elizabeth Boa has noted: "At its most expansionist, *Heimat* ideology justified seizure of *Lebensraum*, strange land to be colonized and turned into homeland" (51). The paradigm for the Nazi colonization of eastern Europe has its roots firmly planted in the soil of Southwest Africa. Indeed, the very titles of the books Frenssen published in the last decade of his life, described by Braun as "of an outright propagandistic nature" (451), indicate his sympathy with Nazi ideology as they use "hot-button" Nazi terminology: for example, *Der Weg unseres Volkes* (The Way of Our Folk, 1938) and *Recht (oder Unrecht)—mein Land* (Right [or Wrong]—My Land, 1940). In April 1935, Frenssen published a brief history of Adolf Hitler in the *Schleswig-Holsteinischen Tageszeitung* in honor of Hitler's birthday; Hitler also awarded Frenssen's novel *Peter Moor* a medal (Griese, 215).

We will return to these links between the genocide of the Herero and the genocide of the Jews in the Third Reich. First, though, a brief glance at other critical responses to *Peter Moor* available to scholars in English. David Kenosian, comparing the work of Gustav Frenssen and German colonial novelist Hans Grimm (who, unlike Frenssen, actually lived in Africa from 1897 to 1911), poses this "crucial question for German colonial literature: How could the Germans represent themselves as culturally superior to the putatively savage.... Africans when they themselves resorted to violent forms of domination?"[19] Focusing on the "internal instability of the discourse of race in these texts which justifies violence as a political praxis" (184), Kenosian traces attitudes toward the black body from Hegel's master/slave dialectic to Franz Fanon and then to Lacan.

Alan Bowyer draws on Homi Bhabha in his highly theoretical analysis of *Peter Moor*. His reading of the semiotics of clothing in the novel is helpful as he points out Frenssen's attention to details such as the buttons on soldiers' uniforms as a distinguishing sign. Similarly, he notes the emphasis in the novel on "order, discipline and labor, and the opposite thereof—a condition of chaos, non-differentiation, carelessness and sloth," the former characterizing the Germans and the latter the black Africans.[20] The common German motto "Ordnung muss sein" (Order must be) is called to mind here as Bowyer reveals frequent instances in the text of the imposition of order by German military on the indigenous population.

Daniel Brückenhaus has analyzed *Peter Moor* as children's literature, or perhaps what we would now call Young Adult (YA) literature.[21] Writing about both British and German children's literature, his focus is the debate among authors during this period about "the role of feelings in imperial relationships. The central issue was whether Europeans should create an emotional connection with non-Europeans and, if so, what the effect would be on the power hierarchies between black and white people" (74). Brückenhaus quotes, as many scholars do, the passage mentioned earlier in which Peter converses with the "old Africans" and Boers about the fate of the indigenous people, likening their struggle for independence to that of the Germans in 1813. This brief passage leads Brückenhaus to erroneously conclude: "the novel seems to accept the fact that from a *moral* standpoint, the Africans are in the right" (86). Frenssen had no such aim in mind in writing the novel and no such affirmation of the African perspective occurs. What Brückenhaus has failed to consider is that the speaker of this passage is *not a German soldier*. Peter in no way agrees with or validates this sentiment.

Brückenhaus does note the *lack* of human emotion on Peter's part toward the Herero and Nama. "However, such acknowledgments [of the just cause of the Herero] are not accompanied by any personal, empathetic connection between black and white characters, or by feelings of compassion. In fact, the protagonist repeatedly and successfully fights against his 'over-emotional' impulses that might diminish his skills as a tough fighter defending German imperial expansion" (86). (It would seem that the inherent contradiction between this observation and his claim about the moral center of the novel would be enough to dissuade Brückenhaus of his opinion regarding the latter.) Brückenhaus concludes, and here we can agree, that the novel "thereby becomes indicative of an especially brutal and 'exterminationist' form of racism" (87). From yet another perspective, then, the presence of the genocidal gaze in Frenssen's work is affirmed.

Reading the novel as an explication of the genocidal gaze is also validated when one learns that the Nazis reprinted the text several times for adult audiences. The novel was originally printed in an edition of 25,000 in 1906. As early as 1908, the text, as Brückenhaus indicates, was required reading in German classrooms.[22] Indeed, the text was so popular with youth that Pathfinder groups (German boy scouts in the early twentieth century) would carry copies of *Peter Moor* on camping trips and read aloud from the novel.[23] By 1933, 233,000 copies were in print and then the Nazis appropriated the text to inculcate the genocidal gaze in schools. The book was re-released in 1933, 1936, and 1938. In fact, the Nazis issued a special edition of *Peter Moors Fahrt nach Südwest* for Wehrmacht soldiers in 1942 and 1944, listed on abebooks.com as *Peter Moors Fahrt nach Südwest. Ein Feldzugbericht. Soldatenbücherei des Oberkommandos der Wehrmacht Abt.Inland Band 34*. This brought the total number of copies in print to 433,000 by 1944 (Warmbold, 67).

I have examined two copies of this Wehrmacht edition of *Peter Moor*, one purchased from abebooks.com and one at the Universitätsbibliothek Johann Christian Senckenberg in Frankfurt, Germany. The text is pocket size, approximately 6"x 4", and has a soft cover, ideal for carrying in a pocket or rucksack. The paper is of rather poor quality, as might be expected in the throes of World War II, and the text is printed in Fraktur. No Nazi insignia was found in either copy. Undoubtedly, *Peter Moor* becomes an instrument for transmitting the genocidal gaze: just as Peter has nothing but scorn for the "barbaric" and "expendable" Africans he encounters, so children and the Wehrmacht, as well as the general reading public, absorbed the "cult of Frenssen" as one critic has called it: the "moral justification" of genocide to acquire land and to maintain the purity of German blood and the racial superiority the Nazis claimed (Warmbold, 68).

Other editions of *Peter Moor* prove instructive as well. A contemporaneous response to Frenssen's text is provided by Herman Babson, mentioned earlier. Babson produced a 1914 edition of *Peter Moor*, in the original German Fraktur, for student use in the United States. He abridged the text by about 50 percent and added a thirty-page introduction, notes, and an appendix of vocabulary. The volume also contains a photograph of Frenssen, two painted images of Schutztruppe, and an elaborate foldout map, with geological features, of the route between Swakopmund and Windhoek. In his preface, Babson states his hope that the "comprehensive account of German colonization activity in Southwest Africa . . . will materially aid in the enjoyment of this *excellent tale of German valor*" (emphasis mine, n.p.). Yet another edition was published in Namibia as recently as 1998. This edition, which curiously has an anonymous editor and is written entirely in German, seems to be created for the significant population of German-speaking descendants of the immigrant settlers still living in Namibia today. The preface, written by Dr. Budack of Windhoek, concludes by hoping that this new edition of Frenssen's "'little book' [*Büchlein*] of which many editions are already out of print, will provide a small but very comprehensible and enthralling report" (my translation).[24] This 1998 edition carries footnotes, photographs, and an appendix that includes battle descriptions and maps excerpted from the 1906 reports by the general's staff and archived in Berlin. *Virtually no paratextual material provides any information about the Herero or Nama themselves.* They have been erased, just as they were almost invisible in the novel itself.

Conclusion

> When we children played soldiers, the inspiration was not the war of 1870/71 and certainly not that of 1866, but rather the Herero uprising in Southwest Africa. In this there was always a long back and forth, who should be a Herero and *who was allowed to belong to the honored and idolized imperial colonial defense forces* [Schutztruppe]. (emphasis mine)[25]

This childhood memory, recalled by Kurt Bittel, who later became an archaeology professor, demonstrates the significant impact that texts such as *Peter Moor* had on German children and the population as a whole. Toy manufacturers in Germany created sets of tin soldiers accurate to the country and ethnicity where conflicts had occurred.

> To capitalize on public interest, such toys were available within weeks of the event portrayed, earning them the nickname "newspapers in tin." Indeed, makers of tin figures stored and recycled molds for this very purpose. With a touch of paint and appropriate scenery, exotic environments and characters could be interchanged at will . . . Boers were repainted as Germans to fight against Indians, themselves repainted as Southwest African Hereros. . . . Battle sets offered explicit lessons in the inevitable and heroic progress of civilization over the less civilized. (Bowersox, 38)

Such "battle sets" also offered lessons in the genocidal gaze, which normalized the idea of mass killings as the inevitable duty of the "higher" races of the world.

Gustav Frenssen's *Peter Moor*, like the tin soldiers, conveyed a message of German valor in the face of the "brutal" and "expendable" races in GSWA. Today, we read *Peter Moor* not only as evidence of the links between German imperialism and the Nazi Holocaust but also as having been *instrumental* in the creation of a mind-set in its German readers regarding racial hierarchies, of justification for the violence of colonialism, and for, when required, *Endlösung*. As Joachim Warmbold has written: "The *Heimatkunst* movement saw itself as an 'educational force for a new German culture' imbued with idealistic and nationalist features. . . . In propagating rejection of industrial urban society, inveighing against 'modernism,' intellectuals, and Jews while, at the same time, evoking a mystical-collective *Volkstum* (national heritage) whose origins were 'rooted in the soil,' the spokesmen for *Heimatkunst* became trailblazers for an ideology that led directly to the *Blut und Boden* mentality of the National Socialist dictatorship" (69).

THREE

Uwe Timm's Critique of the Genocidal Gaze in *Morenga* and *In My Brother's Shadow*

> For me this is not the age of "post-modernism," it is the
> post-Holocaust age. That is the salient marker of our present world.
> SANDER GILMAN | "Why and How I Study the German"

> Memory is treacherous, as distinct from history as emotion from form.
> Every war is fought over memory. Violent nationalism
> is revived memory manipulated as revealed truth.
> ROGER COHEN | *The Girl from Human Street*

As we move from Gustav Frenssen's *Peter Moor* to a consideration of two texts by contemporary German writer Uwe Timm, his colonial novel *Morenga*[1] and his memoir *In My Brother's Shadow*,[2] this observation by David Kenosian serves as a useful comparison and hence transition:

> In a certain sense, a counterversion to the history of the uprising of the Africans appears in Uwe Timm's novel *Morenga*. . . . In contrast to Frenssen's *Peter Moor*, Timm's work historicizes the European, and especially the German efforts to exploit the peoples of Southwest Africa. In *Morenga*, the Germans initiate the cycle of violence that gripped the colony and thus the rebellion of the Africans is portrayed as a response to their brutal subjugation at the hands of the Germans. (195n42)

Kenosian invites us here to grasp the difference in the portrayal of the genocidal gaze by Frenssen and Timm: while the former *inadvertently conveyed* to the reader, in a smug and satisfied manner, the genocidal gaze of the Germans in

GSWA, the latter *intentionally critiqued* the immoral and deadly genocidal gaze as it infected the Schutztruppe.

Uwe Timm's *Morenga* was a revolutionary book upon its release in Germany in 1978 (and subsequently in English in 2003), and it remains so. In writing the novel, Timm inevitably looked back at colonial genocide through the lens of World War II and the Holocaust. Timm's own gaze is cast back against his nation, a critical gaze that sees the harm of colonialism, the tragedy of genocide, and the guilt as falling to the Germans, whose excessive militarism, racism, and violence are depicted in chilling ways in the two texts we will examine in this chapter. Further, these two texts enable the reader to continue to trace the links between imperial genocide and the Nazi Holocaust.

In the 1970s, Germans remained in the thrall of colonial amnesia, which is to say that either they forgot about the brief period of imperialism in their history or they remembered it in glorified fashion, as it had typically been depicted in colonial fiction. How does colonial amnesia (or colonial aphasia, as Ann Laura Stoler has aptly named it), silence about genocide, the failure to remember, to mourn, engender other genocides? How does imperialism itself lead to genocide? These are key questions asked by Uwe Timm in *Morenga*, which examines the genocide of the Herero and Nama people in 1904–7 in GSWA. Using fiction as well as excerpts from actual military reports, soldiers' diaries, and the real diary of the eponymous Morenga, a historical figure who served as leader of the Nama, Timm interrogates the ways in which nineteenth-century Germans perceived Africans, how this contributed to the genocide, and how that genocide compared to, and contributed to, the Nazi Holocaust. "As recently as the 1960's, many Germans did not even realize that their country had once conquered considerable parts of Africa. Only a handful of experts and historians were interested in the subject."[3] Little exists in Namibia today to memorialize the victims.[4] General Lothar von Trotha issued his infamous extermination proclamation in October 1904 after defeating the Herero at the Battle of Waterberg: "I, the great General of the German soldiers, send this letter to the Herero people. The Herero are no longer German subjects. . . . The Herero nation . . . must leave the country. If they do not leave, I will force them out with the *Groot Rohr* (cannon). Every Herero, armed or unarmed, will be shot within the German borders. I will no longer accept women and children, but will force them back to their people or shoot at them" (Steinmetz, "The First Genocide").

German colonial amnesia, or aphasia, is not the only willful forgetting on the part of the German people of the atrocities committed in Africa. The subsequent secrecy surrounding the colonial archives also occluded history; these archives, of the reports, documents, letters, and so forth sent to and from Southwest Africa during the German colonial period there from 1884 to 1918, were closed, unavailable to scholars or the general public during the era of colonialism and subsequently.[5] When the Nazis came to power, they, too, kept the archives closed; during World War II, about 50 percent of the archives were lost to fire and bombs, and a significant portion was taken by the victorious Russian soldiers back to Russia. The files were returned only in the mid-1950s and at that time stored in Potsdam, which was located in the GDR, the communist German Democratic Republic.

One of the first scholars given access to the files was Horst Drechsler, a graduate student who had been trained in East Germany as a Marxist historian. Unlike earlier historians and novelists who had written histories that valorized Germany's colonial era, or similarly self-congratulatory memoirs written by German military leaders after their return to the Fatherland, Drechsler had no problem being critical of Germany and liked to remind his readers that Lenin had written a book defining imperialism as the "highest stage of capitalism" (Drechsler, 3). Drechsler painstakingly reviewed hundreds of documents in the archives, completing his dissertation and then publishing it as a book in 1966 titled *Südwestafrika unter deutscher Kolonialherrschaft. Band 1: Der Kampf der Herero und Nama gegen den deutschen Imperialismus [1884–1915]*; it appeared in English in 1980 as *"Let Us Die Fighting,"* a phrase used by Herero leader Samuel Maherero to spur on his troops in their tragic fight against the Germans. *"Let Us Die Fighting"* would have been one of the few counternarratives available to Uwe Timm as he began his own research for his novel *Morenga* in the 1970s. Indeed, textual evidence suggests that he did avail himself of Drechsler's history as some rather obscure anecdotes about German presence in Southwest Africa, reported by Drechsler, are repeated in the novel.[6] He also cites Drechsler's book as a source at the end of a chapter titled "Concept of the Enemy" (32).

Who Was Uwe Timm and Why Was He Interested in Africa?

Timm was born into a middle-class family in Hamburg in March 1940, as World War II was getting underway. Hamburg, the port city from which steamers to Africa departed, has always had a heightened awareness of German colonies and the city figures in Timm's novel. In an interview, Timm talked about his preparation for writing *Morenga*:

My father was an officer, and I heard many stories at home of this completely strange and different world, about Africa and its totally different customs.... And I always read about Africa and attended lectures about it, about ethnology... I studied the documentary evidence in detail. I visited what was then still South West Africa, Namibia today,[7] worked in the archives, and even interviewed people who had taken part in the uprising, very old people I met personally.[8]

Perhaps most significant, for the analysis that follows, is the fact that Timm's older brother, sixteen years his senior, had volunteered for the Waffen SS and died in a field hospital in Ukraine in 1943. Almost immediately, a kind of apotheosis occurred: his brother became the family hero, eventually leading Timm to write one of his most widely read books, *Am Beispiel meines Bruders*, in 2003, which appeared in English as *In My Brother's Shadow: A Life and Death in the SS* (2005). From the age of three, Timm indeed lived under this shadow. We will turn to this text after our reading of *Morenga*.

Timm's father, also a Nazi soldier, returned from a British POW camp in 1946 and opened a furrier business in which Timm later worked, breaking off his education prior to completing his *abitur*. Eventually he completed the PhD in 1971, writing his dissertation, "The Problem of Absurdity in Albert Camus." As a student, he was politically active, taking part in the radical student movement in Germany in the 1960s. His is the generation that began to ask the question, "What did you do in the war, Daddy?" in the face of the silence surrounding the war and the Holocaust. "Particularly for the generation of '68 the Holocaust became *the* symbol of a negative history of the German nation state."[9] Many writers of this generation and since have engaged in what the Germans named *vergangenheitsbewältigung*, a term coined in the aftermath of the Holocaust that, loosely translated, means "coming to terms with the past."

The Genocidal Gaze in *Morenga*: Timm's Embodied Critique

> The other, the new: the Jumping Bean Tree. Its exact opposite: clicking your heels. Clack. Standing at attention. The German eagle. The abstract. Asking no questions. Saying yes, sir. The love of law and order. Isn't it telling, after all, that we Germans always say: *Geht in Ordnung* when we mean that's fine.
>
> *Morenga* | Gottschalk's diary, 7 September 1905

In the intriguing interview conducted by Rainer Schulte with both Uwe Timm and Breon Mitchell, the translator of *Morenga*, Timm is prompted to talk in very specific terms about his motives, his work process, and his goals for the novel. He describes at some length his attention to detail in research and in the writing, wanting to capture, as far as possible, the mind-set of various German characters in 1904–7. Both Timm and his translator read documents and diaries of that era in order to replicate the differences among the languages of the military, of missionaries, of traders, and of adventurers. In one of the most revealing passages of the interview, Timm talks explicitly about whose gaze he is representing; he also makes absolutely clear his intention to link the genocides of the Herero and Nama and of the eleven million victims of the Holocaust:

> It's a matter of learning about states of consciousness. . . . First of all I don't have the experience to write about Africans, there isn't a single place in the novel where an African is portrayed from within, through some sort of aesthetics of empathy. I would find that inadmissible and naïve, it simply wouldn't do. It's a matter of learning something from the language of the time, of discovering how people came to humiliate others back then, to hold them in such low esteem, to kill other human beings. *It truly resembles a plan for later genocide, one that finds its culmination in Auschwitz, this destruction of the Hereros.* (emphasis mine, Schulte, 4)

In other words, for Timm, the effort of the writer must be to make apparent to the reader how the German mind-set about imperialism and genocide can be traced from GSWA to the Nazis. This must be accomplished through language and what it reveals about perspectives, about the genocidal gaze on the Other. The only representation of African perspective in the novel is the inclusion of short, actual diary entries made by Morenga himself in a notebook he took from a dead German soldier. Even the notebook has now disappeared and Timm relied upon photographs of the handwritten entries included in a German history text for his inclusion of this text in the novel. Timm's unwillingness to create a fictional African mind-set emerges from respect and his reluctance to imagine that for which he has so little knowledge. And this is precisely why it is so important to reclaim authentic African voices such as that of Hendrik Witbooi.

Thus, given both his family history and his generation's history, Timm turned to the subject of genocide for his second novel, *Morenga*, using fiction to look at the history of German genocides, presenting the genocide of the Herero and Nama as a precursor to the Holocaust. *Morenga*, the first full-scale historical novel about GSWA in the post-Holocaust era, anticipated the year 2004, the centenary of the genocide.[10] That centenary was marked in Germany by a major museum exhibition and by a reawakened interest in German colonialism "in an attempt to reinscribe colonialism in German cultural memory and to reflect on its legacy in the postcolonial world of the twenty-first century" (Göttsche, 63). Timm's "reinscription," unlike its early twentieth-century predecessors, is a profoundly critical one.

In order to write the novel, Timm unearthed photographs, letters, military documents, and invaluable diaries. *Morenga* is a pastiche of these documents, creating a postmodern, post-Holocaust, and postcolonial take on the first genocide of the twentieth century, a century in which 170,000,000 people died in a genocide; most of these deaths, as was the case in GSWA and the Holocaust, were perpetrated by their own government.

Let me begin by reviewing the contours of this sprawling, complex, and challenging novel, to be followed by a more complete analysis. The reader is introduced to Veterinary Lieutenant Gottschalk, who arrives in Southwest Africa on 7 October 1904; this is after the decisive Battle of Waterberg on 11 August and the flight of the Herero into the Omaheke Desert. Concentration camps and a death camp are being set up for the remaining Herero. Hendrik Witbooi has just declared, on 1 October, that he is no longer adhering to the Protection Treaty he signed; he will go to war with the Germans as he fears that what happened to the Herero can happen to the Nama people. Gottschalk arrives in Africa with the imperial gaze intact, he grows increasingly eccentric as the novel progresses and his peers take exception to his behavior. He is eventually discharged. Yet, to the reader, he is asking the right questions about what the German military is doing, and he attempts to treat the Nama humanely in spite of the orders he is given. Hence, he embodies Timm's critique of the German genocidal gaze. Timm confirms in his interview with Schulte that "Gottschalk is a fictional character" (1).

Both Theodor Leutwein and Lothar von Trotha, historical figures who played key roles in the colony, are also characters in the novel, thus affording Timm the opportunity to differentiate between their military strategies and theories. While Leutwein favored efforts at getting treaties signed, rather than waging war, to achieve German ends, von Trotha, as we have seen, openly favored annihilation. But lest one think Leutwein was thus a more humane officer, keep in mind that his motive for avoiding destruction of the indigenous people was to save them to serve as a labor force, or rather as forced labor.

This is only one of several links between the Herero and Nama genocide and the Nazi Holocaust in Timm's novel: the use of the victims to further the ends of the

Germans. Timm makes these links vivid. For example, he mentions Shark Island, which was established as a death camp for survivors of the genocide between 1905 and 1907 on an island off the coast. Prisoners were given inadequate clothing, intentionally starved and worked to death, and subjected to medical experiments. Women were systematically raped. It is estimated that 4,000 or more prisoners died there, and this death rate differed significantly from that of the concentration camps inland, prompting historians to note that the Nazi differentiation between concentration and death camps was indeed established in GSWA.[11] Another link can be found in the animal imagery that is rife in the novel. Various German characters perceive the Nama and Herero as animals, a mind-set they shared with the Nazis, who persistently depicted the Jews in propaganda films and cartoons as parasites, diseased rats, and insects, thus justifying their extermination; eventually Gottschalk perceives the Germans themselves as animals.

Despite the title of the novel, Morenga, who was the Nama leader following Hendrik Witbooi's death, appears infrequently in the text. He is referred to as "the Black Napoleon" by the Germans because of his successful guerilla tactics and refuses to be bought off by the increasingly dominant colonizers. Brief excerpts from his actual diary are included in the text; they recount the battles between an indigenous group named the Bondelswarts and the Germans. Morenga's death is described in the closing pages of the novel. "The very fact that Morenga, the symbol of African resistance, provides the novel's title reflects Timm's anticolonial and anti-Eurocentric perspective" (Göttsche, 74). Thus Morenga himself becomes yet another vehicle to carry Timm's critique of German imperialism: the double use of genocide as a "solution" in the twentieth century by Germany and the silence of colonial aphasia in the aftermath.

With that overview, I turn to a close reading of this novel, with an emphasis on the ways in which Timm embodies his critique of the genocidal gaze: through the dissenting hero Gottschalk; in the use of intertextuality in the novel; with the hybridity of narrative technique and textual content; in the deployment of animal imagery as an aspect of the genocidal gaze; and, finally, in the depiction of Morenga.

GOTTSCHALK RECOGNIZES GENOCIDAL INTENT

"Civilization is unthinkable without sacrifices."
OFFICER HARING | quoted in Gottschalk's diary (19)

The novel opens with a chapter titled "Warning Signs." Thirteen brief paragraphs, written as if they are news flashes, alert the reader to indigenous attacks on German settlers, introduce Morenga, and briefly outline the beginning of actual hostilities between the Germans and the Witbooi on 4 October 1904. Immediately following this dry yet rather alarming opening that paints the settlers as victims, Veterinary Lieutenant Gottschalk is introduced as he arrives on African soil. Through a series of flashbacks, the reader learns about his childhood: his father owned a store on the outskirts of Hamburg that sold colonial goods, hence Gottschalk's heightened awareness of, and curiosity about, Africa. His voyage on the *Gertrude Woerman* steamer is sketched, during which he makes the acquaintance of N.C.O. Veterinarian Wenstrup, who is as avid a reader as Gottschalk himself. It is Wenstrup who one day during the crossing announces to Gottschalk that "I think it was the great Moltke who once said: the Prussian army has no room for Jews or dreamers" (12). This proves prescient as we have already been told about Gottschalk's "recurrent dream since childhood: there was no summer" (5). That Gottschalk is a dreamer, recounts his dreams, and becomes a dreamy inventor leads to his eventual discharge from the army.

Gottschalk is a devoted diarist and the reader is given the opportunity to read some of his entries; they provide a window to his consciousness, one of Timm's goals in writing the novel. As Gottschalk is a scientist, many entries simply delineate weather conditions or flora and fauna. Occasionally, however, they provide glimpses of the profound impact that Africa has on him and the profound changes in his values which result. Shortly after his arrival, Gottschalk uses his diary to sketch the exterior and interior of a farmhouse he hopes to construct in GSWA someday. Gottschalk, we are told, is thirty-four years old and, as yet, unmarried. Nonetheless, he engages in reveries about the floor plan of the farmhouse, the rooms it will have, the musical evenings he and his family will enjoy. Nowhere in these reveries is there a hint of concern about who *now* owns the land that Gottschalk intends to acquire. These dreams of the future serve as a kind of baseline: Gottschalk's imperial gaze upon the indigenous people and their rights will morph very soon. On the troop train toward Windhoek, Gottschalk records in his diary what a comrade has told him: "the entire Herero region will be annexed by the crown, i.e.—opened for settlement. The best land in South West Africa supposedly, good pastures and relatively abundant water. It's a fine thought that at some point there will be eyes in this wilderness reading Goethe, ears listening to Mozart" (16). At this point, Gottschalk still adheres to the paradigm of colonialism bringing civilization to the savages. His gaze is imperial: he brings with him the view of the indigenous people inculcated in him through his education and socialization.

But Gottschalk's arrival in Windhoek, today the capital of Namibia and then the location of the central German military fort, will be the first experience that erodes this paradigm. He notes in his diary that "the natives, black (Hereros) and brown (Hottentots [Nama]), as well as numerous half-breeds, called Bastards, look like short, ragged Europeans, only black" (16). So, are the indigenous people savage barbarians? Apparently not. Unlike Peter Moor, who can find no grounds for a relationship with the Herero he meets, and kills, Gottschalk does see resemblance with Europeans. His attitude here is still Eurocentric, but it is evolving.

What Gottschalk next encounters is a kraal (enclosure for animals) built to keep "the cattle, sheep and goats taken from the conquered Hereros" (17). As a veterinarian, he is concerned about the emaciated state of these animals and the number of dead cattle scattered about. "The stench of carrion filled the air" (17). Right next to the kraal, another kraal has been built, this one for "something half way between humans and skeletons. They huddled together, mostly naked, in the piercingly hot sun" (17). His companion proudly announces: "That's our concentration camp . . . a new innovation based on the English experience of the Boer war" (17). "But those are women and children," objects Gottschalk (17).

Later, Gottschalk recounts this experience to Wenstrup, who becomes a kind of mentor to him. The people enclosed in barbed wire, Gottschalk says, die "from dysentery, typhus, and undernourishment. They starve to death" (18). Wenstrup corrects this naiveté: "No, . . . they let them starve to death. That's a subtle but crucial distinction . . . part of a systematic plan. . . . The extermination of the natives. They want the land for settlement" (18). Here, Timm introduces the reader to a definition of the genocidal gaze. Despite Wenstrup's astute comments, Gottschalk persists in believing that the starvation of the prisoners is simply an administrative oversight. He devises a plan: use the dead animals to feed the imprisoned women and children. But when he approaches his superior to propose this plan, he is shouted out of the office with a single retort: "Jungle fever!" (21). Thus, Gottschalk is accused of having lost his sanity to the heat and "savagery" of the jungle. His disenchantment has begun; dawning on him is the reality of the military ideology, the genocidal gaze, of which he has become a part by enlisting. His romantic notions of the Spice Islands, based on his yearning as a child in his father's store for goods forbidden to him, and of the sweet farmhouse he hoped to build in GSWA are dashed. His own imperial gaze begins to change to a harsh critique of the genocidal gaze he perceives in the Schutztruppe. Gottschalk is given orders to proceed south from Windhoek with troops headed "through rebel Hottentot territory" (21).

Together with Wenstrup, Gottschalk is headed into the combat zone of the Nama, led at this moment by the redoubtable Hendrik Witbooi. Wenstrup's behavior is at times odd: he makes noises on the march (yodeling, among other things!), which causes 2nd Lt. Schwanebach to write him up for dereliction of duty and insubordination: "If I understood him correctly, the veterinarian regards imagination and spontaneity as positive values. He compared German civilization to a clubfoot" (48). Whereas Schwanebach declares Wenstrup insane, the reader increasingly sees Wenstrup as completely sane. He takes actions that suggest empathy for the Nama, such as applying for a "bambuse," an indigenous boy, Jakobus, to employ him as a language teacher.[12] Soon Gottschalk joins in the lessons; learning the language of the enemy serves as a recognition of the culture of, and rapprochement with, the Nama. The two men become friends, and discuss government and politics: "It must have dawned on Gottschalk for the first time on this trek that Wenstrup was not as he had thought, a partisan of the Social Democrats, but instead something truly unusual—probably the sole anarchist veterinarian in the German army" (49).

Arriving in Keetmanshoop, the troops prepare to celebrate Christmas, and "Wenstrup surprised everyone by sporting a gray chapeau claque [a top hat that can be collapsed] with a sprig of tamarisk. He was gradually coming to resemble those he had been sent to fight" (53). This sprig features in a dream that Gottschalk subsequently has; it will be described in what follows. Shortly thereafter, Wenstrup disappears; what happened to him is never revealed. But he has left his mark on Gottschalk.

By the midpoint of the novel, Gottschalk "no longer asked himself if the war was unjust. He was now convinced it was, and there were times when he felt it like a physical pain. In his diary he called the war a terrible injustice. Whenever a native was flogged . . . his stomach lurched with the urge to vomit. . . . It gradually became clear to Gottschalk that these people were fighting for their survival as human beings" (195–96). Gottschalk's perception of the genocidal gaze in his fellow soldiers causes physical illness. At this juncture, Gottschalk needs a new horse and selects a powerful white one from the kraal; subsequently, this horse is identified as having belonged to Morenga. Symbolically, this creates a kind of identification between the two, just as Wenstrup is moving in this direction. Gottschalk, thinking back to the battle in which he recently participated, recalls "the brief moment when he'd had the mad notion of joining the enemy" instead of "helping maintain the circulatory system of force and terror" (208). Shortly after this, Dr. Otto examines him because Gottschalk is experiencing stomach pains. Dr. Otto's diagnosis: Gottschalk suffers from "an exaggerated interest in the Hottentots" and "excessive compassion for the fate of this tribe" as well as from "his attempt to learn the highly complex Nama language" (211). His increasingly eccentric behavior is duly noted.

In his role as veterinarian, Gottschalk is asked to experiment with camels as possible beasts of burden for the troops themselves and their military supplies; the ability of camels to go for long periods without water is a distinct advantage in the desert. At first, he considers refusing; he wants no complicity with the unjust war. Reconsidering, he decides that perhaps his experiments will benefit the Nama. Immediately upon his taking this decision, the narrator dryly announces: "Three years later, in 1908, the last rebels were tracked down and defeated in the Kalahari with the help of a German camel corps led by Captain von Erckert" (259). Translation: there is no way to participate in the military without being part of the death machine and the resulting guilt. On his own, Gottschalk is also experimenting with a dental device to give to cows who have lost teeth; this would permit them to continue to chew and produce milk. He imagines this may be helpful to the Herero and Nama as cattle are essential to their culture and survival. Such efforts on his part contribute to his image, in the eyes of his comrades, as a dreamer and too weird to continue to serve in the Schutztruppe. He is called Don Quixote by one of his peers (286).

In August 1905, Gottschalk is assigned to ride his camel with a wagon train bringing supplies south to Ukamas in preparation for a final assault on Morenga and his diminished forces. When the oxen are circled for the evening rest, Gottschalk takes out his diary and makes a brief entry, ending with the ominous "Death: a logic outside us." The narrator then tells us: "That is Gottschalk's last entry in the oilcloth notebook, which was found a year and a half later on one of Morenga's fallen cornets" (297). (Here, "cornet" indicates a military rank no longer in use; it is the equivalent of today's second lieutenant.) The reader rightly senses that the denouement is about to occur. It is a dramatic one, indeed. The wagon train comes under attack by Morenga and his men; Gottschalk's camel is shot out from under him and he remains lying where he fell. In a report he subsequently submits to the military, Gottschalk describes his encounter with Morenga, who finally steps out of the shadows into full view of the reader: "Later I was taken to a man standing off to the side by a wagon, leafing through captured files and maps. It was Morenga. He was strikingly tall and wore a civilian coat with an ammunition belt over it. He asked me where the convoy was headed. . . . He appeared well informed about our troop movements" (300). After Gottschalk informs Morenga that he is a veterinarian, "Morenga asked me to examine him, saying a bullet had lodged in his right hip months earlier. . . . The wound was badly infected . . . I did what I could, painted the wound with iodine, treated it with antiseptic salve, then bandaged it . . . I asked Morenga why he didn't make peace with us . . . Morenga emphasized that he would keep fighting to the last man. And when I asked why, he offered the surprising answer: So that *you* and *we* can remain human" (emphasis in the original, 300–301). Here is Morenga's acknowledgment of and resistance to the genocidal gaze: he will die fighting rather than succumb to the gaze of the Germans that attempts to render him as a subhuman, confine him to a camp in which he must do forced labor, or exterminate him. He will die on his own terms; the Jewish resistance in the Warsaw ghetto and elsewhere manifested this same resolve.

The novel begins to wind down. We are told of Hendrik Witbooi's death in battle on 29 September 1905,[13] the day after Gottschalk meets Morenga (306). We learn that Morenga was also wounded in battle, six months later, shot in the neck and head (304). He subsequently turned himself into English police and was jailed in South Africa, where he was safe from the Germans. In a chapter titled "The End," comprised of an abstract military report, we are told of the pursuit of Morenga to his death, a joint venture of the British and Germans, after he had returned to GSWA. The report concludes with this chilling observation: "The natives of South Africa will now realize they're not fighting the Germans, or the English, or the Dutch, but that *now the entire white race stands united against the black*. The blacks have lost their most important hero, the man they set their hopes on" (emphasis in the original, 337). This passage echoes history: von Trotha wrote to General von Schlieffen, Chief of the General Staff, two days after issuing his infamous extermination order on 2 October 1904: "This uprising is and remains the beginning of a racial war" (Totten and Parsons, 29). The genocide of the Herero and Nama was indeed a racial war, informed by the genocidal gaze, as the Holocaust, to follow in less than three decades, will be.

Our hero—or antihero—Gottschalk turns his attention to meteorology and to inventions as a way to fight the boredom of being a German soldier and to live an alternative life to the violence of imperialism. Having lost his diary in the struggle with Morenga and his troops, Gottschalk begins a new diary, entirely devoted to observations of "the direction and speed of the wind . . . precipitation, sunrise and sunset, cloud cover and cloud formations. These descriptions fill the pocket calendar in a small script, and most incredible is the way in which the clouds are described" (317). It is worth recalling here that early in the novel, as Gottschalk is learning to speak Nama, he inquires, "What lies beyond the stars? Jakobus [the bambuse teaching him Nama] translated the word infinite as cloud" (50). Timm again uses the vehicle of Gottschalk's diary to give the reader a glimpse of his inner self, his consciousness. We are told by the narrator that only twice did Gottschalk deviate from the regular recording of daily weather: once to include "a sketch for the construction of a free balloon, steered by means of dragropes and a balloon sail," and a second time to enter the following: "Learn to understand our inner self as a geological formation. A geology of the soul with its fissures, displacements, sediments, deposits, and erosions" (318).

Gottschalk decides to petition the Schutztruppe for a discharge, which is eventually granted. He ponders what he might do after his return to Germany: he imagines being a country veterinarian, or perhaps pursuing research at a university (315). He travels to the coast of GSWA by camel and one evening, racing the camel, he smiles to himself and chants, "So come! Let us gaze into open spaces, Seeking something our own, no matter how far" (326). On 18 September 1907, having been in GSWA for three years, he boards a ship and heads homeward. His final view is of the death camp, Shark Island.

Our final glimpse of Gottschalk in the epilogue is a potentially baffling one. We see him in a balloon, riding over "the brightly-coloured rag rug of gently folding hills and valleys" of Germany (339). His name is mentioned only once in these three pages; the pilot of the balloon is one Lüdemann. Timm invites several readings of this conclusion. In the preceding few paragraphs, I have endeavored to cite passages that may presage this ending: Gottschalk's growing obsession with meteorology, his sketch of a balloon, his desire for self-understanding and open spaces. Lüdemann calls him "Professor," so perhaps he has chosen the university route of which he dreamed. The narrator tells us: "balloon flight is an art, a work of art in which the pilot, the balloon, the wind and the weather, and the landscape as well, unite. There is no exploitation. . . . No living creature is tormented or mistreated" (338). Perhaps Gottschalk's engagement with balloons is the ultimate escape from his experiences in GSWA, the ultimate expression of his musing there, of the influence of Kropotkin's *Mutual Aid* (about which I include more in the section on intertextuality). Reaching a bit further, we may speculate that Lüdemann's name comes from the Latin *ludens*, "playing." J. Huizinga's well-regarded book, *Homo Ludens: A Study of the Play-Element in Culture* (1944), concludes: "Real civilization cannot exist in the absence of a certain play-element, for civilization presupposes limitations and mastery of the self. . . . True play knows no propaganda; its aim is in itself, and its familiar spirit is happy inspiration."[14] As readers, we may wish this "happy ending" for Gottschalk.

But in a darker mode, we may decide Gottschalk has genuinely lost his sanity due to the horrendous treatment of the Herero and Nama he observed in GSWA;

he returns home with a form of PTSD, having seen the heinous crimes of which humanity is capable. Or worse still, perhaps he embodies here "colonial aphasia": after his return home, he occupies himself in a dream world, imagining fanciful creations, forgetting the horror of the genocidal gaze, doing nothing to prevent a repeat of genocide. Perhaps the epigram that Timm chose for *In My Brother's Shadow* from William Carlos Williams sheds light on the ending of *Morenga*:

> above the battle's fury—
>
> clouds and trees and grass—

INTERTEXTUALITY AS CRITIQUE IN *MORENGA*

> Of all of the Germans in the text, only Dr. Gottschalk questions the scientific justification of the oppressive social relations in the colony. He develops an alternative notion of social development from reading a book on mutual cooperation in nature, Petr Alekseevich Kropotkin's *Gegenseitige Hilfe in der Entwicklung*.
>
> KENOSIAN | "The Colonial Body Politic"

As a literary device, intertextuality is frequently deployed as a strategy for critiquing an earlier text, for revising or correcting it to suit the more recent zeitgeist. Julia Kristeva, the critic credited with coining the term, claims "intertextuality is perhaps the most global concept possible for signifying the modern experience of writing."[15] Intertextuality is seen as a specifically postmodern device and is, according to Sue Vice, the most common literary method in Holocaust fiction.[16] By its very nature, intertextuality illuminates the act of storytelling and makes the reader aware of the author as part of a network of writers. Intertextuality creates metafiction: it is fiction about fiction. For example, fairy tales are often revised as a way to demonstrate that earlier versions were sexist or conveyed inappropriate ideas about class.[17] In fact, Timm devotes an entire chapter in *Morenga* to a text, written by Gottschalk as a report to the German military, with insertions/marginalia/corrections composed of wry and sarcastic remarks by the reader of that report, thus modeling intertextuality. Marginalia also feature in the copy of *Mutual Aid* that Gottschalk reads throughout the novel.

Timm uses intertextuality generously and in several directions in *Morenga*. The novel references external, earlier texts, such as Frenssen's *Peter Moor*, to offer a stinging critique. Timm also includes a kind of internal intertextuality by telling us what books his characters are reading; in doing so, he invites readers to consider the impact of books on individuals and societies. Also internal is the intertextuality among the various narratives, Gottschalk's diary, and his dreams. Finally, we can speak of the intertextual relationship between *Morenga* and Timm's memoir, *In My Brother's Shadow*, written thirty years later, which is discussed later in this chapter.[18]

A comparison of the opening pages of *Peter Moor* and *Morenga* reveals many similarities: they both present an account of the departure from family in Germany in dreary weather, stowing gear in the ship, seasickness, a stop in Liberia, taking on black crew, arrival in Swakopmund in the fog, being ferried to a shore that appears to be barren wasteland, boarding the train for Windhoek, seeing devastated stations along the way where Hereros had attacked, arrival in Windhoek. Both Moor and Gottschalk have enlisted; both eagerly anticipate arrival in this exotic place called Africa. Only time separates their experiences: Moor departs Germany in mid-January 1904, just after the war has begun; Gottschalk departs on 28 September 1904, nine months later, and, significantly, after the Battle of Waterberg has already occurred. Thus, Moor fights in the conflict with the Herero and Gottschalk with the Nama. But, while Gottschalk will dramatically change his attitude about Africa, Africans, and especially about the German military while there, becoming profoundly critical, Moor's experience in the Schutztruppe transforms the imperial gaze with which he arrived into an acceptance of the genocidal gaze.

An incident that occurs in *Peter Moor* and is recapitulated in *Morenga* provides another example of how intertextuality functions as critique. Near the conclusion of *Peter Moor*, a guardsman toys with a Herero man, taking him into captivity and then telling him to run, to escape. As the man does so, the guardsman shoots him in cold blood and he dies before Peter Moor's eyes. Moor offers no objection to this incident except to grumble that the noise of the shot might have alerted "hostile tribes" to their whereabouts.[19] Frenssen is content to present the killing of indigenous people with impunity. A very similar incident occurs in *Morenga* (pages 38–43) but with a very different outcome: the suggestion is that this disturbing incident was one of the causes of Wenstrup's desertion.

Perhaps, when he did his research, Timm also read a memoir by Margarethe von Eckenbrecher based on her experiences as an immigrant to GSWA with her husband; they were part of the settler colony. They departed from Hamburg in dreary weather in late April 1902, and her account of their voyage shares much with that of Frenssen and Timm. She, like Gottschalk, sails on a boat in the Woerman line, is seasick, and stops in Liberia to take on what she calls "Kruboys" (the black men who will assist the passengers in disembarking). Her arrival in Swakopmund happens in the fog, and her "adventure" getting from ship to land in rough seas is quite similar to that recounted by Moor and Gottschalk.

With her husband, she, too, boards a train for Windhoek, stopping along the way at Karibib in order to head to Okombahe, where they hope to acquire land. Eckenbrecher left GSWA with her son, born in Africa, just as the war with the Hereros began. She published her memoir in Germany in 1907 where it became a best seller; she returned to Windhoek in May 1914, a divorcée, with her two sons, where she wrote a second memoir in 1936. It was published in Germany in 1940.[20] So both of these volumes would have been available to Uwe Timm when writing, and though von Eckenbrecher shares some of the Schutztruppe's attitude toward indigenous people, her perspective is that of a woman and a settler, very different from Moor and Gottschalk.

Two symbolically important texts serve as the reading material of Gottschalk and Wenstrup en route to GSWA; both are significant as intertexts. We are told that Gottschalk "brought along three books for the crossing.... A text book on immunology, a South African botany, and a novel by Fontane, *Die* [sic] *Stechlin*" (6). Peter Bowman calls *Der Stechlin* "a novel of extraordinary thematic breadth, treating of the political process, social change, the role of nobility, ideas of nationhood, the position of women, the nature of charity and aspects of artistic life. Above all, though, it is a novel about language."[21] The novel was the final book written by Theodor Fontane; it was published in 1898 so would have been a relatively new novel packed in Gottschalk's bag as he departed Germany in 1904. Bowman further elucidates: "The all-important lake in *Der Stechlin* symbolizes the interconnections between old and new, local and global, and through this it informs the central 'idea' of the novel: *the harmonious coexistence of different discourses and the rejection of dogmatism*" (emphasis mine, 877). Clearly these themes are shared by *Morenga* as well as by the text Wenstrup reads onboard.

That book is Peter Kropotkin's *Mutual Aid: A Factor of Evolution*. Kropotkin, a Russian prince *and* an anarchist, published this work in London in 1902, so this book would also have been new as Gottschalk and Wenstrup sailed from Hamburg. *Mutual Aid* proposes just that: cooperation among groups as a natural state, rather than competition. Kropotkin opens the book with observations about cooperation among animals he studied in Siberia: "even in those few spots where animal life teemed in abundance, I failed to find—although I was eagerly looking for it—that bitter struggle for the means of existence, *among animals belonging to the same species*, which was considered by most Darwinists ... as the dominant characteristic of struggle for life, and the main factor of evolution" (emphasis in the original).[22] Kropotkin's analysis continues with chapters devoted to mutual aid among "primitive" peoples, in the medieval city, and in the concluding two chapters, "mutual aid among ourselves": "The mutual aid tendency in man has so remote an origin, and is so deeply interwoven with all the past evolution of the human race, that it has been maintained by mankind up to the present time, notwithstanding the vicissitudes of history" (223).

Shortly before his mysterious disappearance, Wenstrup gives the book to Gottschalk as a Christmas gift. Gottschalk has been curious about the text that has consumed so much of Wenstrup's time, and he begins to study it carefully. In it, he finds a theory that contradicts the struggle for existence said to be endemic to theories propounded by Social Darwinists, as well as prolific marginalia by Wenstrup. Its appeal to Gottschalk is immediate: it stands in flagrant opposition to the thrust of the Schutztruppe presence in GSWA. The text gives him language for the growing uneasiness he is experiencing about the treatment of the indigenous people of GSWA, about the genocidal gaze of his colleagues. Timm here invites the reader to consider the influence of books on their readers and on society as a whole. The books on German colonialism in 1978, with the exception of that by Horst Drechsler, had failed to provide the critique required, had failed to note the profound power and damage of the genocidal gaze. Timm's aim in *Morenga* is to do just that.

We are told: "Gottschalk always carried this book with him, wrapped in a page of the *Vossiche News* . . . whenever he left his room in Warmbad, he stuck the book in the pocket of his uniform" (122). Timm includes examples of Wenstrup's marginalia in *Mutual Aid*, which fascinate and puzzle Gottschalk. Here is one example: "The only good Herero is not a dead Herero (the butcher Trotha is mistaken there), but one who works for free. The goal of native policy is a well-nourished slave. First iron around the neck, then—a most elegant solution—through the head. The final goal: a slave who affirms his slavery" (122). Wenstrup is writing satirically here, of course, and in doing so, he captures neatly an aspect of the imperial gaze, as well as the conflict between Leutwein and von Trotha. The Germans did thrust the Herero into irons and work them as slaves after the Battle of Waterberg: colonization of the mind was achieved. Practice for the Holocaust, as yet unimagined, occurred.

On patrol, the Germans shoot a Nama man found crouching in the bushes. The following day, Gottschalk experiences a revelation about himself: "They shot a man and all I thought was, I hope no one hears it. What's happened to you, thought Gottschalk, still staring into the mirror shard" he had used to shave (125). "A cold feeling of alienation submerged everything in a clear, bright light: his shock of feeling nothing when he thought about the incident. Shock at his own failure to be shocked, at an indifference that should not be indifferent" (125–26). Gottschalk fears that he, too, is becoming inured to killing with impunity. His roommate, Lt. Haring, notices "with some concern the strange alteration in his roommate Gottschalk" (129): he saves half his rations and surreptitiously feeds the Nama enclosed in barbed wire; he spends "more time with brown riffraff, talking with the kitchen hands and ox-boys" (129); he resumes his language study; and he "was seen several times with a Hottentot named Katharina. . . . That was always the first sign someone was going native" (129). The next entry we are given in Gottschalk's diary reveals the impact of *Mutual Aid*: "Happily enough, competition is not the rule either in the animal world or mankind. . . . Better conditions are created by the elimination of competition by means of mutual aid (Kropotkin)" (131). Not only Lt. Haring notes the changes in Gottschalk: "Soon even men from the lower ranks were openly tapping their heads when Gottschalk walked by" (131).

Gottschalk continues to consult Kropotkin throughout the novel. Once he reaches Keetmanshoop, in late March 1905, when he recognizes that he is moving toward pacifism, he also recognizes that his continuing interest (in *Mutual Aid*) "focused on how his predecessor had read the book, on Wenstrup's marginalia and the passages he had underlined in various colors" (211). For example, Wenstrup has underlined the following passage in red: "One of the greatest pleasures of the Hottentots certainly lies in their gifts and good offices to one another. The integrity of the Hottentots, their strictness and celerity in the exercise of justice, and their chastity, are things in which they surpass all or most nations in the world" (211–12). Thus *Mutual Aid* functions as a counternarrative to the genocidal gaze that Gottschalk has begun to recognize and resist. Wenstrup's trail through the text acts as an affirmation of Gottschalk's growing identification with "the enemy."

Another kind of intertextuality used quite frequently in the novel is the disclosure of Gottschalk's dreams; these dreams are recorded in his diary and serve several functions: they provide a kind of surreal reading of a recent event in Gottschalk's life; they also reveal his unconscious mind-set. As with Gottschalk's reactions to Kropotkin, the dreams become an additional pathway in the text for Timm to signal his critique. Here is the full text of a dream Gottschalk recorded on 19 January 1905, en route to Warmbad:

> Dreamed I had lost my way in the desert. The strange thing was that as I wandered about, I didn't know I'd lost my way, but at the same time I knew, from the outside as it were, that I didn't know it. So I walked on without worrying, but dead tired, climbing sand dunes that stretched away like waves into the interior of the country. Only after seeing a rider in the distance, and then seeing him again drawing nearer,

did I realize I'd lost my way. I felt the sand trickling down into my boots, filling in tightly around my feet, and it was harder and harder to walk. Suddenly, crossing the crest of a dune, I stood before the rider, who wore a German Colonial Guard uniform. I asked him the way, but my questions bounced off him like a wall. Finally he lifted his head. Nothing can be seen beneath the shadowy brim of his hat but a scar: no eyes, no nose, no mouth. A faceless face. On his hat, in place of the black, white and red cockade, he wears a white marguerite. The horse replies in Nama, but in a dialect I can't understand. (80–81)

The dream invites several interpretations. At this point in the novel, *Gottschalk is genuinely lost*, not so much physically as emotionally and intellectually. The assumptions with which he arrived in Africa—the romanticism of colonialism derived from the goods in his father's store, the supposed purity of military motives, the imperial gaze upon the Nama—have been dashed by his experience of Schwanebach and others, by his reading of Kropotkin, and by his friendship with Wenstrup. He is becoming paralyzed by his doubts in the desert of how he should proceed; his walk is slowing. Who is the rider he encounters? The rider is wearing a German uniform and perhaps is thus a figure of death, of the genocidal gaze; but the Herero and Nama would often don the uniforms of slain Germans, so the figure could represent those the Germans are intent on killing; the fact that the horse speaks Nama suggests the rider may be Nama. Yet another reading of this ambiguous dream is that the rider represents Wenstrup. It has been about two weeks since Wenstrup disappeared. In chapter 6, "Wenstrup's Disappearance," we are told he sported a tamarisk sprig in his hat on Christmas Day (53); the figure of death sports a marguerite, a variety of daisy.

Once Gottschalk has admitted to himself and others that he believes the war is unjust, he has another powerful dream of death, dated 25 May 1905, Keetmanshoop. Gottschalk has now been in GSWA for eight months: "Toward morning I woke from a dream: I lay in one of those zinc coffins used to transport corpses back to Germany. But I was not dead. The coffin was screwed down tight and soldered, as usual, to prevent the lid from warping under the pressure of decomposition gases" (259). The coffin is loaded on a ship and during the voyage, Gottschalk is able to converse with bodies in other coffins, including Lt. Schwanebach. Upon arrival in Germany, his coffin is loaded onto a gun carriage. "My zinc coffin bounced and clanged about on the gun carriage until it finally crashed to the ground and sprang open. I woke up" (259). By this time, Gottschalk is making mysterious entries in his journal, which could be interpreted as mathematical calculations needed to plan his escape over the border to English territory (the route Morenga will take). This dream is clearly a dream about his profound need to escape, to leave behind the genocidal gaze of the Schutztruppe. His diary entry for 12 July 1905: "The career officer has his motto: *der Berufsstand zum Tode*—our profession unto death" (266).

Timm deftly uses intertextuality in *Morenga* as one of several vehicles for conveying his critique of the violence of the genocidal gaze as well as for revealing the gradations of Gottschalk's disillusionment with the colonial project. Whether it be citing the books his characters are reading, inviting the reader to peer into Gottschalk's diary, or recounting Gottschalk's dreams, Timm's use of intertextuality calls the reader's attention to the power of words and story to create reality, or change it. Gottschalk's texts and those he reads are part of a network of many texts, versions of German imperialism and its impact on the Schutztruppe, the Africans, and the Germans back home in the Fatherland.

HYBRIDITY OF NARRATIVE TECHNIQUE, TEXTUAL CONTENT, AND FORMAT

It's a historical novel, based on facts . . .
I wanted to write a book that also took a fictional approach to the material.
It was precisely the combination of fact and fiction that interested me.
UWE TIMM | 2003 interview

Morenga is comprised of twenty-seven chapters and an epilogue. The majority of the chapters are written in omniscient, third-person narration, largely focalized through Gottschalk. Nine of the chapters are printed in a smaller font, thus breaking the narration in various ways and interrupting Gottschalk's tale.[23] Some chapters are given titles that represent a sharp change in voice and content. "Battle Report 1," 2, and 3 are such chapters: they report military strategy, battles, and activities of individual soldiers and officers; they are for the most part drawn from the Colonial Archives and can be said to represent the genocidal gaze. "Regional Studies 1" and 2 present flashbacks of supposedly historical men, such as missionary Gorth and trader Klügge, both of whom are surreal and grotesque characters who endeavor to perpetrate hoaxes and scams on the Herero and Nama. "Regional Studies 3: Theodolite or the Usefulness of Sardine Oil" provides the reader with a brief history of the German colonization of GSWA. Timm emphasizes the venal motives for colonization: "the economic sector had finally lived up to its patriotic duty to civilize an underdeveloped and backward land. It was . . . one of the noblest tasks of the country of poets and

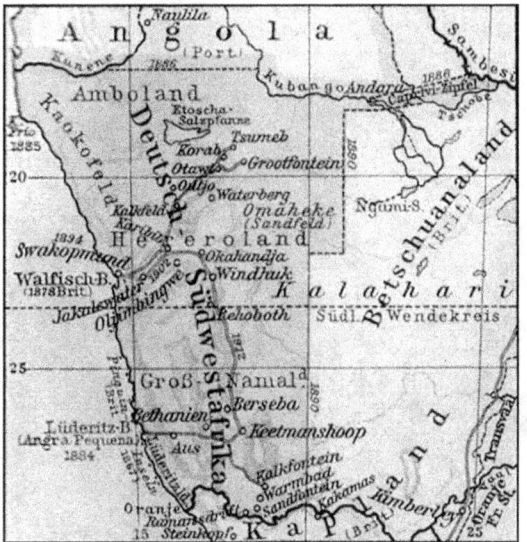

FIGURE 1. "Map of Deutsch Südwestafrika, 1904" (German Southwest Africa). Source: Creative Commons (hereafter CC): CC BY-SA 3.0.

FIGURE 2. "Der Nama-Führer Hendrik Witbooi, um 1900" (The Nama Leader Hendrik Witbooi, around 1900). Note the white scarf covering his hat, a characteristic item of dress for Witbooi and his followers. Source: CC: Public Domain; Regierung von DSWA Regierung von DSWA, www.radiobremen.de /magazin/geschichte/namibia /geschichte_in_bildern.html.

FIGURE 3. "Surviving Herero after the escape through the arid desert of Omaheke, c. 1907." These Herero have escaped, if only temporarily, their intended fate: extermination. Herero who returned from the desert were most often captured, confined to a concentration camp, and put to hard labor. Source: CC: Public Domain; Galerie Bassenge.

FIGURE 4. "Herero chained during the 1904 rebellion." These Herero warriors have been enslaved and put to forced labor on German railways, on farms, or at other tasks. Source: CC: Public Domain; Ullstein Bilderdienst, Berlin.

FIGURE 5. "Samuel Maharero (1856–1923), son of Maharero." Samuel Maherero served as the leader of the Herero during the Battle of Waterberg. It was not unusual for African leaders in German Southwest Africa to appropriate military uniforms from the enemy. Source: CC: Public Domain, Exampapers.nust.na.

FIGURE 6. "Gustav Frenssen, Schriftsteller, Pastor, Deutschland." Frenssen was a Protestant pastor and the author of several bestselling novels, including *Peter Moor's Journey to Southwest Africa* (1906), a colonial novel that valorizes the German military's effort to eradicate the indigenous people in German Southwest Africa. Source: CC BY S-A 3.0 de.

FIGURE 7. Cover design for 1943 edition of Gustav Frenssen's *Peter Moors Fahrt Nach Südwest*. Note thorn design, which may refer to both the vegetation in the German colony and the "martyrdom" of the German soldiers fighting there, a theme in the novel. Photo by Elizabeth R. Baer, of an edition in the collection of the Universitätsbibliothek Johann Christian Senckenberg, Frankfurt, Germany.

FIGURE 8. This edition of Frenssen's *Peter Moor* was created for the Wehrmacht. The book is paperback, measures 6" by 4.5", and is printed in Fraktur on rough paper. Printed by the thousands during the 1940s, this copy is in Elizabeth Baer's personal collection and is dated 1944. A very similar edition is in the collection of the Universitätsbibliothek Johann Christian Senckenberg, Frankfurt, Germany. Photo by Elizabeth R. Baer.

FIGURE 9. "Le major Leutwein lors de son mandat dans le sud-ouest africain (1894–1904)." (Major Leutwein during his Mandate in Southwest Africa). Source: CC: Public Domain.

FIGURE 10. "Portrait of General Lothar von Trotha, ca. 1905." Von Trotha had served in other German colonial massacres previous to his arrival in GSWA in 1904. His infamous "annihilation order," issued in October 1904, made clear the genocidal intent he brought to his engagement with the Herero and Nama. Source: CC: Public Domain.

FIGURE 11. "Photo of the Death Camp at Shark Island, German South West Africa (now Namibia)." Taken circa 1903. This death camp becomes the prototype of the Nazi death camps during the Holocaust. Inmates were systematically starved, raped, worked to death, and allowed to succumb to disease. Source: CC: FAL (Free Art License).

FIGURE 12. "Photo of Lieutenant von Durling at the death camp at Shark Island, German South West Africa (now Namibia)." December 1904. Note that one woman, who is prominently displayed, has her breasts bared. There is evidence, across several photos from this period in German Southwest Africa, that prurient photographers or figures in the photos forced women to remove their clothing from the waist up prior to the photo being taken. Source: CC: FAL (Free Art License).

Eine Kiste mit Hereroschädeln wurde kürzlich von den Truppen in Deutsch-Süd-W.-Afrika verpackt und an das Pathologische Institut zu Berlin gesandt, wo sie zu wissenschaftlichen Messungen verwandt werden sollen. Die Schädel, die von Hererofrauen mittels Glasscherben vom Fleisch befreit und versandfähig gemacht wurden, stammen von gehängten oder gefallenen Hereros.

FIGURE 13. "German Soldiers Packing the Skulls of Executed Namibian Aborigines at Shark Island Concentration Camp, circa 1903." Note that this image was a postcard that was sent by settlers to families back in Germany. Skulls were sent to Germany for eugenic research, to "prove" that the Herero and Nama were a lesser race than Europeans, in the racial hierarchy that underpins the genocidal gaze. Source: CC: FAL (Free Art License).

FIGURE 14. "Kamelreiterpatrouille" (Camel rider patrol). Photo taken sometime between 1906 and 1918. In Uwe Timm's novel *Morenga*, one of the German soldiers, Veterinary Lieutenant Gottschalk, is tasked with experimenting with camels as beasts of burden for both the military and their supplies; the ability of camels to go for long periods without water was seen as an advantage in the deserts of German Southwest Africa. Such camel patrols were, in fact, used in GSWA. Source: CC: BY-SA 3.0 de, Bundesarchiv_Bild_105-DSWA0095/Walther Dobbertin.

FIGURE 15. "Deutsch-Südwestafrika, Herero-Aufstand" (German Southwest Africa Herero Uprising). This photo gives the reader a good idea of the living conditions of the German military during the war with the Herero and Nama. Such living conditions are the source of harsh complaints in Frenssen's *Peter Moor* and are also described in Uwe Timm's *Morenga*. Source: CC-BY-SA 3.0, Bundesarchiv_Bild_183-R18799.

FIGURE 16. "Jacob Morenga, leader of African partisans in the insurrection against German rule." Taken between 1904 and 1907. Morenga is the eponymous hero of Uwe Timm's *Morenga*. Source: CC Public Domain.

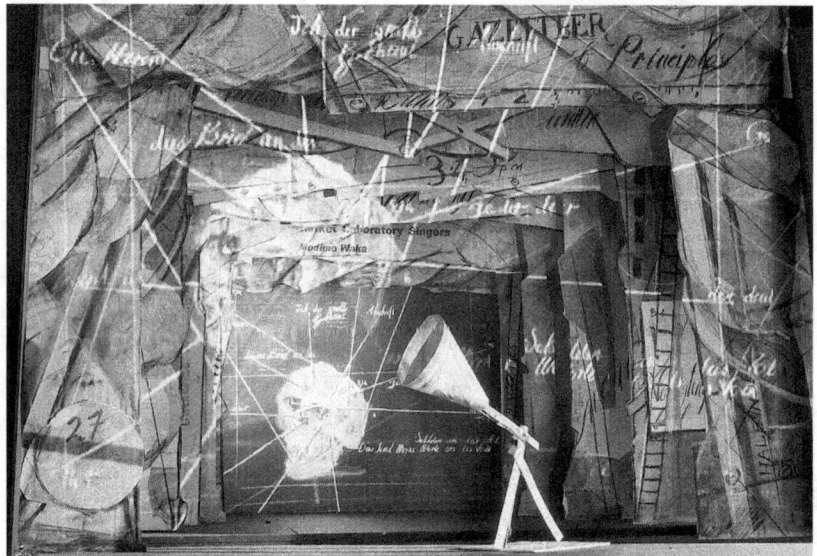

FIGURE 17. William Kentridge's *Black Box*: a still from the 22-minute art installation. This image shows the Megaphone Man puppet, who is the narrator of the piece; the skull, which is a frequent trope in the piece; and the construction of the small stage with "curtains" that form a palimpsest of newspapers, maps, and other documents from the colonial era in German Southwest Africa. Courtesy of the artist and Marian Goodman Gallery, New York/Paris.

FIGURE 18. William Kentridge's *Black Box*: a still from the 22-minute art installation. This image shows the Herero woman puppet at the left, identifiable by the distinctive headdress which Herero women wear. The cattle horn shape of the headdress is an homage to the herds owned by the Herero which historically provided both sustenance and a form of cash. The head to the right references, as does the skull in the previous photo, the genocide and the German practice of severing the skulls and sending them to Germany for "research." Courtesy of the artist and Marian Goodman Gallery, New York/Paris.

FIGURE 19. William Kentridge's *Black Box*: a still from the 22-minute art installation. This image again shows the curtains surrounding the small stage on which the installation takes place. In the center, we see another Herero woman puppet on the left, juxtaposed with an advertisement that reads "üppiger busen," which is German for "ample bosom" or "lush breasts." This is followed by the phrase "Pilules orientales," which can be translated as "oriental pills." Such pills were advertised in the early twentieth century as a method for developing or restoring a firm bust. Such an image of the bosom surely references the German military's obsession with photographing indigenous women bare-breasted. Courtesy of the artist and Marian Goodman Gallery, New York/Paris.

FIGURE 20. Mohrenköpfe. This echo of German colonialism remains widely available in Germany, sold in candy stores and at Christmas markets. These chocolate-covered candies are named Mohrenköpfe, which can be translated as "Moors' Heads." Photo by Elizabeth R. Baer, taken at a Christmas market, Frankfurt, Germany, December 2015.

thinkers to civilize the savages" (214). In other words, the racial hierarchy at the center of the genocidal gaze informs the project from the outset.

And some chapters are given titles that suggest academic essays, such as "Concerning the Milder, More Humane, Yet More Lasting Pedagogical Effects of the Rope," which presents a series of letters debating the usefulness and appropriateness of whipping the indigenous people (chapter 12). Even the chapters that are printed in regular font, and open in the usual narrative style, contain inserted documents in smaller font such as Gottschalk's often heartrending diary entries, letters from a range of authors (including one from Hendrik Witbooi, dated 27 July 1905), military circulars and regulations, the texts of a telegram and a doctor's report, and so forth. The pastiche thus created by Timm allows for wide swings in tone and content: from realistic fiction to apparently authentic military reports, from apocryphal stories about missionaries and wildly inventive stories about traders to abstract, heartless texts that reveal the genocidal gaze of the Schutztruppe.

Following the introduction to Gottschalk in the first twenty pages, Timm inserts a two-page chapter titled "Two Positions." It is comprised of six quotations, in the smaller font, taken from texts in the German Colonial Archives, and attributed to von Trotha, Leutwein, Imperial Chancellor von Bülow, and Colonel-General Count Schlieffen. These texts briefly outline the dispute between von Trotha and Leutwein regarding the disposition of the indigenous people. Von Trotha's belief that "the nation as such must be destroyed" prevailed. The chapter ends with this stark announcement in regular font: "Of approximately 80,000 Hereros, 15,130 survived" (23).

Before the reader is returned to the story of Gottschalk, two more chapters, written in blunt, abstract military language, intervene. The first, "General Situation," further details von Trotha's triumph over Leutwein. It recounts von Trotha's choice of Colonel Deimling (another historical figure) to lead the onslaught against the Nama in the south. Called the White Snake by the Nama, Deimling "didn't intend just to free the encircled villages, he would surround the Witboois and annihilate them. Deimling's typical vocabulary for skirmishes and battles: crush, shatter, smash. Colonel Deimling's plan: to smash the Witboois. Then to march south and smash Morenga and his men too" (26). Timm continues to build, for the reader, an understanding of the genocidal gaze and how endemic it was in the military.

Immediately following is "Concept of the Enemy," a chapter comprised of various quotations from German sources, several of which convey the German perceptions of Morenga: "Jakob Morenga, a Herero Bastard from a small tribe living in the midst of the Hottentots . . . attained a not inconsiderable education for a black . . . he has abstained from the usual bestial atrocities practiced by his northern tribesmen. . . . His unusual importance can be seen in the very fact that although he is a black man, he plays a leading role among the lighter-skinned Hottentots" (28). This racialized description of Morenga, from the Colonial Archives, underscores the centrality of racist hierarchies in the genocidal gaze. Another quotation, attributed to a Cavalry Colonial Guard, continues this racist discourse: "The Hottentots are naturally warlike and have developed a great facility for guerilla warfare. It's true that their most important general—Morenga—was black. Basically, they are all bandits and cattle thieves" (29). These two chapters again reveal that the gaze of the Schutztruppe upon the Herero and Nama is deadly; the enemy is not recognized as human but rather categorized by skin color and slated for destruction.

What is Timm's writerly purpose in mixing fiction, some of it fantastic (for example, when the oxen speak to share with the reader the creation story of both the Nama and of the ox as a beast of burden in chapter 11, "Regional Studies 1"), with such quotations from historical documents and accounts of historical events? If we return to the notion of *Morenga* as a postmodern, postcolonial, and post-Holocaust novel, then one must recall Theodore Adorno's dictum: "To write poetry after Auschwitz is barbaric."[24] Though Adorno subsequently retracted this taboo, controversy remains among Holocaust Studies scholars about the use of the imagination in writing post-Holocaust literature. A Jewish American writer who has considered this dilemma extensively, and who has also written imaginative texts about the Holocaust, is Cynthia Ozick. In a series of essays and presentations during the 1980s, Ozick worked out a formula that allowed for the kind of hybridity Timm is using in post-Holocaust fiction. But she holds such hybridity to a higher standard: "What is permissible to the playfully ingenious author of *Robinson Crusoe*—fiction masking as chronicle—is not permitted to those who touch on the destruction of six million souls, and on the extirpation of their millennial civilization of Europe" (Baer, *The Golem Redux*, 154).

Instead, asserts Ozick: "When a novel comes to us with the claim that it is directed consciously toward history, that the divide between history and the imagination is being purposefully bridged, that the bridging is the very point, and that the design of the novel is to put human flesh on historical notation, then the argument for fictional autonomy collapses, and the rights of history can begin to urge their own force" (Baer, *The Golem Redux*, 154). In other words, a writer must not toy with the facts of a genocide. Ozick criticizes both William

Styron's *Sophie's Choice* and Bernhard Schlink's *The Reader* for having done so.[25] Though Timm wrote *Morenga* before Ozick made these pronouncements, his extensive research in military records, colonial reports, photographs, and the archives in Namibia indicates his desire for authenticity in his use of history. The importation into the text of excerpts from military correspondence, a letter from Hendrik Witbooi, and the pages of Morenga's diary all demonstrate his recognition that "the rights of history" must have their say. In the face of German colonial aphasia, Timm asserts the crucial importance of historical accuracy, with particular attention to the language used by the various forces in conflict with each other—the missionaries, the traders, the Schutztruppe, the Boers, the settlers, and the Africans themselves.

In describing the richness of the hybridity in the novel, Breon Mitchell, who translated *Morenga* into English, notes that such hybridity enables the novel to function on three levels: the first level "recreates the history of the German colonial experience in the war against the Hottentots; . . . there is a second level that is unavoidable: the whole question of genocide and the *Konzentrationslager*. . . . You cannot help but think of what happened during the Nazi period to the Jews; . . . a third level as well: we know there are *Gastarbeiter* [guest workers], Turks and others, in Germany now, and that the country is having a great deal of difficulty in dealing with this" (Schulte, 6).

ANIMAL IMAGERY AS AN ASPECT OF THE GENOCIDAL GAZE

> "How can we expect to colonize a land if we don't take the trouble to understand the natives?" Gottschalk once asked. . . . "With the aid of an interpreter and a hippo-hide whip," Lieutenant Schwanebach replied." (82)

The first forty pages of the novel are rife with German soldiers' references to the Herero and Nama as animals. Here are a few examples of this dominant trope. When the physician onboard is ordered to examine the "natives" who had boarded in Liberia, Schwanebach jokes, "That's a task for our two veterinarians. . . . Everyone laughed" (10). Captain Moll describes the Nama women to Gottschalk as he arrives in Windhoek: "The women are fantastic . . . completely immoral, total animals, but unfortunately syphilitic" (17). As Gottschalk marches toward Rehoboth, a lieutenant who had been in Africa for six years explains: "The Hottentots were much more dangerous than the Hereros. They let themselves be slaughtered in battle, but had few scruples when it came to prisoners. They stuffed a dead man's mouth with his own severed genitals. 'Animals,' Schwanebach said" (37). To which the lieutenant replies, "It was probably because the German troops had raped and mistreated the Herero women during their advance" (37). Yet another incident with Lt. Schwanebach involves his command to Gottschalk to "make sure the baboon [a Nama man] was dead" (40). Gottschalk at first is tempted to demur by saying he was only a veterinarian. "But he . . . said nothing, afraid that Schwanebach might reply, exactly, that's just the point" (40). This pattern of the Schutztruppe not only referring to the Herero and Nama as bestial but actually placing them at the bottom of the racial hierarchy, as less than human, continues throughout the novel. Such language characterizes the imperial gaze and sets up the Schutztruppe for the transition to the genocidal gaze. Viewing other human beings as animals, as unworthy of life, becomes yet another justification of genocide, and another link to the Nazis and their characterization of Jews as subhuman, as parasites.

Schwanebach is often the mouthpiece of the genocidal gaze. Behind his back, he is called Schwinebelly by Gottschalk and others, with the pun carrying heavy irony. Then comes a surreal moment in the novel when Schwanebach reveals himself to be quite "bestial." Unusual rain has arrived in GSWA and the men run outside naked to bathe. "Schwinebelly was seen naked for the first time. They stared at him in shock. He was incredibly hairy, like a black monkey" (52). A joke begins to make the rounds of the officers' mess: Schwinebelly's fourth child went missing at her baptismal ceremony and was found perched on the curtain rod: "There sits the little one, black and hairy as a monkey. And she has prehensile feet" (54). Timm turns the tables on Schwanebach, demonstrating that arraying humans on a racist hierarchy is not only offensive but inaccurate. No distinctions exist between the Germans and the Nama, at least as far as biology is concerned.

When Gottschalk reaches a crucial turning point, acknowledging that he "no longer asked himself if the war was unjust. He was now convinced it was" (195), he also begins to see the Germans as animals, a reversal of the genocidal gaze. He sees Captain Koppy "with his little drunken tapir eyes" while all the officers "break into whinnies of laughter" (192). In a dream, he sees that his own fingers have turned into fish (200). After the battle in the Great Karas Mountains, Gottschalk observes a number of atrocities, including four soldiers raping a Nama woman, and he decides he must "take some action against this human torture" (202). He considers shooting one officer "with his bird-dog face" and another "who also resembled an animal" (202). Finally, Gottschalk begins to voice his doubts aloud: "In Warmbad, Gottschalk once told Doctor Haring he didn't want to be complicit in this war's inhumanity. He wouldn't take an active part in fighting or shooting any Hottentots" (253). So he is assigned a new task: "to test the feasibility of camels as pack animals in German South West Africa" (257). As improbable as this may sound, the Germans actually did import camels for this purpose and, eventually, for the soldiers to ride. Entries in Gottschalk's diary become increasingly cryptic and philosophical. He references the distance to the "English frontier," which would be his destination if he deserts. He tells of dreams about white worms escaping from pine cones and jumping beans with larvae inside.

Timm's use of animal imagery enables him to trace Gottschalk's "conversion" from arriving in GSWA with the imperial gaze to critiquing German values of violence. He begins to see the Germans as engaging in genocidal violence, behaving in a stereotypically "bestial" manner. The use of animal imagery also has a wide referential resonance, signaling the links between the GSWA genocide and the Holocaust. It is a subtle reminder to the reader of the continuity thesis.

THE DEPICTION OF MORENGA: A HEROIC SUBHUMAN?

It was in Keetmanshoop that Gottschalk first heard the name Morenga. (55)

But the reader has already met Morenga, who gives his name to the novel.[26] On page 2, in the first chapter, "Warning Signs," a brief paragraph tells of a "band of armed Hottentots" attacking isolated farms in southwestern GSWA. "The leader of the band is a man named Morenga." "Who is Morenga?" an anonymous voice inquires. Following that query, two paragraphs provide both facts and myths about this heroic leader, suggesting perhaps both the abstract, rational view of Morenga from the military perspective and his heroic stature from the African perspective, which is being ridiculed here in this German report:

> Information provided by the District Office in Gibeon: A Hottentot Bastard (father: Herero, mother: Hottentot). Took part in the Bondelswart Rebellion in 1903. Said to have been reared in a missionary school. The name of school is unknown. Last employed in the copper mines of O'okiep in the northern part of the Cape Colony [now South Africa].
>
> Morenga rides a white horse that can go four days without water. Only a glass bullet polished by an African can kill him. He can see in the dark. He can shoot a hen's egg from a man's hand at a hundred meters. He wants to drive the Germans out. He can make rain. He turns into a zebra finch and spies on German soldiers. (2)

As we have seen, Morenga is also one of the subjects in the chapter titled "Concept of the Enemy." But, considering that his name serves as the title of the novel, Morenga appears relatively infrequently in the novel. His elusiveness is perhaps symbolic of his elusiveness in real life, one of his successful strategies as a guerilla fighter. It is also a function of Timm's unwillingness to enter the consciousness of African characters; he sees this as a kind of neocolonialism.

An account of Morenga's exploits is included in "Battle Report 2: The Siege of Warmbad." Warmbad is located in the very southernmost tip of GSWA. The chapter opens with a complimentary evaluation of Morenga as a soldier, extracted from the German Colonial Archives: "Morenga planned to exploit the German weakness at Warmbad and take the village by storm. He had accurately assessed the town's importance, with its extensive supplies and large prisoner-of-war camps, and as a base for communication with the Cape Colony. As always he set his plan in motion with remarkable speed, energy, and stealth" (75). After five pages of detailed military strategy, the report concludes that "the murderous onslaught of the Hottentots" had failed, thus saving "German prestige" (79). While this report, written in November 1904, acknowledges Morenga's successful guerilla tactics, in the end it valorizes the German military and underscores the German right to steal the land from the Nama.

One hundred pages elapse before any significant coverage of Morenga appears again. "Battle Report 3: Colonel Deimling's Offensive Against Morenga in the Great Karas Mountains, March 1905" informs the reader that Morenga has "been quiet from December to March" as "he lacked ammunition" (177). The account of this siege tracks very closely with that provided by Drechsler (see pages 186–90 of Drechsler), again suggesting Timm's use of *"Let Us Die Fighting."* While the Germans were ultimately the victors, the chapter makes clear the savvy and valiant fighting of Morenga and his wildly outnumbered troops. We learn that Morenga was shot in the hip in one of the skirmishes. We are also given a description of an undated photograph of Morenga with his lieutenants. They are wearing captured Colonial Guard clothing—hats, jackets, shirts, and ammunition belts—and have propped their guns—also captured from the Germans—on the ground. This description does not fit any of the photos that Timm includes in his collection of colonial photographs, *Deutsche Kolonien*, which he put together for publication as a result of his research for *Morenga*.[27] However, a photo taken in 1907 with Morenga and eleven of his followers is similar and does appear in *Deutsche Kolonien* (83).

This chapter also includes the crucially important passage with excerpts from Morenga's diary, the only moment in the novel when we see through African eyes. The reader is told that Morenga captured a chest belonging to the "fallen Lieutenant Edward Fürbringer" (187), which contains a notebook with Fürbringer's diary entries. Morenga appropriates the notebook and uses it to write his own diary.

We know from an interview with Timm that such a diary written by Morenga did exist and is now lost. The novel includes the unpunctuated texts of four entries, with the following dates: "10th [1905] . . . 12th . . . 13.2.1905 . . . Kactchanas 10.3.05" (187–88). These passages detail practical matters: the tribute of a salute and food the Bondels give to Morenga; the inventive use of door nails to shod horses; the Veltshoons (shoes) being made by the Bondels; the capture of cattle and a Boer by a patrol that also yields a cache of ammunition; and an account of a skirmish between the Bondels and the Germans.

The narrator tells us that Morenga's diary was confiscated by the Cape police when he crossed the English frontier to escape and the notebook was later given to the fallen lieutenant's father; from there, all traces disappeared. "Only a few pages reproduced photographically in 1910 have come down to us" (188). The story of these few pages is intriguing. When Timm found them doing research for the novel, he determined to include them in the novel but had to translate them into German for the first edition of the novel. When Breon Mitchell translated *Morenga* into English for the 2003 publication, author and translator decided to use Morenga's original English in reproducing the text (Schulte, 3). While doing research at the Universitätsbibliothek Johann Christian Senckenberg in Frankfurt in December 2015, I discovered the photocopies of Morenga's diary, written in his own hand, tipped into *Deutsche Reiter im Südwest* by Friederich von Dincklage-Camp (Berlin: Bong, 1908) between pages 152 and 153. They carry the title: "Aus dem Notizbuche Morengas" (From the Notebook of Morenga) and read almost identically to the passages in the novel. *Deutsche Reiter* is a big (12" x 8"), glossy book with many plates, rather like a travel book; the illustrations include both drawings and paintings of battles and photographs of soldiers engaged in various activities as well as some who have died. The subtitle of the book describes it well: *Selbsterlebnisse aus den Kampfen in Deutsch Südwest* (Personal Experiences/Adventures of Struggle in German Southwest). Like many other texts about German colonialism from this era, the book valorizes German military behavior and the genocidal gaze.[28]

The chapter "Battle Report 3" closes with a German account of "a remarkable meeting between a titled German officer and a rebel Kaffir" (189), that is to say between Captain von Koppy and Morenga himself. Von Koppy comes to the Nama camp to propose conditions for Morenga's surrender and advises him that he will be "defeated in the long run, and that further resistance would only worsen the situation" (190). Morenga replies that "he knew perfectly well that the Hottentots would perish in the struggle" but the decision is not his alone and he must confer with the Bondels. Subsequently, Morenga does confer but then breaks camp and disappears.

So much of this rich, dense, and sprawling novel remains unexplored here. Timm pokes fun at German proclivities and pretensions: for an obsession with cleanliness (Treptow in chapter 17), with maintaining the purity of the German language (243), and for a compulsive preoccupation with order, "Ordnung muss sein," which is demonstrated throughout the novel. Timm occasionally uses mordant humor to lighten the darkness of his critique. For example, a brief anecdote tells of the invention of the "tropicar," which is a vehicle intended for use in the desert. An early model, however, gets stuck in the sand "where it remains as a monument to this day, nicknamed Luther by the locals: Here I stand, I can't do otherwise" (241)!!! We are given brief glimpses of "fat-handed" Heinrich Göring, Hermann Göring's father (223, 228), and of "the cold deadly nights on Shark Island" (216). A Professor Brunkhorst arrives in GSWA to "measure the heads of the various Nama tribes" (265) and build "an ethnological collection concentrating on Nama and Bushman cultures [including] interesting examples of Hottentot skulls" (267). In these last three references—to a key Nazi henchman, to death camps, and to eugenics—Timm foreshadows the Nazis. Timm even slips in a paragraph referencing his own heady days of rebellion against his father's generation, the generation that initiated and fought World War II and carried out the Holocaust. He depicts a scene in a basement in Hamburg, eighty years after GSWA, in which a conversation about "the use of force against property" ensues, resulting in a decision to "toss into the consulate of the Vietnam murderers" a Molotov cocktail (237). A consistent critique of capitalism is found across the novel, with an inherent accusation of financial gain being the true motive of colonialism.

In reflecting back on the impact of *Morenga*, Timm names three things that have "always pleased me. . . . When this novel appeared, Morenga was rediscovered in Namibia. He had been totally forgotten . . . erased. Historians started studying his life." Timm is equally pleased that *Morenga* "helped open up a discussion in Germany [about] Germany's repressed past" and also helped "to advance a little our sense of the consequences it had, the foreign, the Other, always looked down upon and seen as inferior. Those are the roots buried in this novel" (Schulte, 5).

The Genocidal Gaze: Timm's *In My Brother's Shadow*

> Why do we kill? How can men shoot or hang each other?
> And how can others look on like they're at a fair? Why this indifference
> in the midst of terrible hate? Perhaps there's something they hate in themselves,
> some unlived part of their lives. What kills compassion?
> GOTTSCHALK'S DIARY | 25 September 1905

These existential queries, which Gottschalk confides in his diary after his profound disillusionment with the German colonial project, are also the queries Timm inscribes in his novel *Morenga* and, quite likely, are the queries raised in the minds of his readers. Twenty-five years after writing his critique of the German genocidal gaze upon the Herero and Nama and its horrifying results, Uwe Timm turned to another writing task, one he had consciously waited to undertake until his parents and his older sister had died. Their deaths gave him the freedom to ask questions about his family's behavior during and after the Third Reich and to domesticate his critical gaze. *In My Brother's Shadow* purports to be a memoir of Timm's brother, Karl-Heinz, a Waffen SS soldier who died on the Eastern Front in 1943, after wounds to both legs necessitated a double amputation. And the book does serve in that way, as Timm imports excerpts from his brother's minimalist diary and analyzes them, trying desperately to learn more about this brother he hardly knew; Timm was only three when Karl-Heinz enlisted.

But *In My Brother's Shadow*, though a slender 147 pages, is about much more. Timm asks difficult questions about the values held high by the German nation, particularly nationalism, militarism, and their ensuing violence. He wonders aloud if his brother has been involved in the crimes committed by Nazis on the Eastern Front. He interrogates the impact of all this on himself. *In My Brother's Shadow* looks both backward and forward from World War II and Nazism. Timm investigates "the values of his family background and the various ways in which they were shaped by the social and political history of Germany, and the effects which this process of socialization had on his own values and attitudes."[29] Inevitably, given the work he did on *Morenga*, this backward glance includes German imperialism and its tragic consequences: the history of the genocidal gaze in GSWA. Looking forward from World War II, Timm also investigates "the transfer of authoritarian values from Nazism into the postwar family as a consequence of the public humiliation of these values, portraying the postwar family as a site of containment for the fathers' damaged selves, as well as a sphere of control, latent depression, and violence."[30]

Thus Timm probes his father's life and values, giving credence to use of the label of *Väterliteratur* for the text. "*Väterliteratur* relies on the concept of history as a discourse experienced in the family . . . the father is seen as the representative of the history in the family, the parent that transmits the memory of the Third Reich to the child."[31] Though the title of his memoir would suggest otherwise, Timm in fact focuses on the legacy of violence, denial, and silence in his childhood household; his father is at the center of that legacy; his mother represents the counterexample, the parent by whom Timm hopes he has been most influenced. His brother, given his decision to volunteer for the elite SS Death's Head Division, functions in a shadowy manner as a second father, a second synecdoche for Nazi authoritarian values, a second purveyor of the genocidal gaze, but also as an example of the impact the horrendously misguided German values can have on an individual. In its capacity as *Väterliteratur*, *In My Brother's Shadow* is frequently compared to another popular example of the genre, Bernhard Schlink's *The Reader*.

If *Morenga* demonstrates to the reader the appalling acceptance among the German settlers and military of violence against the indigenous people, if it reveals how the racial hierarchies implicit in the genocidal gaze are used as a justification for genocide, then *In My Brother's Shadow* functions as a kind of sequel. The latter text conveys "the extraordinary conditioning which made the Holocaust possible . . . highlighting the way in which a set of social values can be so internalized, so pervasive, that alternative choices become unthinkable. . . . The normality of the brother's perception of war is clearly presented as the product of a conditioning through his upbringing and army training" (Williams, 76–77). *In My Brother's Shadow* demonstrates the way in which genocide is normalized by the genocidal gaze and how it is transmitted from generation to generation.

In My Brother's Shadow, in fact, is very much like *Morenga*: both texts use a pastiche of other texts, including dreams, in a metatextual way, to call attention to the power of stories to carry cultural ideologies or to critique them. Both books required intensive research on Timm's part: for *Morenga*, he traveled to Namibia, the former GSWA, and used the archives there; for *Shadow*, he followed his brother's route into Russia and read many highly regarded books about the Holocaust as well as German military records. Both books call the reader's attention to how destructive the excesses of German militarism have been: the genocidal gaze is the subject of scrutiny in both books. The story of a soldier under fire who keeps a diary is a focus of each text: the similarities between Karl-Heinz and Gottschalk are compelling. Language, too, is a central concern for Timm as he plumbs the differences among the discourses of the military, settlers, missionaries, and traders in *Morenga* and recalls the way language hid or transmogrified the Nazi past during his childhood while simultaneously creating the apotheosis of his brother. Curiously, despite the many articles written about *In My Brother's Shadow* in English, none has called attention to these connections. The fiction that Timm wrote in the intervening twenty-five years was variously political and comical, with a focus on other themes; it even included some lighthearted children's literature.

Timm had often picked up his brother's diary, returned to the family in a box with other effects after his death, to read. But he could never bring himself to read beyond the entry of 21 March 1943, written in Ukraine:

> Donez
> Bridgehead on the Donez
> 75 m away Ivan smoking cigarettes, fodder for my MG. (12)

Timm feared learning about atrocities his brother may have committed: "It was only with my decision to write about my brother, and thus about myself too, to unleash memory, that I felt free to look closely at what he had recorded there" (12). Timm refers to himself in the text as "the boy" or even as "the afterthought," a way of both distancing himself and revealing how he perceived himself to be positioned in the family drama. His older sister, the firstborn, was also relegated to the periphery. It was Karl-Heinz who held center stage, both during his boyhood and after his death at age nineteen.[32] Timm links his profession as a writer to his father's postwar behavior: "For my father, the end of the war, the Nazi period that ended with unconditional surrender, was not an occasion for grief . . . instead, he reacted with an attitude of morose injury and opinionated carping . . . he put forward arguments to the effect that the Allies were guilty too. . . . An attempt to make the guilt relative, to shift our own guilt to the victors, to make them guilty too. . . . Perhaps that is the deeper reason why the boy, no longer a child now, resisted his father's outrage and started writing" (122–23). Such sharp condemnation of the perpetrator generation, their denial and silence, is a key feature of *Väterliteratur*.

Let us look more closely at these parallels in the two texts. Both texts are characterized by hybridity, by a composition of varying texts that rub up against each other in an intertextual manner and require the reader to compare, to integrate, to judge. Here is a comprehensive list of the kinds of texts found in *In My Brother's Shadow*:

first hand memories, letters from the brother to the father and vice versa, reflections by the narrator from the perspective of the present, interpolated fairy stories, a number of dreams, reflections triggered by photographs or drawings, memories mediated through familiar narratives, the outcome of the narrator's own historical research, the brother's actual diary entries, general reflections on language and its limited capacity to express a reality which is beyond comprehension and hence beyond expression, thoughts prompted by everyday objects, and references to other literary and philosophical texts. (Williams, 75)

The brother's diary entries bear an uncanny resemblance to those of Gottschalk. Both are spare and provide little information about the activity of the war itself, and both diaries form the backbone of the narrative.

One of the earliest intertexts in the memoir is the fairy tale "Bluebeard." Timm confesses to his inability as a child to listen to the grisly details of this tale; he would ask his mother to stop reading at "the moment when Bluebeard's wife tries to enter the locked room after he has gone away, in spite of his prohibition" because this moment was "so sinister" (5). He then includes the passage itself, a paragraph-long quotation from the Brothers Grimm. Just as he cannot bring himself to read beyond the promise of violence in his brother's diary, he could not get beyond the "fearful reluctance" he felt when his mother read "Bluebeard" to him. The theme of hiding, at the heart of "Bluebeard" as he has locked his murdered former wives into a "bloody chamber" in the castle, is also crucial to Timm's memoir. So much is hidden: his brother used to hide in a window seat as a child where his mother could not find him; Karl-Heinz also hides in a cupboard when he comes home on leave and jumps out to surprise his little brother Uwe. More significantly, Timm wonders about the brief diary entries: "What exactly do the words conceal? Armaments?" (11). In glossing the copy of the letter included in the text that his parents received in the box with his brother's effects, Timm muses: "The files, the reports, and the books of the time are full of abbreviations, unintelligible and mysterious sets of letters, usually capitals. Both concealing and revealing the bureaucratic threat of the hierarchical system" (27). Such encryption was endemic in the realm of the Nazis. "They had a keen sense," Timm claims, "of right and wrong and consequently did everything possible to conceal what they had done" (53). Timm cites the example of the 33,771 people killed at Babi Yar: as the Red Army approaches the ravine where they had been shot, the SS used prisoners to dig up the bodies and burn them; then they shot the POWs in order to preserve the sordid secret (53). "The bureaucracy of death" (53), Timm remarks. Similarly, as we know, the

Nazis tried to destroy as many files as possible at the death camps before they fled. Nazi language was full of euphemisms for the tactics of genocide: deported to the East, the Final Solution.

Dreams, too, carry important freight as intertexts, as they did in *Morenga*. Here, they are mostly Timm's dreams; in *Morenga*, the dreamer was Gottschalk. Timm tells us that he dreams of his brother "now and then" and, early in the memoir, he recounts one of these dreams: it is a threatening dream of someone trying to break into his home, a "faceless figure," who is "dark, dirty and covered in mud." Timm braces himself against the door, forcing the man back. "I know for certain [he] is my brother. At last I manage to push the door shut and bolt it. But to my horror I am holding a rough, ragged jacket in my hands" (6). His brother represents threats of various kinds: to the sanctity of his adult home, to his parents' love for him as a child, to the postwar pieties of his father about the Germans as victims. But Timm holds his jacket—evidence of his existence, of his contribution to the war effort as an SS soldier. In another dream, his brother calls out from the end of a passageway. Timm runs along the passage into a garden: "My brother is standing there, black-faced, his suit—or a uniform—light colored" (130). Like the first dream, this one projects an image of a faceless person, which is also reminiscent of one of Gottschalk's dreams. His brother asks him to sing, throws Timm a pear, and "then his voice speaks to me . . . Flower aid, he says" (130). A surreal vision, to be sure, but again like the previous dream, one in which his brother is somewhat hidden from view. Timm's efforts at research and writing fail to re-create his brother's face, his identity: "He mentions no dreams in his diary," no disclosures of wishes or secrets (23).

One of Timm's mother's dreams is also described: "My mother dreamed of a parcel that came by post. When she opened it, it contained bandages, and when she unwrapped them, those long, long white strips of bandaging, a bunch of violets fell out. She really did have that dream on the night he was wounded" (25). A powerful dream that foreshadows death, though days would go by before the family received official notification of Karl-Heinz's wounds. In another dream, Timm finds himself in a bunker with his father, who explains to him how to dive off a ten-meter board; this is one of the feats Karl-Heinz achieved as a child, a source of great pride for his father (136). The final dream recounted in the memoir occurs after Timm's father dies: "I had a recurrent dream," states Timm. "It went like this. The bell on the shop door rings [Timm had taken over his father's furrier business] and he comes in, a tall, shadowy figure. I feel horror. He was only pretending to be dead" (145). This ominous dream conflates the brother and the father as a faceless, threatening figure who returns, a kind of revenant. It also resurfaces the theme of hiding, deception. It encapsulates the tension and hatred between father and son, a central issue in *Väterliteratur*.

Yet another kind of intertext is represented by the more than fifteen "verbal" photographs, inserted in the text as if with black corners in a photo album, in an almost Sebaldian fashion.[33] Most often, these become a prompt for reflection, a spur to a realization about family members. As with the use of dreams, the pattern of photos in the narrative begins almost immediately when Timm describes the photo of his brother, "probably around the time he volunteered for the Waffen SS" (7), which Timm keeps near his desk as he writes the memoir. Other photos are of Karl-Heinz and his father in various playful poses (see, for example, page 6), inciting some jealousy on the part of Timm, who never experienced this kind of close father-son relationship; his father served in the Luftwaffe during World War II and was then a British POW, not returning home until 1946. Many prewar photos of his father are included—in the Freikorps unit in the Baltic in 1919, at a party in a hussar's uniform, a slender ladies' man. Timm's mother kept photos of a postwar trip she took in an album; his sister hid a photo of her fiancé, killed in the war, in a box of mementos; photos of his maternal grandparents' fashionable home are described as well as a portrait of an uncle who declared that "there was nothing wrong with what was happening to the Jews" (121). All of these photos render the memoir itself a family album. But, and this juxtaposition is exactly the point, Timm also includes Lee Miller's postwar photo taken in Dachau of an "SS man drowned in a stream by inmates . . . Lee Miller captioned her photo 'The Evil'" (55). Similarly, gruesome renderings of photos taken by a German photographer of the massacre at Babi Yar are included (129). Despite his father's denials and recriminations, the Holocaust has forcefully entered the family home; Timm gradually comes to recognize it for what it is and to grasp the deceit that has hidden it. The juxtaposition of the photographs—family photos and Holocaust photos—as with the juxtaposition of various texts in *Morenga* demands that the reader grasp the family story in the wider context. This, in turn, reveals what is hidden, what has been the subject of deceit and amnesia. The final photograph, "its surface cracked and brown," shows his father standing outside a peasant's cottage in his army uniform, laughing. "There is a curious likeness to my son and me, at least in this small photograph and from the perspective of the camera," Timm confesses (145–46). It is unlikely that this similarity pleases Timm.

Salted throughout the text are Timm's indictments of German beliefs and values, Nazi ideology, the concept of the Aryan race, the proclivity for violence. Taken together, these passages present as complete a delineation as possible of the genocidal gaze, although, of course, Timm does not use that phrase. I have chosen three to include here as the conclusion of this chapter. The first significant such passage is a somewhat lengthy quotation from a speech Himmler gave in Stettin on 13 July 1941, just prior to the invasion of the USSR, in which Karl-Heinz will die: *"We are involved in a conflict of ideologies and races. In this conflict National Socialism, an ideology based on the value of our Germanic, Nordic blood, stands on the one side, stands for a world as we envisage it—good, decent, socially just.... On the other side stands a nation numbering 180 million, a mixture of races and peoples even whose names are unpronounceable, and whose nature allows them to be shot down without mercy or compunction"* (emphasis in the original, 29). Here is the concept of racial hierarchy justifying genocide. In another passage, after quoting a letter written by his brother in July 1943 about a fierce tank battle in which he was involved, Timm returns to the fact that his brother enlisted in an "elite" unit for which he had to prove his "pure Aryan descent" (52). He continues by further explicating the genocidal gaze: "The chosen ones were to be defined by race, by membership of the nation and not of a social class; as in the nobility, blood was the criterion, not blue but Aryan, German blood, the master race with a vocation to rule... Otto Ohlendorf, a qualified economist, head of Special Action Group D and an expert on statistics, justified the killing of ninety thousand men, women, and children by comparing it to the Children of Israel's annihilation of their enemies in the Bible. The master race" (52–53). Ohlendorf's work as head of Einsatzgruppen D, a mobile killing squad, was responsible for 90,000 deaths in southern Ukraine and Crimea. He was convicted at the Nuremberg Trials and hung in 1951.

After another passage from Karl-Heinz's diary, in which he writes, *"We're demolishing the stoves in Russian houses to build roads"* (83), Timm muses about his brother's inability to see the connections between such destruction of homes in Russia and the Allied bombing of German cities; in fact, Timm's family had been bombed out of their apartment in Hamburg on 25 July 1943. "In Russia," Timm writes, trying to understand his brother's failure to make this connection, "the killing of civilians is normal, everyday work, not even worth mentioning; at home it is murder" (84). The genocidal gaze normalizes such mass killing. "I have now read other diaries and letters of the time; [they] speak of killing civilians—Jews and Russians alike—as the most natural thing in the world. The language they've been taught makes killing easier: inferior human beings, parasites, vermin whose lives are dirty, degenerate, brutish. Smoking them out is a hygienic measure. I find no express justification of killing in my brother's diary, nothing resembling the ideological instruction given to the SS. It is just a *normal* view of daily life in war" (emphasis in the original, 85).

Near the close of the memoir, Timm ramps up his critique, making accusations about Germans in general, not just Nazis. The theme is violence imbued in the mores of the nation. He begins by recalling a beating his father gave him with a leather belt for forgetting something he was supposed to buy. "Violence was *normal*. Children were beaten everywhere, out of aggression, out of conviction, for educational purposes, at school, at home, in the street" (emphasis in the original, 137). Instances of violence become a chorus (he speaks of himself in the third person here, "the boy"): "A cyclist came past and hit him in the face. . . . Violence at school. . . . He also experienced having to learn to write as violence. . . . Violence at home and in the street was licensed by the violence of the state, by political readiness to use violence. *Readiness for war*" (emphasis in the original, 137–38). The repetition becomes almost a verbal violence, form makes content, Timm convincing the reader of this habit of mind in Germany that informs the genocidal gaze.

In one of the passages most specifically alluding to *Väterliteratur*, Timm writes: "My father's generation, the generation of perpetrators, lived by either talking about it or saying nothing at all. There seemed to be only those two options: either you kept discussing it or you never mentioned it, depending on how oppressive and disturbing you felt your memories to be" (93). Timm ends the memoir with the last line of his brother's diary which, in turn, becomes the last line of his book, and which reveals the choice his brother made with regard to disturbing memories: "*I close my diary here, because I don't see any point in recording the cruel things that sometimes happen*" (emphasis in the original, 147). But Timm has made the opposite choice in this astonishing memoir: human beings must talk about the genocidal gaze in order to stem the tide of genocide.

FOUR

William Kentridge's *Black Box/Chambre Noire*

THE GAZE ON/IN THE HERERO GENOCIDE, THE HOLOCAUST, AND APARTHEID

> The past is always an imaginary museum.
> JOACHIM FEST

At Berlin's Martin-Gropius-Bau, in 2012, an art installation created by William Kentridge, a white, Jewish South African, went on display as part of an exhibition called *Art and Press*. Titled *Black Box/Chambre Noire*, this animated miniature theater incorporates early twentieth-century German colonial film clips, mechanized figures, music, photographs, maps, and newspaper clippings; the performance lasts twenty-two minutes. The subject matter of *Black Box* is the 1904–7 genocide of the Herero and Nama people in Africa by the German military.[1] Kentridge gestures in several directions: the work interrogates German guilt; the silence surrounding this genocide; and *Trauerarbeit*, Freud's term for working through grief. Kentridge draws symbolic links between this first genocide of the twentieth century and the Holocaust, initiated less than thirty years later. Kentridge also gestures toward Apartheid: he grew up under this racist regime and, it can be argued, the policies and ideology of Apartheid owed much to the Nazis.

My analysis of this installation piece focuses on Kentridge's exploitation of animation and the ways in which the animation alternately embodies and critiques the *genocidal gaze*. Because of the performative nature of *Black Box*—museumgoers sit on chairs to watch the workings of the miniature theater—and the inclusion of items from the archives of German imperialism, the Holocaust, and Apartheid, *Black Box* dramatically conveys to its audience the lethal nature of the involved ideologies. George Steinmetz argues in *The Devil's Handwriting* that *precolonial* "ethnographic discourse" (i.e., images of Africans disbursed throughout Europe by travel narratives, missionary reports, etc.) created a racist mind-set, the imperial gaze, which in turn shaped colonial policy in German Southwest Africa. The effort of this chapter is, in a sense, to provide a mirror reflection of Steinmetz's work by looking at Kentridge's *postcolonial* "ethnographic discourse" of the genocidal gaze, the colonial policies it shaped, and the subsequent deadly oppressions it begot.

Thus this chapter unpacks the postmodern fragments of *Black Box* in an effort to understand what Kentridge suggests about genocide, silence, mourning, and the role of art/museums in a post-Holocaust world. To provide the proper context, the chapter also attends to the paratextual materials offered by the Martin-Gropius-Bau, as well as to excerpts from Kentridge interviews and from the original catalog for his art installation. I also briefly contextualize *Black Box* in the emerging traditions of Holocaust art. *Black Box* is a palimpsest that emphasizes the profound damage that the genocidal gaze and silence about genocide visits upon subsequent generations.

A Description of *Black Box / Chambre Noire* and Its Archive

For the reader who is unfamiliar with Kentridge, as I was when encountering his installation in Berlin in 2012, or the reader who has not had the opportunity to see *Black Box*,[2] my first dilemma is to describe this work. I turn to the catalog for *Black Box/Chambre Noire* published by the sponsor of the piece, Deutsche Guggenheim. This catalog appeared in 2005, well before the Martin-Gropius-Bau exhibit, when the work was first displayed in Berlin, in the gallery of Deutsche Bank, a partner with the Solomon R. Guggenheim Foundation; the partners present three or four exhibits per year in the bank gallery. Here is how the piece is described in the foreword to the catalog, written by Dr. Tessen von Heydebreck, a member of the board of directors of Deutsche Bank AG:

> Over the course of more than three years, the artist has been developing his *Black Box*—an installation of animated film, mechanized figures, and drawings all situated in a miniature theater. Formally, the focus is on the technical development of the theater and visual reproduction procedures, but the contents deal with Germany's colonial history in Africa, in particular the massacre of the Hereros in 1904. This abominable chapter of German history was recently the subject of a commendable

exhibition in the neighboring German Historical Museum. The German Colonial Exhibition of 1896, which Kentridge refers to, treated similar themes, albeit with a completely different perspective, and was also in Berlin.[3]

This brief description of *Black Box* is a useful one, combining as it does the physical aspects of the installation, its themes, and its historical context. It also hews closely to Kentridge's own assessment of German violence during the colonial era in German Southwest Africa between 1884 and 1919.

By contrast, here is the curatorial label of the piece as it appeared in the Martin-Gropius-Bau exhibit in 2012 (note that the label appeared in both German and in an English translation, which I quote here):

> William Kentridge (b. 1955) gained recognition through his drawings and animations and as a stage designer. *Black Box* encompasses animated films, sculptural objects, and drawings, and can have three meanings: Black Box as theatre, as photographic "dark room," and as flight recorder, registering the course of events and causes of catastrophes. With his *Black Box* Kentridge, a South African, documents the course of history, the process of mourning, guilt, and atonement. The work combines photographs, newspaper articles, and excerpts of German films dating to the era of colonialism, with the artist's own drawings and films.

A second label, provided only in German, lists the materials used and the sponsors of the commission.

It is *stunning* that this curatorial label contains no specific reference to the Herero and Nama, GSWA, or the genocide committed there by German colonizers in 1904–7. Stunning for several reasons. First, as noted in the catalog quoted above, the German Historical Museum mounted an exhibition titled *Namibia-Deutschland: Eine geteilte Geschichte* that ran November 2004–April 2005; genocide (*Völkermord*) is specifically named in the opening sentences of the exhibit description:

> The hundredth anniversary of the outbreak of the German colonial wars in Namibia took place in January 2004. The war lasted from 1904–1908 and went down in history as the first genocide of the twentieth century. For Namibia, at that time German Southwest Africa, this was one of the first wars of resistance of the African population against foreign rule and colonization.[4]

Second, scholars have begun to publish widely on this genocide and to call the Germans to account for their silence:

It was, after all, in the colonies that the European "*Gewaltmensch*" [a Nietzschean term for "strong man" born to dominate] learned his handiwork of extermination. Nevertheless, this war of annihilation has been largely forgotten in Germany and pushed into the background by the catastrophes of two World Wars and the Holocaust. Yet concentration camps and genocide in the German colony foreshadow the crimes committed later during the Third Reich. (Zimmerer and Zeller, xiv)[5]

Third and most significant, such silence is precisely what Kentridge himself is addressing in *Black Box*: the failure to come to terms with the past, to acknowledge particularly the Herero and Nama genocide as a kind of precursor to the Holocaust, to publicly undertake *Trauerarbeit*, the work of mourning, as a bulwark against repetition of such crimes against humanity. One can only imagine Kentridge's anguish upon reading such a label.

Black Box: The Genocidal Gaze, the Camera, and Apartheid

William Kentridge was born on 28 April 1955 into a comfortable, middle-class family in Johannesburg, South Africa. Apartheid was seven years old and Johannesburg housed the largest township for black South Africans, Soweto, which today has more than two million inhabitants. Kentridge's parents were both attorneys who worked in the anti-Apartheid movement; his mother co-founded an important public-interest law firm in South Africa. His family is of Lithuanian Jewish descent, Kentridge himself being third generation.[6] After attending primary and secondary school in Johannesburg, Kentridge earned his bachelor's degree from the University of Witwatersrand in Politics and African Studies in 1976.

Kentridge recounts a formative childhood experience, a discovery made in his father's study:

> At the time, I was six years old and my father [Sydney Kentridge] was one of the lawyers for the families that had been killed [at the Sharpville Massacre].[7] I remember coming once into his study and seeing on his desk a large, flat yellow Kodak box, and lifting the lid off of it—it looked like a chocolate box. Inside were images of a woman with her back blown off, someone with only half her head visible. The impact of seeing these images for the first time—when I was six years old—the shock was extraordinary. I understood that the world was not how I had imagined it at all, that things happened in the world that were inconceivable.[8]

The camera thus becomes an instrument of both trauma and epiphany for Kentridge. Certainly one of the multiple meanings of *Black Box* is the black box camera, an early style of camera shaped like a black box; more recent terminology often links black box cameras with veiled observation and spying. The stage of Kentridge's miniature theater becomes just such an instrument of surveillance and denigration,[9] revealing the very genocidal gaze that leads to the murder of thousands of "expendable" indigenous people, to the murder of six million Jews and five million other victims, and to the massacres during Apartheid.

Thus, while *Black Box* is certainly about the ideological and methodological connections between the Herero genocide and the Holocaust, it is also about Apartheid. These events are linked by attitudes toward racial/racist hierarchies that the Apartheid government reconfigured as whites/Indians/coloreds/blacks. Other links include support of totalitarian ideologies; relocation of peoples according to race and ethnicity; large-scale murder of those deemed genetically inferior; use of concentration camps and military tactics to confine people; institution of laws that defined citizenship, chose who could receive an education and who could vote; and the delusion of "Aryan supremacy." Apartheid was rooted in fascism: the primary architect of Apartheid, Hendrik Vervoerd, studied in Germany in the 1920s as the Nazi Party was forming, as did several of the future leaders of Apartheid, and they used many of the principles and tactics of Nazism in the creation of the Apartheid state.[10] The secret organization of the Afrikaners, the Broederbond, espoused Nazi principles, particularly nationalism, antisemitism, opposition to intermarriage, and insistence on the purity of language in educational settings.[11] While the transition in South Africa from Apartheid to a democracy with Nelson Mandela elected as its first president is often praised as a "bloodless revolution," it should be noted that thousands died in the anti-Apartheid struggle.[12] In sum, *Black Box* is a raw accusation of the genocidal tendencies/gaze of the German people, who provide the connections among these three historical moments.[13]

Black Box: Animation and Memento Mori

In the following section, I will briefly describe the entire twenty-two-minute performance, emphasizing specific instances of Kentridge's use of animation to reference genocide and the genocidal gaze: his use of puppets; drawings and a film of rhinos; and drawings of skulls, which are omnipresent in the piece. The movement of the puppets and the use of animation to create the rhinos and skulls in effect perform aspects of the genocide and present to the viewer the unremembered and unlamented victims. The focus here is on images of the

Herero and Nama genocide and images of the Holocaust. Many of these images apply equally well to Apartheid. Kentridge has said: "I have never tried to make illustrations of apartheid, but the drawings and films are certainly spawned by and feed off the brutalized society left in its wake. I am interested in a political art, that is to say an art of ambiguity, contradiction, uncompleted gestures and uncertain endings."[14]

The first sequence of the piece displays an image of a typewriter, drawn in white crayon on black, and the typewriter "types" a scrawled cursive sentence that reads, in part, "Worte an das Volk der Herero," an excerpt from the infamous statement by German General von Trotha: "Das sind meine *Worte* an das *Volk der Herero*" (These are my words to the Herero People), one of his orders for extermination of the Herero.[15] The typewriter then transforms into a rhinoceros, also drawn in white on black. The rhino is a frequent image in *Black Box*, symbolizing GSWA; both the human and animal inhabitants there were an endangered species under German control. Through the use of animation, the rhino transforms into other objects or from other objects. Finally, a camera on a tripod flashes by in this opening sequence, an instrument of surveillance, control, and denigration when used by German imperialists. Thus Kentridge dramatizes the genocidal gaze immediately, calling the viewer's attention to the use of the *worte* (word) to inform the Herero of the intent to exterminate.

The viewer then sees a series of "curtains" open, as if the performance is to begin; the curtains are made of newsprint, written in German. Semiotically, these curtains continue to highlight the use of language—texts, treaties, orders, lies—to dominate the indigenous people. The sequential openings create a palimpsest, as if the viewer is being drawn back in time, through layers of texts, in order to discover what really happened, what has been silenced, consigned to oblivion. The first puppet appears: it looks to have been constructed of the kind of compass used in geometry, but it clearly has resonances with the calipers Germans used in both GSWA and the Holocaust to measure heads and skulls. Such a device gestures toward eugenics and the devious and completely spurious effort to use such measurements as evidence of Aryan superiority. This puppet always carries a baton, almost invariably performs acts of violence or directs them to be performed, or invokes symbols and images of death; he is Kentridge's synecdoche of the genocidal gaze. Here, he conjures up a drawn image of the Nazi eagle who is poised on top of the world, another image of both domination and the aspirations of the Third Reich.

It is perhaps the puppets that are the most menacing aspect of Kentridge's use of animation. Kentridge describes them thus:

The six characters are a Megaphone man who's the narrator; a transparent Herero woman defined by the head-dress: she's actually a spring with a piece of transparent gauze on her head. A mechanical running man: a cut-out piece of paper that runs; a pair of dividers, that's the measuring arm, measuring skulls and geography; an exploding skull that makes a brief appearance; and a second Herero woman based on a German postal scale from 1905, a scale for weighing letters.[16]

These puppets move to a metronome-like sound, which might be heard as a typewriter or a telegraph, both tools of death in GSWA, and they move in an accompanying jerky motion. Occasionally their movements are timed to the music in the piece, which includes excerpts from Mozart and Namibian praise songs recorded in Namibia. The puppets are eerily humanoid, despite their robotic movements, and they are *unheimlich*, uncanny: they carry resonances of Kafka's torture device in "The Penal Colony."

Following this sequence, the screen behind the curtains begins to move from right to left, and intersecting lines appear, suggesting the links between Berlin and Windhoek (both words appear in script) and between the genocide of the Herero and Nama and the Holocaust. A camera lens opens and closes and an image of three men hung from trees appears, which is based on an actual photograph taken by the Germans, who often photographed their cruel actions and their victims, another "gaze" of manipulation and control.

Next, the running man appears and signals to von Trotha's extermination order, inscribed above on another layer of the palimpsest (and not visible on all YouTube iterations). The mechanical running man seems to represent the fleeing Herero, the effort to escape from the German violence. Then two puppets beat a third into oblivion; Kentridge describes the origin of this image: "In *Black Box* there's a sequence of two men beating each other or a third object based on postcards the Germans made and sent home of people being whipped, a prurient violence assumed to be a thrill that wasn't hidden away. The mechanical figures are based on those postcards."[17] Note that when Kentridge visited Namibia to do research for *Black Box*, he visited an antique store where he found a trove of Nazi memorabilia[18] as well as documents, maps, and other ephemera from the German colonial era; he purchased some of these materials, which were then incorporated into the installation. As these two puppets flog a third, the victim falls into pieces, is reconstituted, and then falls apart again, an image of a merciless death. As we saw in the opening pages of the introduction, such flogging was routine and completely unregulated in GSWA and led to many deaths.

After this rather frenetic phase of the *Black Box*, the viewer sees more intersecting lines and then a text appears, reading "Walfisch Bai" (often spelled Walvis Bay), a body of water south of the Namibian coastal town of Swakopmund, where one of several concentration/death camps was established by the Germans in the aftermath of the Battle of Waterberg. These camps were created to both exploit the labor of the Herero and Nama and intentionally exterminate them through starvation and disease; again, an obvious link to the Holocaust is made here. The word "Waterberg" then slides into view; this mountain located in northern GSWA was the site of the key battle between the Germans and the colonized Hereros in August 1904. During this sequence, one of the Herero women puppets appears, made of a spring and some gauze, and wearing the characteristic Herero headdress for women. This headdress resembles two cattle horns atop a large, fabric-covered hat; as cattle were highly valued by the Herero, the headdress is an honorific. The woman puppet bends back and forth as if quietly grieving; her movements are seen against black-and-white footage of the actual site of the battle of Waterberg, filmed by Kentridge himself.

Now comes a louder, somewhat dizzying sequence in which a spinning disk delivers images in split seconds: a bull's-eye target riddled with bullets, animals that metamorphose, drawings of Africans with bullet holes, a text that reads "Zwischen den Rassen" (between the races) and another that advertises a cream for a "Shone Buste" (a well-cared for bust/breast). The latter undoubtedly references the German imperial gaze upon black African women and the proclivity for photographing them bare-breasted. Some such photographs, in books published after the genocide, show evidence that the women's clothing has been rudely torn down so as to reveal their breasts for the photographer. The running Herero man appears again, against various backdrops including one with bold letters "Welt-Detektive," a reference to a magazine titled *Aus den Geheimakten des Welt-Detektiv*, which began circulation in Germany in January 1907, the time when the genocide was subsiding.[19] Then a roughly hewn, sketched telephone pole transforms into a swastika and then into a gibbet, or gallows. A hanging light appears from which a shower head grows, and a full-on shower pours down on the running man, an overt symbolic reference to the Holocaust and the use of "showers" for gassing at death camps. He runs in place here for several seconds, then proceeds through a landscape full of abstract, linear drawings, robotic-looking calipers.

The skull—a symbol of the victims of the genocidal gaze and thus a powerful memento mori—appears in varying positions and transformations throughout *Black Box*. The viewer first sees the skull when the compass puppet reappears after the sequence of the running man and the shower. The compass puppet turns a clay pot into a skull; this is followed by a drawing of the head of Hendrik Witbooi (the subject of chapter 1), which turns into a skull, and then by a globe that turns into calipers holding a skull. This is a particularly laden metamorphosis—again reminding viewers of the tools of the Schutztruppe and the Nazis. Kentridge has commented: "This links the Herero of 1904 with the genocides of the 20th century. I had archival images of those heads that were sent to Berlin and references to the measuring of skulls. There's a character in *Black Box* whose main job is to measure skulls" (www.postmedia.net/06/kentridge.htm). Shortly after this skull sequence, the skull reappears and a series of intersecting lines is drawn from the skull to other objects; such intersecting lines, which again function as a visible reminder of the linkages (and the silence) that are the overall message of *Black Box*, are commonplace in Kentridge's work.[20] Finally, the skull appears atop the compass puppet, exploding again and again.

At this point, viewers have seen about two-thirds of *Black Box*. We have seen the representative of the genocidal gaze—the compass/calipers man—and the symbols of the victims—the Herero running man, the Herero woman, and the rhino. Now, suddenly, a new puppet appears—the Megaphone Man. He is made of sticks topped by a megaphone, and he carries a sign affixed to his front that carries the capital letters "TRAUERARBEIT." He serves in this final section of the installation/performance to command the audience to grieve for the forgotten victims of German genocides and Apartheid. He performs a kind of metafunction, reminding viewers that they are in a museum, that the work of art they are watching serves as a memorial, and that their participation in this mourning and memorialization is required; it is their responsibility to end the forgetting.

As the Megaphone Man crosses the stage, a clip of a 1912 film made during Germany's colonial era in Cameroon comes into view under the Megaphone Man, who soon sallies off the stage. The audience sees white hunters, dressed in classic khaki safari garb, shoot a rhino at close range.[21] The viewer watches as the rhino painfully thrashes about in the throes of death. The hunter then bounds lightly over the tall grasses and cuts off the foot of the rhino, his trophy. Use of the rhino as an image no doubt references the plight of the rhino in Africa now: as a result of drought and poaching, the rhino faces extinction/erasure in several areas.[22] The rhino thus serves as one of many reminders of the fragility of life, of mortality, of the impact of the colonizers for whom wresting the natural resources of Africa—minerals, rubber, diamonds, gold, and the labor of human beings to extract these resources—was the real goal. The colonial project was, in its essence, hypocritical: its outcomes were profoundly antithetical to the so-called goal of bringing "civilization" to the "heathens."

The two figures that flogged a man previously now flog a skull that is beaten into oblivion, to be replaced onstage by the exploding skull Kentridge mentions in his list of puppets. The skull is then manipulated in various ways by the compass puppet, being bandaged, becoming a severed head, having characters written on it, including a "J," most likely a reference to the Nazi use of "J" for Juden, which was marked on passports and identity cards during the Third Reich. The Herero woman reappears, bending over, swaying, grieving, while behind her is flashed "Totenliste II und Nachtrag" (list of the dead and a supplement [to the list]). The music slows and the movement, almost like davening, becomes excruciatingly slow. Another series of intersecting lines intervenes, and then the rhino appears for the final time, moving in the direction of the Megaphone Man puppet. He indicates his commands by turning his megaphone head. The rhino stands on his hind legs, and then his forelegs, turns into a drafting compass, then into two geometric forms beating each other, and finally, becoming a rhino again, soars over Megaphone Man. The piece ends with the Megaphone Man, boasting his "Trauerarbeit" sign, alone on the stage; he is briefly illuminated and then eases off the stage, which falls into darkness. The credits for the piece begin to roll.

What Kentridge Has to Say

> The history that looms largest in Kentridge's work is the complex,
> deeply entwined relationship between Europe and Africa,
> the rhino in the room, so to speak [a reference to the rhino in
> "Black Box"], a presence that can never be ignored.
>
> MARIA-CHRISTINA VILLASENOR

In his own essay in the original catalog for the *Black Box* exhibit in 2005 (a full seven years before the *Art and Press* exhibit with the inexcusably bland label quoted earlier), Kentridge makes it abundantly clear what his emphasis is:

> I am particularly interested in the Germans in southern Africa, what was then known as German Southwest Africa, now Namibia. German missionaries and traders came to colonize Southwest Africa in the later part of the nineteenth century and asked Bismarck for support. Reluctantly at first, Germany sent in troops to support them, and, eventually, Southwest Africa was declared a colony. . . . In the first years of the twentieth century, there was an enormous massacre, primarily

of the Herero tribe, in southwest Africa. Although *it is now mostly forgotten, overshadowed by other German massacres and genocides later in the century, there are many ways in which the mechanisms of those later European massacres were already underway in southwest Africa at the turn of the century* [emphasis mine].²³

Kentridge goes on to delineate some of the links between the Herero genocide and the Holocaust, including the measurement of skulls.²⁴

When Kentridge determined to make the Herero genocide and its links to the Holocaust and Apartheid the center of his installation, he not only read widely on these topics, but he traveled to Namibia to see the actual locations of the brutality and violence. Specifically, he visited the site of the Battle of Waterberg and studied the memorial there. In an interview conducted by Cheryl Kaplan in New York in 2005 while Kentridge was still creating the installation, and later in Kentridge's studio in Johannesburg, he commented:

> I'm looking at German colonization in reference to Namibia for the exhibition. I went there to look at the place where there was a great massacre of the Herero by the Germans from 1904–1907. Some of that archival material and footage shot in the mountain where the genocide began is in the final piece. . . . At the site where the battle first happened, the Hereros, in anticipation of the attack, retreated with their families and cattle to a mountain where there was water, called Waterberg. They waited there for the attack. The German forces fought under General Lothar von Trotha and the Herero forces under Samuel Manharero [*sic*]. The Germans took months getting ready, building railway lines, and then a great battle took place. The Hereros were driven into the desert where most of them died of thirst, ambushed at water holes. 85% perished in three years. The site is now a national park in Namibia. At the bottom of the mountain, there's a German war cemetery where 23 German soldiers are buried. It's well maintained with a visitor's book, where German tourists write things like: "thanks for keeping such good care of the graves" and "please can there be no more wars in our times and you do such honor to these people." In the campsite dining room there are photographs of the Kaiser and his wife and of German troops, but *nowhere is there any word of what happened there.* It's as if you had Auschwitz and a few Germans who died of dysentery while they were working there and then had a sign where they were buried, but not a word else about what happened in Auschwitz. (emphasis mine, www.postmedia.net/06/kentridge.htm)

In this illuminating midrash on *Black Box*, Kentridge again emphasizes what I have termed the genocidal gaze. He traces the fatal consequences of the German perception of indigenous Africans and Jews as subhuman. He also notes the

German failure to come to terms with the past, to engage in *Vergangenheitsbewältigung* about imperialism in GSWA, and the ways in which such silence led to the Holocaust.

The Genocidal Gaze in *Black Box* and Animation as Transformation

Standard texts on animation almost invariably define the term "to animate" as "to bring to life" and they reference its etymology as the Latin word *anima*, meaning soul or life.[25] This emphasis on animation as life-giving was at the heart of the early Disney studio. In writing their famous book on that studio, two of Disney's animators, Ollie Johnston and Frank Thomas, noted that "truly the age of the animator arrived with the first crude evidence of *life* in the single drawing."[26]

By contrast, Kentridge sees the technique as one of *transformation*, metamorphosis not limited to bringing life to the inanimate. In creating his animations, Kentridge begins with one or two images in his head and makes a large charcoal drawing in his studio, where he has set up a 35mm camera on a tripod some distance from the drawing. He makes a new mark on the drawing or erases an existing mark, steps to the camera, shoots two frames of the drawing, and then repeats. These still shots are then connected to create for the viewer a sense of a moving drawing, not unlike flipbooks enjoyed by children. Kentridge has commented:

> There is *a sense of animation as a field of transformation*, of depicting transformation, that has always been at the heart of it and that continues today. Charcoal is very fortuitous material to be working with for animation because its tonal range kind of is very good for photographic film but also because of the speed of its transformability. It's very easy to erase so you can kind of change it as quickly as you can think. *I suppose it became a way of thinking rather than a physical movement* [emphasis mine].[27]

In an interview filmed in 2005, the year *Black Box* was completed, Kentridge provided salient details of his creative process.[28] He noted that his animated films generally run between four and nine minutes. He uses only twenty to thirty pieces of fresh paper to create the entire film, redrawing, erasing, and redrawing as he goes. His laborious process means that he makes forty to fifty seconds of material in a week; the full film thus takes months to complete. He acknowledged that "each day I keep a crazy animation log" to track his progress. Watching Kentridge perform this process in his studio is rather astonishing. His facility with the charcoal means that with a few strokes he can change an entire facial expression, make a bodily movement, or cause a bird to fly. This kind of faculty was acquired through years of practice: as an art student he was taught that charcoal drawings were the prelude to oil painting—considered the "real" art—and so he diligently perfected his charcoal technique. Now he uses that skill exclusively.

Kentridge's process of "animation," by virtue of the nature of charcoal and his approach of erasing lines and reinserting them at a slightly changed angle to create movement, gestures toward the erasure of the Herero and Nama genocide from memory and from German history for almost a century. And yet, traces are left behind: Kentridge's reuse of the same paper, rather than cels (the traditional process for animation), creates a visual palimpsest that becomes form, content, and synecdoche. Kentridge employs neither script nor storyboard, considered to be de rigueur steps in the process of animation; instead, his charcoal becomes "a way of thinking rather than a physical movement" and it leads him toward discovery. When asked by an interviewer about his work on *Black Box*, "What did your research reveal that you didn't know at the start?" Kentridge replied tellingly:

> *The big thing was the invisibility of the story in Namibia.* It would be very hard to imagine our relationship and the history of WWII in the absence of records, books, writings, films, memorials, museums, debates. *Those are absent here, though not completely.* I by no means am the first person to look at this material. My ongoing interest is the question of Enlightenment and Colonialism, it's a very current question in the world today. The Kaiser wiped out a whole population for the sake of Germany's honor. Those questions are not so far from us still. (emphasis mine, www.postmedia.net/o6/kentridge.htm)[29]

Kentridge's desire to make visible the heretofore invisible, to make the absent present, to memorialize the Herero and Nama, is also the impulse behind much Holocaust art. This is true whether the art was produced by victims during the Holocaust—such as that by Felix Nussbaum, Nelly Toll, and Charlotte Salomon—or by survivors after the Holocaust, or by the second generation, the children of survivors. It is also true of post-Holocaust art created by artists—such as Kentridge—who have no direct connection to the Shoah. Many contemporary artists, endeavoring to represent memories or create them, have also used installations, as Kentridge has. For example, American artist Shimon Attie is famous for the site-specific installations he produces; in the work titled *The Writing on the Wall*, he used slides to project photographs of Jewish life in pre–World War II Berlin onto the same or nearby buildings. His work functions as a memorial by making the absent present and engendering memory. Anselm Kiefer, a German artist who now lives in France, creates enormous installations that often reference decay and degeneration. One of his installations, *Breaking of the Vessels*, is a twelve-foot-high bookshelf filled with giant books in a state of decay; broken glass surrounds the installation. *Breaking of the Vessels* alludes to the Kabbalah; the installation has also been read as a memorial to the People of the Book, a common designation for Jews and Judaism, given the centrality of the Torah; the broken glass may reference the Night of Broken Glass, the first full-scale Nazi attack against Jews in Germany. Kentridge is somewhat unique in that he has used his installation to represent "man's inhumanity to man" over the entire twentieth century.

Holocaust art "moves freely between history and memory."[30] The same kinds of debates discussed in chapter 3 regarding "poetry after Auschwitz" are also a source of controversy in Holocaust art. How faithful to history should such art be? Can it be beautiful? Are people without a direct connection to the Shoah "authorized" to represent it? Can the horrors of the Holocaust ever be truly represented? What are the ethical responsibilities of artists creating work about the Holocaust? What about the use of "popular" culture? Many survivors were deeply offended by Art Spiegelman's *Maus* books because of their use of the medium of comics, yet they have become classics in the field. "The visualization of the Holocaust remains one of the quandaries of Holocaust representation" (Zelizer, "Gender and Atrocity," 1), and yet to both honor and re-create personal and collective memory, as Kentridge has done in *Black Box*, is essential as the survivors, the witnesses, pass away.

It is also instructive to think of the similarities between *Black Box/Chambre Noire* and the two texts by Uwe Timm, *Morenga* and *In My Brother's Shadow*, discussed in chapter 3. All three of these pieces are post-Holocaust, postmodern, and postcolonial. All three are comprised of bits and pieces that somehow make a whole, fragments of various texts, photographs, imagined and historical characters, dreamlike images, military orders. As these fragments rub against each other in the work of art and in the mind of the reader/viewer, they cause comparison, disruption, accusation, understanding, and mourning. This frisson calls attention to the ways in which the genocidal gaze is carried from generation to generation and to the damage it inflicts.

Conclusion

"Each sheet of paper has built into it the history of the sequence of movements," remarks Kentridge in the 2005 film. Just as the history of the charcoal is embedded inside the visible movements of the head or the bird on the film, so are the historical connections among the Namibian genocide, the Holocaust, and Apartheid that Kentridge is endeavoring to make visible. These events are reconnected in *Black Box*, with the title here suggesting the disclosure of the disaster that the black box in an airliner records. The secrets of the catastrophe are hidden until the black box can be retrieved and decoded. Kentridge's postcolonial art serves the same function: to impart to the viewer the details of the Herero genocide and make visible its relationship through both ideology and methodology with the Holocaust and Apartheid. The palimpsest of Kentridge's technique is the synecdoche for the palimpsest of history. "The process itself brings certain kinds of meaning to the work . . . if one is working with a cel image, you have a perfectly clean image; when working with charcoal, it shows traces, the passage of time," continues Kentridge in the film. So, for Kentridge, the use of animation is about transformation: the sobering, inhuman impulses seemingly transformed by geography, time, agency, motive, culture, and outcome, and yet repeated again and again.

Kentridge uses animation not to suggest life, to animate the inanimate, as is the usual sense of animation, but rather, in a counterintuitive manner, to create multiple images and symbols of death, a palimpsest of mortality and genocide. The use of his automatons in *Black Box* often results in death or in reminders of mortality. The kinds of metamorphoses imposed by/upon the puppets are at the heart of Kentridge's use of animation. Such an approach is inevitable, according to Alan Cholodenko, professor of art history at the University of Sydney, Australia, and author of theoretical books on animation:

> Animation cannot be thought without thinking loss, disappearance and death, that one cannot think the endowing with life without thinking the other side of the life cycle—the transformation from the animate to the inanimate—at the same time, cannot think endowing with motion without thinking the other side of the cycle of movement—of metastasis, deceleration, inertia, suspended animation, etc.[31]

The installation poignantly reminds viewers of the *lack* of mourning and grief work after the GSWA genocide; nothing comparable to the development of *Vergangenheitsbewältigung* following the Holocaust occurred in GSWA or Germany itself. In a real sense, *Black Box* becomes the memorial for the Herero and the Nama, demanding words, names, noise, music, a reminder of what happened and who the perpetrators were. The Megaphone Man *shouts*; he *insists on* the importance of mourning; he engenders memorialization where little has occurred. Meanwhile, in Windhoek, the capital of Namibia, the infamous *Reiterdenkmal*, a fifteen-foot-high bronze equestrian statue mounted by a German soldier, continues to serve as a powerful indicator of the devastating German presence in Namibia.[32]

As one critic has commented: "Though it seems unlikely that Freud, Mozart, colonialism, Nazism, pseudoscientific justifications for racism, the nature of perception, and the histories of photography and moving pictures could be woven into a single work, Kentridge succeeds at just that in *Black Box/Chambre Noire*" (Dubin, 157). Kentridge deploys animation to interrogate the cruelty of human beings toward one another, to make visible a history that has been silenced, to demonstrate the power of the genocidal gaze as an instrument of destruction linking events of the twentieth century that were "justified" by the racial/racist hierarchies of imperialism. His palimpsest succeeds in representing the passage of time and the consequences of the failure to do the work of mourning. *Black Box* becomes the memorial for all who died even as it is also a warning to museumgoers of their responsibility to remember, to speak, and to resist the tools of oppression.

FIVE

Ama Ata Aidoo's *Our Sister Killjoy*

THE AFRICAN GAZE OF RESISTANCE TODAY

> All Europe contributed to the making of Kurtz.
> JOSEPH CONRAD

> Travel implicitly involves looking at,
> and looking relations with, peoples different from oneself.
> E. ANN KAPLAN

As we turn to Ama Ata Aidoo, we listen again to black African voices as they parse the impact of colonialism on the continent. *Our Sister Killjoy, or, Reflections of a Black-eyed Squint* was published in 1977, almost one hundred years after Hendrik Witbooi began his archive. The intervening century had seen the Nazi Holocaust and the struggle for independence from colonialism in Africa. The title of Aidoo's novel invites the reader to consider again the African gaze—the squint—upon the Western imperialists. Aidoo, too, depicts the genocidal gaze, as did Hendrik Witbooi, hers a backward gaze, his an intuitive anticipatory gaze.

In his iconic novel *Heart of Darkness*, published in 1899, Joseph Conrad endeavored to capture the colonial intervention in what was then the Belgian Congo. His novel remains controversial despite its status as a classic: Chinua Achebe, the great Nigerian writer whose novel *Things Fall Apart* (1958) is seen as a founding text of postcolonial African fiction, famously termed the text "racist" while others read *Heart of Darkness* as a critique of the racial hierarchies that were an inherent part of colonialism.[1] While the novel, given its date of publication, would not be defined as strictly "*post*colonial," it remains a staple of courses in postcolonial literature and part of the "canon" of books a scholar of postcolonial studies should know.

Heart of Darkness has also provoked several intertexts: in a gesture of what is often termed "writing back" from the Empire (or its post-equivalent), novelists have riffed on Conrad's title, his journey structure, and his depiction of the "Dark Continent." Recent examples of such riffs stretch from Nadine Gordimer's *July's People* (1981) to a video game titled *Heart of Darkness* (1998) to Anne Patchett's best-selling novel *State of Wonder* (2012). Such deployments of intertextuality are often made by writers to signal their disapproval of a particular fiction and their subsequent re-vision of that text as a correction. For the purposes of this chapter, I will be using the following definition of intertextuality: "The fundamental concept of intertextuality is that no text, much as it might like to appear so, is original and unique-in-itself; rather it is a tissue of inevitable and to an extent unwitting, references to and quotations from other texts."[2]

Intertextuality calls into question the viability of originality and stability in literary texts; in turn, it calls upon the reader to trace references, quotations, or allusions to other texts. Intertextuality allows for the re-vision and appropriation of older texts to suit new situations and meanings, and presents the opportunity to critique outmoded assumptions. Intertextuality makes us aware of the ways in which the author of the book we are reading is morphing an earlier text and creating a new one.

In disrupting our sense of the text as a reflection of reality and positing instead the postmodern paradox that texts "both enshrine the past and question it,"[3] intertextuality as a concept can be said to instantiate the disruption of our notions of human nature, evil, and "history-as-progress," of meaning itself. I read intertextuality more broadly than simple influence; I read it as dialogue among a network of texts that at once destabilizes meaning and enables the writer to render ideological commentary.

One of the African writers who has engaged in such an intertextual appropriation of Conrad's novel is Ghanaian Ama Ata Aidoo. Aidoo is a late twentieth-century writer who has spent considerable time in the West. My reading of Aidoo occurs at the intersection of Postcolonial and Genocide Studies, the theoretical location of much of *The Genocidal Gaze*. *Our Sister Killjoy* is Aidoo's most well-known novel. Though brief (134 pages), this novel is challenging in that it includes unorthodox page formatting as well as several genres and a shifting narrative voice, which are frequent features of Ghanaian literature.[4] Like Uwe Timm's *Morenga* and William Kentridge's *Black Box*, *Our Sister Killjoy* uses pastiche to deliver its complex message. It is also highly intertextual, incorporating references to fairy tales, Charlotte Brontë's *Jane Eyre*, historical events, and the gesture of "writing back" to Joseph Conrad's *Heart of Darkness*. While a few scholars have noted this link with Conrad, none has made the connection between imperialism and genocide in Africa and genocide in Germany that Aidoo is interrogating. Her novel thus provides a very useful case study for this emerging field.

Aidoo has reversed the trajectory of *Heart of Darkness* by focalizing the novel through Sissie, a college student who leaves Africa to visit Germany on a foreign exchange program. While recognizing the privilege and opportunity of such travel, Sissie encounters a very different Germany than she had expected. Physical traces of the Holocaust, the constant experience of being "othered," and an unwelcome lesbian advance all conspire to make her stay a dark and frightening one.

Thus Aidoo establishes Germany, rather than the Congo, as the heart of darkness in the twentieth century. The critique Aidoo offers is this: the very people—white Europeans—who came to Africa with the avowed purpose of "civilizing" indigenous Africans in the nineteenth century in fact demonstrated then, as well as a half century later, that they were capable of the most heinous crimes *against* humanity and "civilization." Europeans have long called Africans savages, and this, as Chinua Achebe has taught us, is certainly the view propounded by Conrad. Yet a mere fifty years after the 1885 Berlin Conference that parceled out Africa to colonization, Hitler had already established the first concentration camps in Germany. As we have seen in the preceding chapters, the continuity thesis establishes the links between savage European behavior in colonialism and in the Holocaust. While Aidoo uses many of the tropes of postcolonial writing such as mimic men, "new englishes," and colonization of the mind, she also references chimneys/smoke, Hitler, racial hierarchies, and other tropes of the Holocaust, thus creating a pioneering novel that has puzzled some critics unfamiliar with the intersection of Postcolonial and Genocide Studies. While other scholars have also noted the intertextual relationship between Conrad and Aidoo, none specifically links Aidoo's critique to Germany's extermination of six million Jews and five million other victims who did not meet the standards of the "Master Race" and "Aryan supremacy" set by Nazi ideology.[5]

Previous Critical Readings of *Our Sister Killjoy*

The critical response to Aidoo's oeuvre falls quite neatly into three categories that are largely chronological. In the 1980s, the first phase of response to her work, which includes plays as well as fiction, was feminist. This approach to Aidoo was encouraged by several early interviews in which she identified herself as a feminist. In her article "The African Woman Today" (1992), Aidoo declares:

When people ask me rather bluntly every now and then whether I am a feminist, I not only answer yes, but I go on to insist that every woman and every man should be a feminist—especially if they believe that Africans should take charge of our land, its wealth, our lives, and the burden of our own development. Because it is not possible to advocate independence for our continent without believing that African women must have the best that the environment can offer. For some of us, this is the crucial element of our feminism.[6]

Almost twenty years later, in a 2010 interview conducted at Brown University, Aidoo again affirmed her commitment in the importance of feminism. While she believes that she "grew up among women who can be described as strong in terms of an understanding of their own lives and what is expected of them and how they should negotiate their own existence," nevertheless, "women have always been marginalized in every way—from the beginning of societies."[7]

Scholars have examined her women characters in terms of their awakening consciousness, which often results from transnational travel and encounters with the West. Chiomo Opara, appropriating the tropes of Sandra Gilbert and Susan Gubar's *Madwoman in the Attic: The Woman Writer and the Nineteenth-Century Literary Imagination* (1979), reads the oppression of African women as a central theme in Aidoo's work. Opara concludes her somewhat confusing essay with the declaration that Aidoo is "a militant female writer [who] strives to arouse our consciences while taking a critical glimpse at the newly awakened African woman."[8] A more effective and, hence, persuasive feminist analysis of Aidoo can be found in Kofi Owusu's essay "Canons under Siege: Blackness, Femaleness, and Ama Ata Aidoo's *Our Sister Killjoy*."[9]

The second phase of critical response might be termed nationalist. Critics such as Anuradha Needham and Ranu Samantrai labeled Aidoo as too nationalist and even as racist.[10] Elizabeth Willey's article, which looks at Aidoo's oeuvre in terms of her dialogue with the political discourse of Kwame Nkrumah, is perhaps representative of this category of critical approaches to Aidoo. Incorporating some of the earlier feminist insights on Aidoo, Willey asks about the "possibility that women and men experienced the colonial condition differently."[11] She answers the query in the affirmative, pointing out the compromised position of women under colonialism, "an emasculating enterprise" (Willey, 4) as well as in the postcolonial era. In this era, women are often viewed as the site of cultural authenticity of the African tradition as Ghana, in its newly found independence, sought to recover its African identity. Willey reads *Our Sister Killjoy* as Sissie's quest to find out "what it means to be a true African woman" (15), which is embodied in the question of "how to define a 'life relevantly lived.' For Sissie, relevance involves a person's obligations to self, country, and Africa" (13). Willey devotes very little time to discussing Sissie's sojourn in Germany.

The most recent approach to Aidoo has been postcolonial, beginning about the time in which the field of Postcolonial Studies became robust in the 1990s.[12] Yogita Goyal's detailed analysis of *Our Sister Killjoy* serves as a fine example. Goyal opens her chapter on Aidoo with a meditation on Frantz Fanon and she reads the novel through that lens, focusing on the transnational consciousness of the narrative. "Aidoo stands firmly against the celebration of mobility, migration and hybridity, interested instead in how a neo-colonial world order comes into being in the wake of decolonization."[13]

None of these essays is necessarily "wrong," but they are too limited. While some identify Aidoo's intertextual appropriations, none specifically speaks to her attention to genocide. An example of a particularly problematic essay is Hildegard Hoeller's "Ama Ata Aidoo's *Heart of Darkness*."[14] Hoeller names her own subject position near the beginning of the article "as a Westerner and, more specifically, as a German" (132). She then immediately relegates herself to the *role of victim* by accusing Aidoo of racist depiction of her German characters: "Reading *Our Sister Killjoy*, I saw myself . . . reduced; like Achebe reading Conrad, I was forced to identify not with the central figure, the traveler and explorer, but with the crude, stagnant background characters, the 'black figures' and their caricatured history and culture" (132). Like the Austrians who greeted the arrival of the Nazis in their country with wild enthusiasm, and then, after the defeat of Germany, styled themselves as "Hitler's first victims," Hoeller wants to claim victim status for herself and deem Aidoo a "racist."[15] Though Hoeller's article goes on for another fifteen pages, she does not once mention the word "Holocaust" (or any of its synonyms such as "Shoah"), nor does she acknowledge the overt references in Aidoo's novel to this horrific genocide.

Hoeller also fails to mention the prevalent fairy tale tropes in the novel. Since these tropes have been used often by other novelists as well as survivors writing their Holocaust memoirs,[16] and since the German Grimm Brothers collections are some of the key sources of fairy tales, such intertextuality is just as crucial to analyze as that with Conrad. Instead, after some perceptive analysis of the textual links between *Heart of Darkness* and *Our Sister Killjoy*, Hoeller concludes that "Aidoo's heart of darkness is *Heart of Darkness*" (141), a gross simplification of Aidoo's work and one that completely ignores the critique Aidoo is offering: that the racial hierarchies established by Europeans as justification for their colonial crimes are, at once, false and yet also a leading cause of the genocide gaze.

In his recent essay "Reading *Heart of Darkness* after the Holocaust," Robert Eaglestone concludes by confessing: "This essay has tried to explore what it means to read other works of literature with eyes oriented by the Holocaust."[17] After those twelve devastating years between 1933 and 1945, can we do otherwise? Isn't it incumbent upon us to use our "eyes" to see the "genocidal gaze" and what its consequences have been? To recognize that when racial hierarchies are established, genocide will follow, whether in Berlin or German Southwest Africa or Rwanda or Darfur?

Our Sister Killjoy, or, Reflections of a Black-eyed Squint: The Trajectory to Genocide

Our Sister Killjoy is divided into four chapters: "Into a Bad Dream," "The Plums," "From Our Sister Killjoy," and "A Love Letter." The novel opens with three pages printed with only a few words and then a fourth page with a narrative voice that seems to be that of a black African speaking disparagingly about how misleading white perspectives on Africa are.[18] First, the narrator decries the colonization of the mind of the average black African worker who "regurgitates" "white" issues, such as the population explosion, and values, such as the sanctity of the UN charter. The narrator continues: "The academic-pseudo-intellectual version [of Africa] is even more dangerous, who in the face of the reality that is more tangible than the massive walls of the slave forts standing along our beaches, still talks of universal truth, universal art, universal literature, and the Gross National Product."[19] Postcolonial theory has, of course, pointed out that "universality" is almost always a code word for the supposed superiority of Western art. This jibe is directed at both African and Western scholars.

The narrative voice continues in a call-and-response pattern:

> Yes, my brother,
> The worst of them
> these days supply local
> statistics for those population studies, and
> toy with
> genocidal formulations.
> That's where the latest crumbs
> Are being thrown! (7)

Certainly for the white postcolonial studies scholar, this passage serves as a warning, much as the concluding pages of Chinua Achebe's *Things Fall Apart* do by presenting a satiric portrait of the colonizer writing a condescending book about the tribal life he has observed. Aidoo's passage also calls to mind the short essay by Binyavanga Wainaina titled "How to Write about Africa," originally published by *Granta*, which went viral on the Internet a few years ago. Wainaina parodies journalists and academics who fall into stereotypes with their alarming depictions of Africa, all presented as a "how to" guide to such writing. "Always use the word 'Africa' or 'Darkness' or 'Safari' in your title. . . . Establish early on that your liberalism is impeccable. . . . If you are a woman, treat Africa as a man who wears a bush jacket and disappears off into the sunset. Africa is to be pitied, worshipped or dominated. . . . Be sure to leave the strong impression that without your intervention and your important book, Africa is doomed."[20]

So, I take Aidoo's warning to heart. But it is undoubtedly significant that she has signaled to her readers in this passage that genocide is under consideration in what follows and that readers will be presented with a "genocidal formulation" that is more accurate, more appropriate than that drummed up by the "academic-pseudo-intellectuals." The remainder of Aidoo's opening chapter provides details of Sissie's selection to study in Germany; the fawning of the German ambassador in his Mercedes-Benz; her encounter with Sammy, a classic mimic man; and her departure by plane for Europe.

Arriving in Frankfurt, Sissie is taken to the train station for transfer to a small village and there experiences interpellation for the first time, resulting in an epiphany. Overhearing a German woman say to her daughter, "**Ja, das Schwartze Mädchen**" (Yes, the black girl), she "was made to notice differences in human colouring" (bold in original text, 12). Indeed, this passage clearly echoes Fanon's own experience, as described in *Black Skin, White Masks*:

> "Look, a Negro!" It was an external stimulus that flicked over me as I passed by. I made a tight smile.
>
> "Look, a Negro!" It was true. It amused me. . . .
>
> "Mama, see the Negro! I'm frightened!" Frightened! Frightened! Now they were beginning to be afraid of me.[21]

Such interpellation leads Sissie to new insights. Puzzled by the epithet, she looks around herself carefully: "And it hit her. That all that crowd of people going and coming in all sorts of directions had the colour of pickled pig parts that used to come from foreign places to the markets at home" (12). Just as in Timm's

Morenga Gottschalk begins to see the Germans as animals as his grasp of the genocidal gaze expands, so Sissie sees the Germans as pigs and understands that their gaze has racialized her.

She also comes to an important realization about colonization: "But what she also came to know was that someone somewhere would always see in any kind of difference, an excuse to be mean."

> A way to get land, land, more land . . .
> Gold and silver mines,
> Oil
> Uranium . . .
> Jewels to adorn, . . .
> Power, Child, Power.
> For this is all anything is about.
> Power to decide
> Who is to live,
> Who is to die, (13)

And then, for emphasis, Aidoo gives an entire page to each of her next three words: Where, When, How (14–16). Again, she has signaled that genocide is one of her themes and that arrival in the Fatherland has awakened Sissie's consciousness to the exploitation of African natural resources and the genocide of its peoples.

Chapter 2, "The Plums," is devoted to Sissie's experiences while in Germany. Sissie has been assigned to live in a youth hostel that is actually a huge old castle, bringing the tropes of fairy tales into the novel; the fairy tale intertext is enhanced by the occasional use of the phrase "Once upon a time" and a series of short tales in stanzas. Almost immediately, Sissie meets Marija, "a young mother pushing her baby in a pram" (19). Marija inquires whether Sissie is an Indian and confides in her that "my Mann is called A D O L F and zo is our little zon" (23), the first clear reference to the Holocaust. Many such references follow. Sissie's visit is sponsored by an international volunteer organization, INVOLOU, and she is assigned to work in the Bavarian woods, tending seedling Christmas trees. Hitler, of course, lived in Bavaria, and Munich, the capital of Bavaria, was the birthplace of Nazism. The students work along with Nazi war widows:

> The blood of their young men was
> Needed to mix the concrete for
> Building the walls of
> The Third Reich. (36)

As the students work, they wonder:

> They wonder if, should they
> Stop cultivating the little pine trees, would
> Something else,
> Sown there,
> Many many years ago,
> In
> Those Bavarian woods
> S P R O U T?

As the title of this chapter suggests, plums become a central symbol of the storyline here. Marija grows them and feeds them to Sissie in their daily rendezvous at Marija's archetypal little cottage near the castle. The plums, described as possessing a "skin-colour almost like [Sissie's] own" (40), take on the lure of the apple in the Garden of Eden and as proffered by the wicked stepmother in "Snow White and the Seven Dwarfs." Marija provides bags of the fruit for Sissie to take back to her peers in the youth hostel. Marija's activities arouse the suspicion of her nosy neighbors, who treat Sissie as the exotic other. Their little village, we are told as the omniscient narrator weighs in, was the site of a chemical plant built by the Leader (i.e., Hitler) where "experiments were done on herb, animal and man. But especially on man, just hearing of which should get a grown-up man urinating on himself" (44). Thus, as Sissie is still learning about what happened in Germany, the narrator interjects information that reveals the genocidal gaze and its results.

One evening, Marija comes later than usual to fetch Sissie and informs her that she has baked a plum cake. The narrator contrasts the two characters as they walk through the village: Marija is "A daughter of mankind's / Self-appointed most royal line, / The House of Aryan" (48) while Sissie is "A Little/Black/Woman who / [should] . . . Not / Have been / There / Walking /Where the / Führer's feet had trod— /A-C-H-T-U-N-G!" (48). After several pages devoted to a blistering presentation of the corruption of postcolonial governments in West

Africa by the narrator, often in stanza form, the storyline returns to Marija and Sissie. Marija suggests they go upstairs to see Little Adolf sleeping and Sissie agrees; what follows is rife with fairy tale motifs. Climbing the stairs, Sissie feels as if "she was moving not up, but down into some primeval cave" (62). She enters the bedroom, which "indeed looked as if it was cut out of a giant rock" (63) and is dominated by "a giant white bed, laid out smooth, waiting to be used" (63). The tale of "Bluebeard" comes immediately to mind as does the passage early in *Jane Eyre* in which Jane finds herself in a red and white bedroom, also a riff on Bluebeard. Such foreshadowing proves accurate as suddenly Sissie feels "Marija's cold fingers on her breast . . . while her other hand groped round and round Sissie's midriff" (64). Sissie quickly shakes off this unwanted sexual advance and thinks longingly of home, of "how she always liked to be sleeping in the bedchamber when it rained her body completely-wrapped-up in her mother's akatado-cloths" (64), an image of safety. But the narrator intrudes with a far darker connection with the Holocaust: "And now where was she? How did she get there? What strings, pulled by whom, drew her into those pinelands where not so long ago human beings stoked their own funeral pyres with other human beings, where now a young Aryan housewife kisses a young black woman with such desperation, right in the middle of her own nuptial chamber?" (64). The reader is made to see the Einsatzgruppen doing their grisly work across Europe, shooting Jews into pits the Jews themselves have dug.

This scene has been interpreted in widely different ways by literary critics. For example, Yaw Asante notes that Sissie "returns to Africa unscathed because she shows restraint in her rejection of a death-dealing lesbian sexual relationship proffered by her German friend,

Marija . . . for Marija, Sissie is a sexual object just like Kurtz's savage Amazon in Conrad's *Heart of Darkness*. What Aidoo does is to evoke the stereotypical image of the black woman as represented in colonial fiction in order to subvert it" (n.p.). Cheryl Sterling reads the passage in terms of African perceptions of homosexuality.[22]

After her rejection by Sissie, Marija begins to weep and Sissie is prompted to contemplate the links between colonialism and the Shoah. She begins by reflecting on the trope of smoke from the ovens of the Holocaust.

> Suddenly Sissie knew. She saw it once and was never to forget it. She saw against the background of the thick smoke that was like a rain cloud over the chimneys of Europe,

L
O
N
E
L
I
N
E
S
S

Forever falling like a tear out of a woman's eye.

And so this was it?
Bullying slavers and slave-traders.
Solitary discoverers.
Swamp-crossers and lion hunters.
Missionaries who risked the cannibal's pot to
bring the world to the heathen hordes.

Speculators in gold in diamond uranium and
copper
Oil you do not even mention—
Preachers of Apartheid and zealous educators.
Keepers of Imperial Palace and homicidal
plantation owners.
Monsieur Commandant and Madame the
Commandant's wife.
Miserable rascals and wretched whores whose only distinction in life was that at
least they were better than the Natives. (65–66)[23]

In this passage, Aidoo brings together the various systems of oppression that stem from white supremacy and racial hierarchy, deeming one group subhuman: slavery, colonialism, genocide. She names the oppressors: slavers and slave traders, missionaries, speculators, preachers of Apartheid, zealous educators and homicidal plantation owners, Monsieur and Madame Commandant. All derive satisfaction from deeming themselves "better than the Natives," even the "miserable rascals and wretched whores." Sissie has grasped the concept of the genocidal gaze and seen the connections among these various systems.

In the remaining fifteen pages of this chapter, the story of a white female missionary to Africa is introduced with the classic fairy tale opener "Once upon a time" (66). It is a story of child abuse and homophobia. Sissie and Marija return to the kitchen and make a vain effort to eat a cake topped with "the melting dark purple of jellied plums" (68). Sissie departs from Marija's cottage, having experienced an initiation of sorts.

Sissie is taken with the other INVOLOU students on a round of visits to various sites in Bavaria, setting off a speculation about medical experiments done on women in Global South countries to control overpopulation, with the observation that "we would rather / Kill / than / Think / or / Feel" (71), another reference to genocide, here presented as the "efficient" solution (71). Again, a linkage is made between colonialism and the Holocaust, eugenics and genocide as a means of controlling undesirable populations.

Sissie breaks the news to Marija that she will be departing from Bavaria shortly to travel to other sites in Germany and Europe, and then return home to Africa. The pending separation causes Marija, who was planning a rabbit supper for Sissie, much grief, and Sissie is surprised to discover within herself pleasure at hurting Marija. "It hit her like a stone, the knowledge that there is pleasure in hurting" (76). Another epiphany: the human capacity for cruelty. Marija alternately goes white and then red as strong emotions surge through her; Sissie calls this her "blushing and blanching" (72), and she is prompted to wonder about the danger of being white: "It made you awfully exposed, rendered you terribly vulnerable. Like being born without your skin . . . is that why, on the whole [whites] have had to be extra ferocious?" (76).

Marija arrives on the train platform early in the morning as Sissie departs. She urges Sissie to spend a little time in Munich: "Because München, Sissie, is our city, Bavaria" (79). But Sissie rejects this advice, and the narrator summons the historical links between Munich and Nazism:

> Munich, Marija,
> Is
> The Original Adolf of the pub-brawls
> and mobsters who were looking for
> a
> Führer—
>
> Munich is
> Prime Minister Chamberlain
> Hurrying from his island home to

> Appease,
> While freshly-widowed
> Yiddisher Mamas wondered
> What Kosher pots and pans
> Could be saved or not. (81)

Here Aidoo includes a reference to the Munich Agreement of September 1938, when leaders from England, France, and Italy met with Adolf Hitler in that city to discuss the future of Czechoslovakia. These discussions ended in ceding portions of Czechoslovakia to Hitler in an effort of appeasement to avoid war, an effort that was, of course, futile.

This reference is followed by one about a Jewish mother packing pots and pans in preparation for deportation, also a futile gesture as most women with children were directed immediately to the gas. With Sissie's refusal to see the sites of ignominious Munich, chapter 2 draws to a close.

The focus of chapter 3, "From Our Sister Killjoy," is also a postcolonial theme: the diaspora engendered by colonialism. Sissie travels next to England: "If anyone had told her that she would want to pass through England because it was her colonial home, she would have laughed," a reference to the British as colonizers of Ghana (85). But pass through she does, encountering far more people of color than she had anticipated, many of whom are students being exploited by the academic system:

> For a few pennies now and a
> Doctoral degree later,
> Tell us about
> Your people
> Your history
> Your mind.
> Your mind.
> Your mind.
>
> They work hard for the
> Doctorates—
> They work too hard,
> Giving away
> Not only themselves, but
> All of us—

> The price is high,
> My brother,
> Otherwise the story is as old as empires. (87)

Here are the familiar tropes of fiction from West Africa about the "been to's"—that is, those who have immigrated to Europe to realize a dream, to earn money to send back home, to live in the imagined metropolitan paradise. Sissie sees her countrymen and women shabbily dressed, poorly employed, living in below-ground hovels, and yet lying to everyone back home in Africa, not able to admit that being part of the diaspora has been humiliating and disillusioning. The Irish and Scots try to depict themselves as fellow travelers, that is, fellow victims of the British Empire, but Sissie is having none of it: "the world is not filled with folks who shared our sister's black-eyed squint at things" (93). Her black-eyed squint, becoming more critical and astute as her journey continues, returns the gaze of resistance to the imperial gaze that would diminish her.

Sissie encounters a German-born professor now living in America who tries "to convince her of one thing. That this thing binds the Germans, the Irish and the Africans—in that order naturally—together. And that this thing is, OPPRESSION. 'Ja, our people have been oppressed for many many years, since the First World War,' he said. Our Sister's own mouth caught so rigidly open with surprise, and wide enough for a million flies to swarm in and out" (93). Sissie is so taken aback by the professor's attempt to claim that Germans were victims that:

> She forgot to ask
> Her Most Learned Guest
> If he had heard of
> Buchenwald,
>   or come across
> Dachau
>   even in his reading? (93–94)

Colonial amnesia, or aphasia, becomes genocidal amnesia here as the German professor attempts to claim victim status and align himself with the colonized. Aidoo devotes the remaining several pages of this chapter to the visit of a mimic man named Kunle, originally African, who has lived in London for seven years. He is boasting about the recent heart transplant performed in South Africa. (The first successful heart transplant was performed by Dr. Christiaan Barnard, an Afrikaner, on 3 December 1967 in Cape Town; the heart of a black South

African man was transplanted into a white South African man.) Kunle runs on about how such a surgery "is the / type of development that can /solve the question of apartheid / and rid us 'African negroes and all other negroes' of the / Colour Problem" (96). Sissie is deeply skeptical of this claim, pondering the medical racism involved: "the Christian Doctor has himself said that in his glorious country, niggerhearts are so easy to come by, because of the violence those happy and contented bantus perpetrate against one another, in their drunken ecstasies and childlike gambols" (100). Aidoo closes this chapter dealing with the diaspora by recounting Kunle's death in a car accident upon his return home to Nigeria. The chauffeur he insisted on hiring drives too fast on the rough roads and Kunle's heart is "wasted," too far from South Africa to become a transplant.

The final chapter of the novel, "A Love Letter," recalls *Heart of Darkness* once again. Just as Marlow carries a letter to Kurtz's "Intended" back in Europe, Sissie writes a letter, in the first person, to her "Darling" that recounts whole blocks of conversations they have had about race and racism, slavery, language, colonialism, neocolonialism. Gradually it becomes apparent to the reader that Sissie and her lover have had a falling out. Both are African, but the lover has lived abroad for a lengthy period. Sissie challenges her lover to rethink his notions of what an African woman should be: "No, My Darling: [she writes] it seems as if so much of the softness and meekness you and all the brothers expect of me and all the sisters is that which is really western. Some kind of hashed-up Victorian notions, hm? Allah, me and my big mouth!!" (117). In recounting the suffering African women have endured, Sissie names the sins of colonialism:

> When she did not have to sell [her children] to local magnates for salt, rampaging strangers kidnapped them to other places where other overlords considered their lives wasted unless at least once before they died, they slept with an African woman. . . . Meanwhile, those who grew up around Mother woke up in forced labour and thinly-veiled slavery on colonial plantations. . . . Later on, her sons were conscripted into imperial armies and went on to die in foreign places, all over again or returned to her, with maimed bodies and minds. (123)

Sissie criticizes her lover, identified as a physician, and other Africans who remain in the West while Africa needs their talents, and their families need them to return. She recounts a student union meeting at which she railed against her fellow Africans for finding myriad excuses to remain in the West, thus providing one reason why the novel is titled *Our Sister Killjoy*. As Marlow attempted and failed to bring Kurtz back to "civilization," Sissie has endeavored to bring her fellow Africans home from the "heart of whiteness."

The novel closes with a narrative return to the third person. Sissie is on a plane, returning home to Africa, and it is on the plane ride that she has been writing this extended missive to her former lover. Significantly, the passengers have been watching "a bleary film of the American Wild West, dating from the early days of motion pictures" (132). Genocide of the American Indian serves as "lite entertainment," as do the sweets and liquor being served, the "familiar duty-free rubbish" being hawked, and the gossip going around. Sissie imagines that she feels the welcome warmth of the African continent as passengers are alerted by an announcement that the coastline is visible below. She decides she will not mail the letter; "she was back in Africa. And that felt like fresh honey on the tongue: a mixture of complete sweetness and smoky roughness. 'Oh, Africa. Crazy old continent,'" Sissie intones, not caring if the person in the seat next to her thinks she's crazy (133–34).

Aidoo leaves the reader there, with the journey not quite complete. Sissie returns a wiser, more sober woman, one who has recognized the links between the racial hierarchies of colonization and the German genocide of eleven million people whose "blood" did not meet Aryan standards. She has experienced the diminishment of the imperial gaze and grasped its evolution into the genocidal gaze. But Aidoo does not intend for the conclusion of the novel to be entirely bleak. In an interview, she noted: "*Killjoy* doesn't end on a note of despair. I want to say that we struggle through, in spite of the almost overwhelming nature of our grief, the horrors around us, we struggle through. One keeps looking for hopeful signs and invariably one finds them; however tiny."[24]

Afterword

At the core of the genocide of the Herero and Nama, and of the Nazi Holocaust, was the acceptance, indeed the fervent embrace, of the concept of racist/racial hierarchies. In his sober and sobering book, *When Victims Become Killers: Colonialism, Nativism and the Genocide in Rwanda*, Mahmood Mamdani notes: "The horror of colonialism led to two types of genocidal impulses. The first was the genocide of the native by the settler. . . . Faced with the violent denial of his humanity by the settler, the native's violence began as a counter to violence [the second impulse]. . . . The genocide of the Herero was the first genocide of the twentieth century. The links between it and the Holocaust go beyond the building of concentration camps and the execution of an annihilation policy and are worth exploring." Mamdani notes other links, such as the influence of Social Darwinism on the "cleansing" of the African tribes, the critique by von Trotha of the missionaries for "inciting the Herero with images 'of the bloodcurdling Jewish history of the Old Testament,'" and the medical experiments of Eugen Fischer, who returns to Germany to become Josef Mengele's teacher. However, the link Mamdani emphasizes most strongly "is *race branding*, whereby it became possible not only to set a group apart as an enemy, but also to exterminate it with an easy conscience" (emphasis in the original, 9–13). The construction of the target of genocides as subhuman, as vermin, as cockroaches, as barbarians lacking in civilization, religion, and history crosses the boundaries of centuries and continents.

The Genocidal Gaze strives to demonstrate these deadly linkages between imperialism and genocide, between the genocide of the Herero and Nama people and that of the victims of the Holocaust, and between German colonialism in Africa and that in eastern Europe during the Third Reich. It endeavors to do so by careful reading of texts written both during colonialism and in the post-Holocaust era, with an emphasis on the idea of *race branding*, or racist hierarchies, which give rise to the genocidal gaze. It traces the impetus that enables the imperial, or colonial, gaze to evolve into the genocidal gaze. These linkages, which have been termed "the continuity thesis" by historians such as Jürgen Zimmerer, Joachim Zeller, Jan-Bart Gewald, Casper Erichsen, and others, are explored here beyond the realm of the discipline of history.

Such a tracing of the continuity thesis—into letters, fiction, memoir, and art installation—functions to further validate the idea of connections across decades among genocides. This extension also demonstrates the potential, and real, impact of literary and artistic texts to serve as both a goad to the acceptance of racist hierarchies as the norm (with all the horrifying consequences of that acceptance) and a critique of such acceptance. By its location at the intersection of Holocaust and Genocide Studies and Postcolonial Studies, this book seeks to find connections among various transnational oppressions, methodologies of persecution and extermination, and ideologies of perpetrators.

As this book was going to press, in March 2017, I traveled to Europe to see two exhibits on the Herero and Nama genocide. These exhibits were remarkable in many ways, not the least in that they, too, sit at the crossroads of Holocaust and Genocide Studies and Postcolonial Studies. The first exhibit, at the Mémorial de la Shoah in Paris, was titled *Le Premier Génocide du XXe Siècle: Herero and Nama dans le Sud-Ouest africain allemande 1904–1908*. A modest catalogue was produced in connection with the exhibit. The images and text of the exhibit are notable for several reasons. First, this genocide is clearly named as the first of the twentieth century; until recently, this designation was almost always given to the Armenian genocide, which took place a decade later. Second, von Trotha's extermination order is quoted in full. Third, the exhibit takes a gendered approach, discussing and demonstrating the Schutztruppe proclivity for photographing women's exposed breasts. In addition, an offensive German cartoon from the period, titled "Die Macht der Gewohnheit" (The Force of Habit) and originally published in *Simplicissimus* in 1904, is displayed. The cartoon shows a soldier being intimate with an indigenous woman, a whip at his side; arriving home to his white wife; painting her with stove blacking until she resembles the indigenous woman; and then proceeding to whip her with distinct relish. Such a cartoon calls to mind topics discussed in *The Genocidal Gaze*, including the permission for "paternal chastisement" (see the introduction) and the sexual violence against Herero and Nama women. It also starkly demonstrates the manner in which colonial violence travels back to the Fatherland, changing perceptions and behaviors.

Hendrik Witbooi plays an important role in the exhibit. His photo is centrally displayed, as is a model of his distinguishing mark: his hat and white scarf.

Quotations from his letters (the subject of chapter 1) are frequently incorporated into the curatorial information in order to provide history and context. I was particularly pleased to see that the bookstore in the museum carried a new edition of his letters, translated into French, with an introduction by novelist J. M. Coetzee, a Nobel Prize winner from South Africa. A similar edition, translated from Witbooi's original Cape Dutch, or a reprint of Brigitte Lau's translation, is urgently needed in English to make more widely available Witbooi's wise and poignant archive.

Other items in the exhibit include an example of a "Gibeon Pass," the oval metal tag with a personal number that the indigenous people were required to wear in the aftermath of the genocide; the cover of the British "Blue Book," which was quoted in chapter 1, is there, too. A considerable examination of the concentration camps and Shark Island, including several photos, is a centerpiece of the exhibit. The museumgoer can see a chilling German document that lists inmates in each of the camps: "Männer, Weiber, Kinder" (men, women, children); this document closely resembles the lists of prisoners arriving at Nazi concentration and death camps. While no specific reference is made to the continuity thesis—the drawing of connections between this first genocide of the twentieth century and that of the Holocaust—a Nazi poster is prominently displayed toward the end of the exhibit. A huge flag with swastika flies over a map of Africa, on which the German colonies are outlined in red. The motto says: "Auch hier lieght unser Lebensraum!" (Also here lies our living space). As I have discussed, the Nazis hoped to regain control of the colonies they lost at the end of World War I, and to that end, maintained a presence in the country we now call Namibia.

The final image in the exhibit is a photograph of a memorial stone erected in Swakopmund in 2007, which reads: "In memory of the thousands of heroic Ovaherero/OvaMbanderu who perished under mysterious circumstances at the realm of their German colonial masters in concentration camps in Swakopmund/Otjozondjii during 1904–1908. Rest in peace. Suvee Mohange Kavitondema. 31 March 2007. Swakopmund-Namibia." In this way, the Paris exhibit serves not only to teach museum audiences about the genocide but also as a fitting memorial to the victims of the genocide.

When I began work on *The Genocidal Gaze* in 2008, such an exhibit was almost unimaginable. The genocide of the Herero and Nama had been forgotten: colonial amnesia in Germany, certainly, and complete lack of awareness in other European countries and in the United States. The spirit of the Parisian exhibit was imbued with a certain French satisfaction at pointing out the genocidal behavior of its twentieth-century enemy, Allemagne/Germany. By contrast, the spirit of the second exhibit I saw, this one in Berlin at the Deutsches Historisches Museum, was one of guilt and apology.

That exhibit, titled *Deutscher Kolonialismus: Fragmente seiner Geschichte und Gegenwart* (German Colonialism: Fragments Past and Present), was spectacular, both as an exhibit and as an admission of guilt for the genocide in Africa. Boldly printed in white on a blood-red column near the entrance was the title of one section of the exhibit: "Der Genozid an Den Herero und Nama." No double-talk, no colonial amnesia. All the signage appears in both English and German. A certain metalevel to the exhibit makes it clear that the curators were cognizant not only of the historical events themselves, and the history of the objects, but also of their representation in Germany during the last century. Material from all Germany's colonies is included.

A beautifully produced catalogue, carrying the same title as the exhibit, runs to 335 pages and costs only 25 euros, a price made possible by state subsidy. It is laden with color photographs and a clear-eyed text. In addition to recapitulating the eight sections of the exhibit and their highlights, the catalogue contains sixteen essays by major scholars. These extend the meaning and value of the exhibit itself. For example, Jürgen Zimmerer, an early advocate of the continuity thesis, presents an essay that traces the torturous history of German colonial amnesia, repression, and denial of the genocide. He recounts the negotiations that have occurred between the German state and Namibia. He notes that as recently as "March 2016, the Bundestag rejected a motion from the Left Party, DIE LINKE, which called for recognition of the genocide of the Herero and Nama and for apology and compensations" (143). So the Deutsches Historisches Museum bravely acknowledged the genocide while the lawmakers were still stalled.

The number and the range of artifacts are staggering: the catalogue lists eighty-three institutions that loaned objects for the exhibit. One can view the original Treaty of Berlin with the signatures of Bismarck and other European leaders, as well as the extermination order issued by Lothar von Trotha in October 1904. The latter is typed, reminding me of the opening of Kentridge's *Black Box/ Chambre Noire*, in which a typewriter types an excerpt from this order. Kentridge came to mind again when I spotted a small metal figure of a German soldier whipping an indigenous man, bent backward under the beating. The curatorial label reads: "With the acquisition of colonial territories, toys specifically related to the colonies became popular in Germany. They served as *a medium for subtly disseminating stereotypes and as an indirect way of creating acceptance for the disparity between the colonized and the colonizers*—including the normality of violence against Africans" (emphasis mine). That is exactly the "race branding" of which Mamdani writes and it is inscribed in a toy. Nearby is an actual sjambok from the period, a whip made from hippopotamus hide, and Hendrik Witbooi's personal Bible, captured by the Schutztruppe.

Many, many photographs of the colonial era are available for the viewer. One of the photos in *The Genocidal Gaze* (identified as #3, "Surviving Herero") is on display, described as "a matchless icon of the German genocide against the Herero and Nama," which "is rightly criticized as an example of the photography of unwilling subjects, reproducing the power relations between the subjects and the photographer and exposing the people yet again *to a degrading gaze* onto their desperation" (emphasis mine). Fascinating photographs from the Colonial School for Women, located in Germany, reveal how women were trained as helpmeets for their spouses when sent out to settle in Africa.

The contents of the entire study of one Heinrich Schnee are behind a glass partition. His collection of ethnographic artifacts and objects from nature are described on the accompanying label as "the heedless appropriation of other cultures and the idea of conquering the wildness of nature . . . allowing the colonizer to reassure himself of his own superiority while putting the colonized on the lowest rung of the ladder of civilization." Race branding again. Clothing, posters, a colonial clock, hand-carved *colon* figures, and so many other items prompt the onlooker to wonder at the project of amassing and storing such a quantity of objects. To what end? The catalogue entry for this section of the exhibit suggests: "Many museum collections are closely entangled with colonial power relations. . . . The collection stocks grew rapidly, guided by ideas of completeness and the prevalent impetus among ethnologists to pre-empt an anticipated extinction of 'primitive peoples'" (219). "An anticipated extinction"—and one that was indeed carried out.

Near the end of the exhibit, displays deal frankly with issues of language and the presence of Africans in Germany as a result of colonization and the world wars. Another section looks at attitudes toward Africa in the German Democratic Republic, and yet another traces the Namibian fight for independence from South Africa, finally successful in 1990. Having spent several hours in the exhibit, I came away sensing that Germany is moving toward a new *Vergangenheitbewältigung*: this one a coming to terms with their colonial history. Other colonial powers—England, France, and the United States—would do well to follow this example. I hope that *The Genocidal Gaze* will contribute to such a project.

Notes

Introduction

Sartre's slim volume, *Black Orpheus*, served originally as the introduction to an anthology of works by African and West Indian poets, edited by Leopold Sédar-Senghor. Published in French in 1948, the text of the introduction became available in an English translation by S. W. Allen (Paris: Présence Africaine, 1951) as a separate volume. Thus the text appeared at the dawn of African decolonization. Though the passage quoted in the epigraph, largely from the first page, is arresting and anticipates later theories of the gaze, much of the sixty-four-page essay is problematic. Sartre valorizes Negritude, now a discredited idea owing to its reliance on essentialism. Though he was a radical opponent of colonialism and engaged in the Algerian conflict, his analyses of specific verses in the anthology are also essentialist.

1. Jeremy Silvester and Jan-Bart Gewald, eds., *Words Cannot Be Found: German Colonial Rule in Namibia: An Annotated Reprint of the 1918 Blue Book* (Leiden: Brill, 2003), 95, 159.

2. See ibid., 197–98, for a statement made under oath by a Herero about his service as a "police-boy" at Omarurn in 1905. He provides dramatic and disgusting details of the work he was forced to do in flogging his fellow Hereros.

3. The details regarding Cramer that follow are taken from Horst Drechsler, *"Let Us Die Fighting": The Struggle of the Herero and Nama against German Imperialism (1884–1915)*, trans. Bernd Zöllner (London: Zed Press, 1980; originally published in German in 1966), 234–37, and Silvester and Gewald, part 2, chapter 2.

4. George Steinmetz, *The Devil's Handwriting: Precoloniality and the German Colonial State in Qingdao, Samoa, and Southwest Africa* (Chicago: University of Chicago Press, 2007), 150.

5. Mahmood Mamdani, *When Victims Become Killers: Colonialism, Nativism, and the Genocide in Rwanda* (Princeton: Princeton University Press, 2001).

6. Jürgen Zimmerer, "War, Concentration Camps and Genocide in South-West Africa: The First German Genocide," in *Genocide in German South-West Africa: The Colonial War of 1904–1908 and Its Aftermath*, ed. Jürgen Zimmerer and Joachim Zeller, trans. E. J. Neather (Monmouth, Wales: Merlin Press, 2008), 59.

7. Volker Langbehn and Mohammed Salama, eds., *German Colonialism: Race, the Holocaust, and Postwar Germany* (New York: Columbia University Press, 2011).

8. Birthe Kundrus, "German Colonialism: Some Reflections on Reassessments, Specificities, and Constellations," in *German Colonialism: Race, the Holocaust, and Postwar Germany*, ed. Volker Langbehn and Mohammed Salama (New York: Columbia University Press, 2011).

9. Kitty Millet, "Caesura, Continuity, and Myth: The Stakes of Tethering the Holocaust to German Colonial Theory," in *German Colonialism: Race, the Holocaust, and Postwar Germany*, ed. Volker Langbehn and Mohammed Salama (New York: Columbia University Press, 2011).

10. This list of the primary causes of the Holocaust is generally accepted by historians and can be found in early histories of the Shoah such as Raul Hilberg, *The Destruction of the European Jews* (Chicago: Quadrangle Books, 1961) and more recent histories such as Doris Bergen, *War and Genocide: A Concise History of the Holocaust*, 3rd ed. (Lanham, MD: Rowman and Littlefield, 2016).

11. Laura Mulvey, "Visual Pleasure and Narrative Cinema" (1975), reprinted in *Visual and Other Pleasures* (New York: Palgrave Macmillan, 2009). This classic essay claimed that the male gaze upon women actors was the dominating "look" of the camera/audience in Hollywood films as well as of the male actors on screen. Such a gaze results in objectifying women. Critiques of Mulvey's theory have pointed to its failure to deal with the issue of female, gay, and lesbian filmgoers; Mulvey subsequently published an article that responded by expanding her ideas. Feminist theory has insisted upon the notion of the resisting gaze or the resisting reader.

12. E. Ann Kaplan, *Looking for the Other: Feminism, Film, and the Imperial Gaze* (New York: Routledge, 1997).

13. One must note, however, that despite Foucault's stint in Tunisia, his work is solidly grounded in Western institutional practices. See *Discipline and Punish: The Birth of the Prison*, trans. Alan Sheridan (London: Penguin, 1991).

14. See Robert Irwin, *Dangerous Knowledge: Orientalism and Its Discontents* (Woodstock, NY: Overlook Press, 2006).

15. Gustav Frenssen, *Peter Moor's Journey to Southwest Africa*, trans. Margaret May Ward (Boston: Houghton Mifflin, 1908), 233–34.

16. John Noyes, *Colonial Space: Spatiality in the Discourse of German South West Africa, 1884–1915* (Chur, Switzerland: Harwood Academic Publishers, 1992), 163–64.

17. As we will see in chapter 2, this is one of the mantras used by Frenssen in *Peter Moor's Journey to Southwest Africa*.

18. I am indebted to George Steinmetz for this section title. See *The Devil's Handwriting: Precoloniality and the German Colonial State in Qingdao, Samoa, and Southwest Africa* (Chicago: University of Chicago Press, 2007), 6.

19. This statistic comes from David Maybury-Lewis, "Colonial Genocide," in *Genocide: A Reader*, ed. Jens Meierhenrich (Oxford: Oxford University Press, 2014). The remarkable

story of King Leopold, his Congo colony, and the abusive and deadly treatment administered to the forced laborers there, which went largely unpunished, is told by Adam Hochschild in his deservedly admired history *King Leopold's Ghost: A Story of Greed, Terror, and Heroism in Colonial Africa* (New York: Houghton Mifflin, 1999).

20. Samuel Totten and William S. Parsons, *Century of Genocide: Critical Essays and Eyewitness Accounts*, 3rd ed. (New York: Routledge, 2009), 19.

21. Sebastian Conrad, *German Colonialism: A Short History*, trans. Sorcha O'Hagan (Cambridge: Cambridge University Press, 2012), 3.

22. Susanne Zantop provides lavish details about these images in *Colonial Fantasies: Conquest, Family, and Nation in Precolonial Germany, 1770–1870* (Durham: Duke University Press, 1997).

23. For examples of such "Protection" treaties, and how they varied among ethnic groups, see Arthur J. Knoll and Hermann J. Hiery, eds., *The German Colonial Experience: Select Documents on German Rule in Africa, China, and the Pacific, 1884–1914* (Lanham, MD: University Press of America, 2010).

24. Jon Bridgman and Leslie J. Worley, "Genocide of the Hereros," in *Century of Genocide: Critical Essays and Eyewitness Accounts*, 3rd ed., ed. Samuel Totten and William S. Parsons (New York: Routledge, 2009), 21.

25. See, for example, Karla Poewe, *The Namibian Herero: A History of Their Psychosocial Disintegration and Survival* (Lewiston, NY: Edwin Mellen Press, 1985).

26. George Steinmetz, "The First Genocide of the 20th Century and Its Postcolonial Afterlives: Germany and the Namibian Ovaherero," hdl.handle.net/2027/spo.4750978.0012.201.

27. Benjamin Madley, "From Africa to Auschwitz: How German South West Africa Incubated Ideas and Methods Adopted by the Nazis in Eastern Europe," *European History Quarterly* 35:3 (2005): 432–33.

28. Casper Erichsen has written the definitive study of these camps, particularly Shark Island. See *"The Angel of Death Has Descended Violently among Them": Concentration Camps and Prisoners of War in Namibia, 1904–1908* (Leiden: African Studies Centre, 2005).

29. See www.bbc.com/news/world-europe-15127992 and www.dw.com/en/germany-to-return-skulls-of-colonial-victims-in-namibia/a-18575293.

30. Rene Lemarchand, ed., *Forgotten Genocides: Oblivion, Denial, and Memory* (Philadelphia: University of Pennsylvania Press, 2011).

31. See, for example, Patrick Furlong, *Between Crown and Swastika: The Impact of the Radical Right on the Afrikaner Nationalist Movement in the Fascist Era* (Hanover, NH: Wesleyan University Press, 1991).

Chapter One

1. Werner Hillebrecht, "Hendrik Witbooi and Samuel Maharero: The Ambiguity of Heroes," in *Re-Viewing Resistance in Namibian History*, ed. Jeremy Silvester (Windhoek: University of Namibia Press, 2015), 39.

2. Kaplan, *Looking for the Other*, xix.

3. The term "Hottentot" is now heard largely in connection with the "Hottentot Venus." See Steinmetz, *The Devil's Handwriting*, chapter 2, for more information on this topic.

4. Steinmetz, *The Devil's Handwriting*, 114–15. Steinmetz includes a thorough analysis of precolonial German conceptions of the indigenous groups of Southwest Africa, with a focus on the Nama, the Herero, and the Rehoboth Basters. Steinmetz has meticulously combed precolonial travel narratives, early anthropology studies, missionary reports, and other primary documents to create these portraits.

5. Herman Babson, introduction to Gustav Frenssen, *Peter Moors Fahrt nach Südwest*, ed. Babson (New York: Henry Holt, 1914), xxiv.

6. Brigitte Lau, ed., *The Hendrik Witbooi Papers*, 2nd ed., trans. Annemarie Heywood and Eben Maasdorp (Windhoek: National Archives of Namibia, 1996), i. Biographical information in this section is taken largely from Lau and Steinmetz, *The Devil's Handwriting*.

7. Hillebrecht notes that the extent of "continuous tribal wars between mutually hostile ethnic groups" has been exaggerated by German historians; the reality, he continues, "is much more complex, as it must be realized that 'pre-colonial' Namibia was already a colonial frontier zone" due to the impact of indigenous peoples from South Africa relocating in Namibia ("Hendrik Witbooi and Samuel Maharero," 41).

8. www.unesco.org/new/en/communication-and-information/flagship-project-activities/memory-of-the-world/register/full-list-of-registered-heritage/registered-heritage-page-5/letter-journals-of-hendrik-witbooi/.

9. Contents of all three journals, plus invaluable appendices, were published in an English edition in 1989 in Windhoek. *The Hendrik Witbooi Papers* was edited by Brigitte Lau and translated by Annemarie Heywood and Eben Maasdorp. Werner Hillebrecht gives an ample account of the various segments of the Witbooi archive, which ones have been lost, which recovered, and where they are now housed.

10. Another instance of Witbooi's use of his archive by forwarding a letter as proof of his claim can be found in letter 28, dated 3 January 1890, and addressed to the Rev. Olpp, a mentor of Witbooi's who remained loyal to him until the end.

11. Witbooi was correct about this type of punishment. Indeed, the Germans took photographs of each other administering this kind of beating.

12. See the exchange of correspondence between Samuel Maharero and Hendrik Witbooi as they negotiate this peace in Lau, *The Hendrik Witbooi Papers*, 115–18.

13. See Steinmetz, *The Devil's Handwriting*, 157–79 for a fuller examination of the relationship between Leutwein and Witbooi between 1894 and 1904.

14. Helmut Bley, *South-West Africa under German Rule, 1894–1914* (Evanston, IL: Northwestern University Press, 1971), 155–63.

15. Although 29 October is the date usually cited for Witbooi's death, Steinmetz (*The Devil's Handwriting*, 170n129) gives the date of 22 November 1905, citing a telegram of 11 December 1905 in the Berlin Archives.

16. Leutwein employs the term "brother-in-arms" because Witbooi had signed the "Protection Treaty" and its addendum that obligated him to fight on the side of the Germans until he ultimately decided to fight against them again, causing his own death in battle; Leutwein uses the term "little Captain" in what is perhaps a descriptive rather than derogatory term. Hillebrecht tells us that Witbooi was "so small in stature that it earned him the nickname 'Kort,' which could be translated as 'Shortie'" ("Hendrik Witbooi and Samuel Maharero," 51). A photo of Witbooi and Leutwein standing together shows Witbooi to be about a head shorter than Leutwein (47).

17. This book, which appeared in 2003, is a reprint, with new scholarly material, of the British 1918 publication, *Report on the Natives of South-West Africa and Their Treatment by Germany*, commonly known as the Blue Book of 1918.

18. For a fascinating account of the publication of the Blue Book, the accuracy of the eyewitness reports, and the German objections to it, which included the German publication of a White Book recounting alleged British atrocities in their own colonies, see the introduction to *Words Cannot Be Found*. Additionally, for an account of the animosity between German settlers and the British settlers who arrived after 1914, see Margarethe von Eckenbrecher, *Africa: What It Gave Me, What It Took from Me, Remembrances from My Life as a German Settler in South West Africa*, trans. and ed. David Crandall, Hans-Wilhelm Kelling, and Paul Kerry (Bethlehem, PA: Lehigh University Press, 2015). Her memoir was written and published in two volumes: her initial stay in GSWA stretched from April 1902 to March 1904; she departed for Germany to escape the 1904 war and remained in Europe for a decade during which time she published book 1 of her memoirs. After divorcing her husband, she returned alone to the colony with her two sons in May 1914 and remained on the continent until her death. In 1936, she completed book 2 of her memoirs, and it was first published in 1940.

19. Lieut. Fred C. Cornell, *The Glamour of Prospecting* (New York: Frederick A. Stokes Company, 1920).

20. Cornell's memoir is 334 pages long and I quote or reference here all the passages relevant to German military behavior and treatment of the Herero and Nama. Thus my emphasis is *not* representative of the text as a whole, which devotes pages and pages to landscape descriptions and mishaps in trekking. Cornell's purpose was not a political one but rather intended as a kind of valorization of the prospector. He cautions the reader in the preface that the book "is in no wise intended to serve as a handbook to the would-be prospector" but rather depicts the prospector as "the true pioneer; his pick and hammer open up the wild places of the earth (usually to the benefit of those who follow him more than to his own)" (*The Glamour of Prospecting*, vii). The book also includes almost forty black and white photographs of Cornell and his companions in barren landscape, with their various kinds of transportation, and of dramatic river gorges, mountains, and vegetation.

21. Marengo is an alternate spelling of the name of a Nama rebel. Uwe Timm's novel *Morenga* uses the other spelling. These brief passages from Cornell are useful in analyzing Timm's work.

22. It is impossible to tell from Cornell's book whether he saw Shark Island while it was still in operation. The camp closed in April 1907, and Cornell dates his adventures in German Southwest Africa as occurring from "the latter part of 1907" (*The Glamour of Prospecting*, 2) to 1914. But he certainly saw the coast of Lüderitzbucht where the camp was located, he experienced the extremes of weather and wind there that made the camp so deadly, and he heard details from the Boers who had themselves seen the camp in operation. Thus he was a witness to the difficulties of climate and rocky landscape but perhaps a secondary witness to the atrocities committed by the Germans against the Herero and Nama in the camp.

23. See Mel Gussow, "W. G. Sebald, Elegiac German Novelist, Is Dead at 57," *New York Times*, 15 December 2001, C16.

24. Ann Laura Stoler, "Colonial Aphasia: Race and Disabled Histories in France," *Public Culture* 23:1 (2011): 121–56. Stoler differentiates amnesia from aphasia thus: "Aphasia, I propose, is perhaps a more apt term, one that captures not only the nature of the blockage but also the feature of loss.... In aphasia, an occlusion of knowledge is the issue. It is not a matter of ignorance or absence. Aphasia is a disremembering, a difficulty speaking, a difficulty generating a vocabulary that associates appropriate words and concepts with appropriate things" (125).

25. Studies of Holocaust photographs, particularly those of women, can be found in Andrea Liss, *Trespassing through Shadows: Memory, Photography and the Holocaust* (Minneapolis: University of Minnesota Press, 1998), and Barbie Zelizer, "Gender and Atrocity: Women in Holocaust Photographs," in *Visual Culture and the Holocaust*, ed. Barbie Zelizer (New Brunswick, NJ: Rutgers University Press, 2001). For a full treatment of the fate of women during colonization, see Ann Laura Stoler, *Carnal Knowledge and Imperial Power: Race and the Intimate in Colonial Rule* (Berkeley: University of California Press, 2002).

26. This image brings to mind Claude Lanzmann's film *Shoah*, in which a barber in Israel recounts the immense pain he experienced as a barber in the anteroom to gas chambers. Friends from his hometown arrive and he must maintain silence regarding what is about to occur as he cuts their hair. In both instances, victims are made to do the grisly work of the perpetrators on people they are likely to know.

27. Anna Heywood, Brigitte Lau, and Raimund Ohly, eds., *Warriors, Leaders, Sages, and Outcasts in the Namibian Past* (Windhoek: Michael Scott Oral Records Project, 1992).

Chapter Two

The epigraph source is Medardus Brehl, "'The drama was played out on the dark stage of the sandvelt': The Extermination of the Herero and Nama in German (Popular) Literature," in *Genocide in German South-West Africa: The Colonial War of 1904–1908 and Its Aftermath*, ed. Jürgen Zimmerer and Joachim Zeller, trans. E. J. Neather (Monmouth, Wales: Merlin Press, 2008), 101.

1. Sander Gilman, "The Image of the Black in the German Colonial Novel," *Journal of European Studies* 8 (1978): 1–11, quote on 3.

2. *New York Times*, 2 March 1907.

3. Frenssen, *Peter Moor's Journey to Southwest Africa*, trans. Ward, 6. All further quotations cited in the text are from this edition.

4. Wilhelm Alberts, *Gustav Frenssen* (Berlin, 1922) and Numme Numsen, *Gustav Frenssen* (Stuttgart, 1938), as cited by Frank X. Braun, "Gustav Frenssen in Retrospect," *Monatshefte* 39:7 (1947): 449–62.

5. "Freitisch" (literally, "free table") can be described as a kind of free board for children from impoverished families.

6. *Heimat* is a complicated and emotionally laden term in German that loses much in the translation to the term "regional literature." *Heimatkunst* might be translated literally as "Home Art." But that still does not do the term justice. Here is a definition that gets at the nuances: "Heimat designates a felt relationship enduring over time between human beings and places that can extend metaphorically to connote identification with family or nation, cultural tradition, local dialect or native tongue." See Elizabeth Boa, "Some Versions of Heimat: Goethe and Hølderlin around 1800, Frenssen and Mann around 1900," in *Heimat: At the Intersection of Memory and Space*, ed. Frederike Eigler and Jens Kugele (Berlin: De Gruyter, 2012), 34.

7. Frenssen, *Peter Moors Fahrt nach Südwest*, ed. Babson, vii; apparently Babson had contact with Gustav Frenssen during the editing of *Peter Moor* as he thanks him explicitly in his preface for permission to publish this edition.

8. Effie Louise Pratt, *A Comparative Study of the Literary Technique of Theodor Storm and Gustav Frenssen* (Chicago: University of Chicago Press, 1925).

9. Volker Griese, *Die drei Leben des Gustav Frenssen: Eine Frenssen Chronik* (Münster: Verlagshaus Monsenstein und Vannerdat, 2011), 85.

10. "Peter Moors Fahrt nach Südwest," *Journal of the Royal African Society* 6:23 (April 1907): 322.

11. "Peter Moor's Journey to Southwest Africa," *Advocate of Peace* 70:10 (November 1908): 248.

12. Andrew Henshaw Ward came from an illustrious New England family of writers. See Andrew Henshaw Ward, *Ward Family; Descendants of William Ward who settled in Sudbury, Mass in 1639* (Boston: S. G. Drake, 1851).

13. Sander Gilman notes: "The vision of the Black as a non-productive animal is even reflected in the justice of German South West Africa which punished the thievery of milk (i.e. real property) with six months imprisonment and fifty lashes while the poisoning of a Black by Blacks was punished by twenty-five lashes!" ("The Image of the Black in the German Colonial Novel," 4), quoted from Fritz Ferdinand Müller, *Kolonien unter der Peitsche* (Berlin: Rütten and Loening, 1962), 90–91.

14. See Steinmetz, *The Devil's Handwriting*, for a full and fascinating account of what he calls the "ethnographic discourse" about the various indigenous groups living in Southwest

Africa when the Germans colonized it. Steinmetz has made a thoughtful study of travel narratives, missionary reports, visual images, and the like from the precolonial era. This ethnographic discourse informed the German perceptions of the Herero and Nama and, ultimately, contributed to the genocidal gaze of the Germans.

15. The railway from Swakopmund to Windhoek was completed in 1900 and covers a distance of 237 miles (Babson introduction, xx).

16. "Hottentot," now considered a racist term, is the designation given by the Dutch to the Khoikhoi people in southwestern Africa. They are more frequently referred to now as the Nama.

17. See Stoler, *Carnal Knowledge and Imperial Power*, for gendered analysis of colonialism and attitudes toward both female colonists and indigenous women.

18. John K. Noyes, "National Identity, Nomadism, and Narration in Gustav Frenssen's *Peter Moor's Journey to Southwest Africa*," in *The Imperialist Imagination: German Colonialism and Its Legacy*, ed. Sara Friedrichsmeyer, Sara Lennox, and Susanne Zantop (Ann Arbor: University of Michigan Press, 1998), 88.

19. David Kenosian, "The Colonial Body Politic: Desire and Violence in the Works of Gustav Frenssen and Hans Grimm," *Monatshefte* 89:2 (1997): 183.

20. Alan Bowyer, "'Narrating the Nation': Homi Bhabha and Gustav Frenssen," *JLS/TLW* 9:3/4 (December 1993): 261.

21. Daniel Brückenhaus's essay "Ralph's Compassions" appeared in Ute Frevert et al., *Learning How to Feel: Children's Literature and Emotional Socialization, 1870–1970* (London: Oxford University Press, 2014), 74–93. Dr. Brückenhaus replied to an e-mail I sent in February 2015 to seek clarification of this categorization of *Peter Moor*. He sent the following helpful reply: "About Gustav Frenssen's book: among the co-authors of the volume, we had many discussions about which works to include in our chapters. In the end, we decided to use 'children's literature' in a broad sense, encompassing all books whose main character(s), and main intended audience, were people who, according to the legal and cultural norms of the period, had not fully 'come of age' yet. For Germany during the 'Kaiserreich' period that means those under 21 years old. This includes Frenssen's character Peter Moor, who is in his late teens. In German, there actually is a separate term for books that are written for teenagers specifically (as opposed to younger children), called '*Jugendbuch*'—'Youth Book'; that is the category under which *Peter Moors* is frequently discussed in the German secondary literature."

22. Joachim Warmbold, *Germania in Africa: Germany's Colonial Literature* (New York: Peter Lang, 1989), 67.

23. Jeff Bowersox, *Raising Germans in the Age of Empire: Youth and Colonial Culture, 1871–1914* (Oxford: Oxford University Press, 2013), 175.

24. Gustav Frenssen, *Peter Moor's Fahrt nach Südwest: Ein Feldzugsbericht* (Windhoek, Namibia: Druck and Verlag, 1998), 8.

25. Quoted in Bowersox, *Raising Germans in the Age of Empire*, 52.

Chapter Three

1. Uwe Timm, *Morenga*, trans. Breon Mitchell (New York: New Directions, 2003). All references in the text are to this edition.

2. Uwe Timm, *In My Brother's Shadow: A Life and Death in the SS*, trans. Anthea Bell (New York: Farrar, Straus and Giroux, 2005). All references in the text are to this edition.

3. Dominik Schaller, "'Every Herero Will Be Shot': Genocide, Concentration Camps, and Slave Labor in German South-West Africa," in *Forgotten Genocides: Oblivion, Denial, and Memory*, ed. Rene Lemarchand (Philadelphia: University of Pennsylvania Press, 2011), 53.

4. See Henning Melber, *Understanding Namibia: The Trials of Independence* (London: Hurst and Company, 2014), 28–31, for an account of the building of Heroes Acre and some of the problems associated with its construction by a Korean firm, as well as the monuments and texts at this war memorial built in 2002.

5. For a history of the archives, see both Drechsler, *"Let Us Die Fighting"* and Julia Hell and George Steinmetz, "The Visual Archive of Colonialism: Germany and Namibia," *Public Culture* 18:1 (2008): 147–84.

6. For example, on page 13, note 28, Drechsler describes the intentional deception by Lüderitz of the indigenous people when reaching an agreement in a treaty about land; Lüderitz used geographical miles to indicate distance, rather than English miles, thus grabbing much more territory. Lüderitz's nephew, an historian, subsequently ignored this deception in his writing, although records available to him at the time make it clear what happened. This is an obscure fact, to be sure, but one adopted by Timm in *Morenga*.

7. Namibia did not gain its independence until 1990—it was the last country in Africa to do so—and at that time took the name Namibia.

8. Rainer Schulte, "Interview with Breon Mitchell and Uwe Timm: Collaboration between Translator and Author," *Translation Review* 66:1 (2003): 2.

9. Lothar Probst, "'Normalization' through Europeanization: The Role of the Holocaust," in *German Culture, Politics, and Literature in the Twenty-First Century: Beyond Normalization*, ed. Stuart Tabener and Paul Cooke (Rochester, NY: Camden House, 2006), 62.

10. While *Morenga* was the first post–World War II novel to openly criticize the German colonial project, a short story, *Weltreise auf deutsche Art*, by Alfred Andersch was published in a collection of his short stories titled *Geister und Leute: Zehn Geschichten* (1958). This collection is available in English under the title *The Night of the Giraffe and Other Stories*. See Dirk Göttsche, *Remembering Africa: The Rediscovery of Colonialism in Contemporary German Literature* (New York: Camden House, 2013), for a useful summary of the story, which recounts the experiences of a young German clerk conscripted to fight colonial wars in China and GSWA: the experience leaves him "disillusioned, traumatized and 'increasingly silent'" (68). Like *Morenga*, the story "clearly sets the traumatic memory of colonial violence and genocide against colonial narratives of cultural superiority and imperial nostalgia" (69).

11. See Erichsen, *"The Angel of Death Has Descended Violently among Them"* for his thoroughgoing analysis of fatality statistics in the various concentration and death camps. Steinmetz, "The First Genocide," estimates that the mortality rate at Shark Island was over 90 percent.

12. Bambuses usually functioned as servants to the Schutztruppe and were given tasks such as polishing shoes and cleaning house.

13. Witbooi's death is usually dated 29 October 1905.

14. Johan Huizinga, *Homo Ludens: A Study of the Play-Element in Culture* (1944; Boston: Beacon Press, 1968), 211.

15. Julia Kristeva, "Intertextuality: An Interview with Julia Kristeva," conducted by Margaret Smallen, www.msu.edu/user/chrenkal/1980/INTEXINT.HTM.

16. Sue Vice, *Holocaust Fiction* (New York: Routledge, 2000).

17. For greater detail about the deployment of intertextuality in post-Holocaust fiction, see Elizabeth Baer, *The Golem Redux: From Prague to Post-Holocaust Fiction* (Detroit: Wayne State University Press, 2012).

18. Though I do not work with it in this book, another stunning intertextual relationship exists between *Morenga* and Thomas Pyncheon's *Gravity's Rainbow*, published in 1973, five years prior to *Morenga*.

19. Frenssen, *Peter Moor's Journey to Southwest Africa*, trans. Ward, 231–32. All further references in the text refer to this edition.

20. See von Eckenbrecher, *Africa: What It Gave Me, What It Took from Me*. This edition carries both volumes as well as very helpful paratextual material.

21. Peter Bowman, "Fontane's 'Der Stechlin': A Fragile Utopia," *Modern Language Review* 97:4 (October 2002): 877–91.

22. Petr Kropotkin, *Mutual Aid: A Factor of Evolution* (New York: Garland, 1972), vii.

23. It is intriguing to learn that the change in font size was introduced first in the Breon Mitchell translation to English: "The New Directions designer decided to put some of the collage-like material into smaller type, thinking it would be easier to read," remarks Mitchell. Timm responds: "I must say that the English edition is much better than the German one. That's because of the typography . . . it's an excellent solution" (Schulte, "Interview," 6).

24. See Theodor Adorno, *Can One Live after Auschwitz? A Philosophical Reader* (Stanford: Stanford University Press, 2003).

25. For a much more detailed analysis of Ozick's arguments regarding the use of the imagination and of history in post-Holocaust fiction, see Baer, *The Golem Redux*, 152–69.

26. The spelling of his name varies. Sometimes it is Marengo. About Timm's decision to use Morenga, Göttsche says: "The very fact that Morenga, the symbol of African resistance, provides the novel's title reflects Timm's anticolonial and anti-Eurocentric perspective. However, the use of the German variant of his name, 'Morenga,' rather than the more accurate form 'Jakob Marengo,' illustrates that Timm's literary reconstruction does not claim to represent African perceptions of German colonialism, aiming in-

stead to remind the German public of Germany's forgotten colonialism" (*Remembering Africa*, 74).

27. Uwe Timm, *Deutsche Kolonien* (Köln: Verlag Kiepenheuer and Witisch, 1986).

28. A few other books of this ilk, which celebrate the German victories in GSWA, include the following: (1) *Heisse Tage: Meine Erlebnisee im Kampf gegen die Hereros* by Conrad Stülpnagel (Berlin, 1905). Written in Fraktur, this text is 126 pages and contains several black-and-white photos, mostly of landscape; there is also a photo of a typical supply wagon such as is referred to in *Peter Moor*. (2) *Im Kampf* by von Salzmann, who served as an Oberleutnant in the Schutztruppe. Published in Berlin in 1908, this must have been an expensive book. It is printed on fine paper and contains many black-and-white photos, which give an excellent idea of a soldier's life. There is also a two-page spread of naked Herero and "Hottentot" women, standing in provocative poses in doorways. Many of the books from this era about GSWA have such photos, always showing bare-breasted women. (3) *Der Krieg* by R. Schwabe, published in Berlin in 1907, is a 440-page book, boasting photographs and paintings, including the seemingly mandatory photo of bare-breasted "Feld Herero." The author served in an infantry regiment. The cover of the book is an attractive Art Nouveau design. (4) *Unsere Helden in Sudwestafrika* by Paul Kolbe, published in Leipzig in 1907, contains many headshots of soldiers, a foldout map, a photo of the use of a termite mound for cooking, and a chart showing the numbers of wounded and dead.

29. Rhys Williams, "'A Perfectly Ordinary Childhood': Uwe Timm's *Am beispiel meines Bruders*," in *Uwe Timm (Volume II)*, ed. David Basker (Cardiff: University of Wales Press, 2007), 71–84.

30. Helmut Schmitz, ed., *A Nation of Victims? Representation of German Wartime Suffering from 1945 to the Present* (Amsterdam: Rodopi, 2007), 80.

31. Erin McGlothlin, *Second-Generation Holocaust Literature: Legacies of Survival and Perpetration* (Rochester, NY: Camden House, 2006), 18–19.

32. The sense in which Timm believes himself to have been almost absent from his father's consideration, overshadowed by his dead brother, mirrors, obversely, the experience Art Spiegelman describes in *Maus I & II* (1986, 1992).

33. See pages 7, 16, 37, 42–43, 47, 55, 57, 76, 79, 80, 104, 121, 125, 129.

Chapter Four

1. The Germans began wresting land from the indigenous Herero and Nama in Southwest Africa in the late nineteenth century, shortly after the shameful Conference of Berlin (1884–85). A war ensued and ultimately, 80 percent of the Herero and 50 percent of the Nama died, making this the first genocide of the twentieth century.

2. URLs for *Black Box* on YouTube: There are various filmic versions of "Black Box" to be found on YouTube. The most complete are presented in three separate sections: part I, http://www.youtube.com/watch?v=Nn38eZC8400 (6:53 minutes);

part II, http://www.youtube.com/watch?v=Ogru_gg9R2Y (5.13 minutes); part III, http://www.youtube.com/watch?v=Yd2q9XkVt3c (9:43 minutes). A version that better shows the colors but is cut by about seven minutes, can be viewed at www.youtube.com/watch?v=w6COnGRIFsw.

3. *William Kentridge: Black Box/Chambre Noire* (New York: Guggenheim Museum Publications, 2009), 15.

4. "Im Januar 2004 jährte sich zum hundertsten Mal der Ausbruch des deutschen Kolonialkrieges in Namibia. Er dauerte von 1904–1908 und ging als erster Völkermord des 20. Jahrhunderts in die Geschichte ein. Für Namibia, das damalige Deutsch-Südwestafrika, gilt dieser Krieg als einer der ersten Widerstandskriege der afrikanischen Bevölkerung gegen Fremdherrschaft und Kolonisierung." www.dhm.de/ausstellungen/namibia/ausstellung.htm (my translation).

5. See Bridgman and Worley, "Genocide of the Hereros," a concise summary that includes brief eyewitness narratives from Herero.

6. The majority of Jews in South Africa descend from immigrants from Lithuanian shtetls, and the Jewish Museum in Capetown offers a full-scale re-creation of such a shtetl. See A. Sarid, *There Once Was a Home: Memories of the Lithuanian Shtetls . . .* (Cape Town: Jewish Publications, South Africa, 2015).

7. The Sharpville Massacre occurred on 21 March 1960. It began as a demonstration by black Africans against the pass laws, the requirement under Apartheid that black Africans carry a pass at all times that controlled their movements from town to town; the primary goal of the pass laws was to control the labor of black Africans, specifically for work in mines. (This represents yet another link between GSWA, where pass laws were instituted in 1907, and Apartheid.) During the demonstration at Sharpville, the police turned their guns on unarmed demonstrators, killing 69 people and injuring 180.

8. Carolyn Christov-Bakargiev, *William Kentridge* (Brussels: Société des Expositions du Palais Des Beaux-Arts de Bruxelles, 1998), 28. See also Marianne Hirsch, "Surviving Images: Holocaust Photographs and the Work of Postmemory" for discussion of similar encounters with traumatic photographs in childhood experienced by Susan Sontag and Alice Kaplan. The essay is in Barbie Zelizer, ed., *Visual Culture and the Holocaust* (New Brunswick, NJ: Rutgers University Press, 2001).

9. See William Kentridge, *Six Drawing Lessons* (Cambridge, MA: Harvard University Press, 2014), 45–52 for his conceptualization of the stage as a camera.

10. T. Dunbar Moodie, *The Rise of Afrikanerdom: Power, Apartheid and the Afrikaner Civil Religion* (Berkeley: University of California Press, 1975), 154. Moodie traces the influence of European nationalism, in the form of neo-Fichtean philosophy, on the architects of Apartheid.

11. J. H. P. Serfontein, *Brotherhood of Power: An Exposé of the Secret Afrikaner Broederbond* (Bloomington: Indiana University Press, 1978). The influence of Nazi ideology on Apartheid, and on specific Apartheid leaders, is a controversial topic outside the scope of

this essay. In his book, Serfontein provides documentation of visits to Nazi Germany by the "brothers," including a consultation with Göring. A dissenting perspective is offered by Christoph Marx in "Hendrik Verwoerd's Long March to Apartheid: Nationalism and Racism in South Africa," in *Racism in the Modern World: Historical Perspectives on Cultural Transfer and Adaptation*, ed. Manfred Berg and Simon Wendt (New York: Berghahn Books, 2011), 281–302. Marx has undertaken extensive research into Verwoerd's private papers in archives and, while he acknowledges Verwoerd's racism, he endeavors to deny undue Nazi influence.

12. Nadine Gordimer's novel *July's People* envisions a bloody revolution as the end of Apartheid. Figures as to the total number of deaths in the struggle vary widely but by no means constitute genocide. See Nancy Clark and William Worger, *South Africa: The Rise and Fall of Apartheid* (Harlow, England: Pearson, 2011).

13. For a useful analysis of the similarities and differences between Apartheid and the Holocaust, see Juliette Peires, *The Holocaust and Apartheid: A Comparison of Human Rights Abuses* (Sea Point, South Africa: Union of Jewish Women, 2006).

14. Reena Jana, ed., *Vitamin D: New Perspectives in Drawing* (London: Phaidon Press, 2005), 160.

15. The full text of von Trotha's statement is as follows: "I, the great General of the German soldiers, send this letter to the Herero people. The Herero are no longer German subjects... The Herero nation... must leave the country. If they do not leave, I will force them out with the *Groot Rohr* (cannon). Every Herero, armed or unarmed, will be shot within the German borders. I will no longer accept women and children, but will force them back to their people or shoot at them." Steinmetz, "The First Genocide."

16. www.postmedia.net/06/kentridge.htm.

17. Ibid.

18. The Nazis were active in the former colony during the Third Reich, though Southwest Africa was then under the control of the British Mandate in South Africa. Nonetheless, the Nazis celebrated Hitler's birthday there with parades and swastikas, formed bund organizations for boys and girls, and carried on a covert propaganda campaign. See Benjamin Bennett, *Hitler over Africa* (London: T. Werner Laurie, 1939).

19. See de.sherlockholmes.wikia.com/wiki/Aus_den_Geheimakten_des_Welt-Detektivs for an image of this journal and more information on it.

20. See, for example, his film *Automatic Writing* (2003).

21. For a useful survey of films made in Africa by German filmmakers, see Guido Convents, "Film and German Colonial Propaganda for the Black African Territories to 1918," in *Before Caligari: German Cinema, 1895–1920*, 9th ed., ed. Paolo Cherchi Usai and Lorenzo Codelli (Pordenone, Italy: Edizioni Biblioteca dell'Immagine, 1990).

22. For more information about the fate of the rhino as a result of human predation, see www.savetherhino.org. See also Steven C. Dubin, "Theater of History: William Kentridge's *Black Box/Chambre Noire*," *Art in America* (April 2007): 128–31, 157. Dubin amplifies

the intertextual references of the rhino: "Kentridge had a number of ideas in mind when he drew his version of the animal—depictions of the bestiaries of Albrecht Dürer (1515) and Pietro Longhi (1751), for example, each of which was shaped (and misshaped) by travelers' tales. He was also alluding to Eugene Ionesco's absurdist play of 1959, as well as to a conservation campaign to save the white rhino" (131).

23. Kentridge in Elizabeth Levy, ed., *William Kentridge: Black Box/Chambre Noire* (Berlin: Deutsche Guggenheim, 2005), 50–51.

24. Some of these skulls have only recently been returned to Namibia. See BBC article "Germany Returns Namibian Skulls Taken in Colonial Era," 30 September 2011, www.bbc.co.uk/news/world-europe-15127992. Reports suggest that Herero women were forced to remove the skin with glass shards from these decapitated heads before they were shipped to Germany.

25. For example, see Charles Solomon and Ron Stark, *The Complete Kodak Animation Book* (Rochester, NY: Eastman Kodak Company, 1983), and Richard Williams, *The Animator's Survival Kit* (London: Faber and Faber, 2001).

26. Frank Thomas and Ollie Johnston, *Disney Animation: The Illusion of Life* (New York: Abbeville Press, 1981), 146.

27. William Kentridge on his process, www.youtube.com/watch?v=s_UphwAfjhk.

28. "William Kentridge: Art from the Ashes," from the series *Video Artists, Video Art: Film at the Fringes of Experience* (Princeton, NJ: Films for the Humanities and Sciences, 2005). It is noteworthy that the subtitle "Art from the Ashes" was used here; this is the title of a well-regarded anthology of Holocaust literature, edited by Lawrence Langer.

29. Kentridge's interest in Enlightenment principles, and their contradiction by the violence promulgated in the colonies in the name of such principles and "civilization," is another key theme in *Black Box* that has been explored by critics. See, for example, Andrew Hennlich, "The Shadows of History: Photography and Colonialism in William Kentridge's *Black Box/Chambre Noire*," in *German Colonialism Revisited: African, Asian, and Oceanic Experiences*, ed. Nina Berman, Klaus Mühlhahn, and Patrice Nganang (Ann Arbor: University of Michigan Press, 2014), 259–70.

30. Shelley Hornstein and Florence Jacobowitz, eds., *Image and Remembrance: Representation and the Holocaust* (Bloomington: Indiana University Press, 2003), 3.

31. Quoted in Paul Flaig, "Life Driven by Death: Animation Aesthetics and the Comic Uncanny," *Screen* 54:1 (Spring 2013): 1–19. Flaig's article is an excellent example of analysis of animation as gesturing toward death; he uses Freudian and Lacanian theory to analyze *Toy Story* and early Disney animation.

32. In 2002, Heroes' Acre was created as a memorial for the fallen in the Herero and Nama genocide as well as Namibia's struggle for independence. It is located near the capital of present-day Namibia, Windhoek. The erection of the memorial remains controversial as the contract for building the site was given to North Korea, rather than local

workers, and there were significant cost overruns. For an excellent account of Heroes' Acre and the *Reiterdenkmal*'s recent relocation, see Melber, *Understanding Namibia*, 28–32, 132.

Chapter Five

1. See Chinua Achebe, "An Image of Africa: Racism in Conrad's *Heart of Darkness*," in *Heart of Darkness*, ed. Paul Armstrong (New York: W. W. Norton, 2006), 336–49. Achebe says: "*Heart of Darkness* projects the image of Africa as 'the other world,' the antithesis of Europe and therefore of civilization, a place where man's vaunted intelligence and refinement are finally mocked by triumphant bestiality.... The point of my observations should be quite clear by now, namely that Joseph Conrad was a thoroughgoing racist... Conrad saw and condemned the evil of imperial exploitation but was strangely unaware of the racism on which it sharpened its iron tooth" (338, 343, 349).

2. Graham Allen, litencyc.com.

3. Linda Hutcheon, "Historiographic Metafiction: Parody and the Intertextuality of History," in *Intertextuality and Contemporary American Fiction*, ed. Patrick O'Donnell and Robert Con Davis (Baltimore: Johns Hopkins University Press, 1989), 6.

4. See Helen Gilbert's introduction to Aidoo's play *Anowa* in which Gilbert states: "By drawing upon the Ghanaian oral tradition's fusing of narrative techniques, [Aidoo] is able to synthesize these different forms, which are generally split among different genres in Western literary traditions." Helen Gilbert, ed., *Postcolonial Plays: An Anthology* (New York: Routledge, 2001), 97.

5. Critics who briefly mention the references to the Holocaust in *Our Sister Killjoy* include: Yaw Asante, "'Good Night Africa. Good Morning Europe': Europe's (Re)Discovery by a Black African Woman: Ama Ata Aidoo's *Our Sister Killjoy*," www.ucalgary.ca/uofc/eduweb/engl392/yaw-aid.html, and Gay Wilentz, "The Politics of Exile: Ama Ata Aidoo's *Our Sister Killjoy*," in *Arms Akimbo: Africana Women in Contemporary Literature*, ed. Janice Liddell and Yakini Kemp (Gainesville: University Press of Florida, 1999), 159–73.

6. Ama Ata Aidoo, "The African Woman Today," *Dissent* (Summer 1992): 319–25.

7. Anne V. Adams, ed., *Essays in Honor of Ama Ata Aidoo at 70: A Reader in Cultural African Studies* (Oxford: Ayebia Clarke Publishing Limited, 2012), 31.

8. Chioma Opara, "Narrative Technique and the Politics of Gender: Ama Ata Aidoo's *Our Sister Killjoy* and *No Sweetness Here*," in *Writing African Women: Gender, Popular Culture and Literature in West Africa*, ed. Stephanie Newell (Atlantic Highlands, NJ: Zed Books, 1997), 144.

9. Kofi Owusu, "Canons under Siege: Blackness, Femaleness, and Ama Ata Aidoo's *Our Sister Killjoy*," *Callaloo* 13:2 (1990): 341–63.

10. Anuradha Needham, *Using the Master's Tools: Resistance and the Literature of the African and South-Asian Diasporas* (New York: St. Martin's Press, 2000); Ranu Samantrai,

"Caught at the Confluence of History: Ama Ata Aidoo's Necessary Nationalism," *Research in African Literatures* 26:2 (1995): 140–57.

11. Elizabeth Willey, "National Identities, Tradition, and Feminism: The Novels of Ama Ata Aidoo in the Context of the Work of Kwame Nkrumah," in *Interventions: Feminist Dialogues on Third World Women's Literature and Film*, ed. Bishnupriya Ghosh and Brinda Bose (New York: Garland, 1997), 3.

12. For examples of these three phases, in addition to essays already cited, see the following: for feminism, Chimalum Nwankwo, "The Feminist Impulse and Social Realism in Ama Ata Aidoo's *No Sweetness Here* and *Our Sister Killjoy*," in *Ngambika: Studies of Women in African Literature*, ed. Carole Boyce Davies and Anne Adams Graves (Lawrenceville, NJ: Africa World Press, 1986), 151–59, and Sara Chetin, "Reading from a Distance: Ama Ata Aidoo's *Our Sister Killjoy*," in *Black Women's Writing*, ed. Gina Wisker (New York: St. Martin's Press, 1993), 146–59; for nationalism, see Kwaku Larbi Korang, "Ama Ata Aidoo's Voyage Out: Mapping the Co-ordinates of Modernity and African Selfhood in *Our Sister Killjoy*," *Kunapipi* 14:3 (1992): 50–61; for postcolonial approaches, see Kwadwo Osei-Nyame, "Toward the Decolonization of African Postcolonial Theory," *Matatu* 35 (2007): 71–92.

13. Yogita Goyal, *Romance, Diaspora, and Black Atlantic Literature* (Cambridge: Cambridge University Press, 2010), 185.

14. Hildegard Hoeller, "Ama Ata Aidoo's *Heart of Darkness*," *Research in African Literatures* 35:1 (2004): 130–47.

15. Books that are often cited as suggesting that Germans were victims after World War I, due to the stringent terms of the Treaty of Versailles and again under Hitler, include Günter Grass, *Crabwalk*, trans. Krishna Winston (New York: Harcourt, 2003) and W. G. Sebald, *On the Natural History of Destruction*, trans. Anthea Bell (New York: Random House, 2003).

16. For example, see Louise Murphy's Holocaust novel *The True Story of Hansel and Gretel* (New York: Penguin, 2003) and Magda Denes's Holocaust memoir *Castles Burning: A Child's Life in War* (New York: Touchstone, 1997).

17. Robert Eaglestone, "Reading *Heart of Darkness* after the Holocaust," in *After Representation? The Holocaust, Literature, and Culture*, ed. R. Clifton Spargo and Robert Ehrenreich (New Brunswick, NJ: Rutgers University Press, 2010), 206.

18. This voice is called a "chorus" by Goyal: "The chorus of the novel sounds a collective voice that functions as a community of village elders" (*Romance, Diaspora, and Black Atlantic Literature*, 189).

19. Ama Ata Aidoo, *Our Sister Killjoy, or, Reflections from a Black-eyed Squint* (London: Longman, 1977), 6. All further quotations included in the text are from this edition.

20. granta.com/How-to-Write-about-Africa/.

21. Frantz Fanon, *Black Skin, White Masks* (New York: Grove Press, 1967), 111–12.

22. Cheryl Sterling, "Can You Really See through a Squint? Underpinnings in Ama Ata Aidoo's *Our Sister Killjoy*," *Journal of Commonwealth Literature* 45:1 (2010): 132–50.

23. Note that Jamaica Kincaid also asserts that loneliness is at the heart of colonialism. She calls it a "European disease" (80) at the conclusion of her searing book about colonialism, *A Small Place* (1977; New York: Farrar, Straus and Giroux, 1988).

24. Adeola James, ed., *In Their Own Voices: African Women Writers Talk* (Portsmouth, NH: Heinemann, 1990), 18.

Bibliography

Achebe, Chinua. "An Image of Africa: Racism in Conrad's *Heart of Darkness*." In *Heart of Darkness*, ed. Paul Armstrong, 336–49. New York: W. W. Norton, 2006.
Adams, Anne V., ed. *Essays in Honour of Ama Ata Aidoo at 70: A Reader in Cultural African Studies*. Oxford: Ayebia Clarke Publishing Limited, 2012.
Adorno, Theodor W. *Can One Live after Auschwitz? A Philosophical Reader*. Stanford: Stanford University Press, 2003.
Aidoo, Ama Ata. "The African Woman Today." *Dissent* (Summer 1992): 319–25.
———. "Ghana: To Be a Woman." In *Sisterhood Is Global*, ed. Robin Morgan. New York: Doubleday, 1984.
———. "Nowhere Cool." *Callaloo* 13:1 (1990): 62–70.
———. *Our Sister Killjoy, or, Reflections from a Black-eyed Squint*. London: Longman, 1977.
Alexander, N. E. "Jakob Morenga and Namibian History." *Social Dynamics* 7:1 (1981): 1–7.
Alloula, Malek. *The Colonial Harem*. Minneapolis: University of Minnesota Press, 1986.
Andersch, Alfred. *The Night of the Giraffe and Other Stories*. Trans. Christa Armstrong. New York: Pantheon, 1964.
Arendt, Hannah. *The Origins of Totalitarianism*. Orlando: Harvest Books, 1976. Original German edition, 1951.
Asante, Yaw. "'Good Night Africa. Good Morning Europe': Europe's (Re)Discovery by a Black African Woman: Ama Ata Aidoo's *Our Sister Killjoy*." www.ucalgary.ca/uofc/eduweb/engl392/yaw-aid.html.
Atmore, Anthony. "Südwestafrika unter deutscher Kolonialherrschaft: Der Kampf der Herero und Nama gegen den deutschen Imperialismus (1884–1915) by Horst Drechsler; Kolonialismus Und 'Humanitätsintervention': Kritische Untersuchung der Politik Deutschlands gegenüuber den Kongostaat (1884–1908) by Henrich Loth." *Bulletin of the School of Oriental and African Studies* 30:3 (1967): 738–39.
Azodo, Ada, and Gay Wilentz, eds. *Emerging Perspectives on Ama Ata Aidoo*. Trenton, NJ: AWP, 1999.
Baer, Elizabeth. *The Golem Redux: From Prague to Post-Holocaust Fiction*. Detroit: Wayne State University Press, 2012.

———, and Myrna Goldenberg, eds. *Experience and Expression: Women, the Nazis, and the Holocaust*. Detroit: Wayne State University Press, 2003.

Basker, David. *Uwe Timm (Volume II)*. Cardiff: University of Wales Press, 2007.

Basualdo, Carlos, ed. *William Kentridge: Tapestries*. New Haven: Yale University Press, 2008.

Batrop, Paul R. *Encountering Genocide: Personal Accounts from Victims, Perpetrators, and Witnesses*. Santa Barbara, CA: ABC-CLIO, 2014.

Behdad, Ali, and Luke Gartlan, eds. *Photography's Orientalism: New Essays on Colonial Representation*. Los Angeles: Getty Research Institute, 2013.

Bennett, Benjamin. *Hitler over Africa*. London: T. Werner Laurie, 1939.

Berman, Nina, Klaus Mühlhahn, and Patrice Nganang, eds. *German Colonialism Revisited: African, Asian, and Oceanic Experiences*. Ann Arbor: University of Michigan Press, 2014.

Bley, Helmut. *South-West Africa under German Rule, 1894–1914*. Evanston, IL: Northwestern University Press, 1971.

Boa, Elizabeth. "Some Versions of Heimat: Goethe and Hølderlin around 1800, Frenssen and Mann around 1900." In *Heimat: At the Intersection of Memory and Space*, ed. Frederike Eigler and Jens Kugele, 34–52. Berlin: De Gruyter, 2012.

Boemeke, Manfred, Roger Chickering, and Stig Forster, eds. *Anticipating Total War: The German and American Experiences, 1871–1914*. Cambridge: Cambridge University Press, 1999.

Bonn, M. J. *Wandering Scholar*. New York: John Day Company, 1948.

Booker, M. K. *The African Novel in English: An Introduction*. Portsmouth, NH: Heinemann, 1998.

Bowersox, Jeff. *Raising Germans in the Age of Empire: Youth and Colonial Culture, 1871–1914*. Oxford: Oxford University Press, 2013.

Bowman, Peter. "Fontane's 'Der Stechlin': A Fragile Utopia." *Modern Language Review* 97:4 (October 2002): 877–91.

Bowyer, Allan. "'Narrating the Nation': Homi Bhabha and Gustav Frenssen." *JLS/TLW* 9:3/4 (December 1993): 250–65.

Braun, Frank X. "Gustav Frenssen in Retrospect." *Monatshefte* 39:7 (1947): 449–62.

Brehl, Medardus. "'The drama was played out on the dark stage of the sandvelt': The Extermination of the Herero and Nama in German (Popular) Literature." In *Genocide in German South-West Africa: The Colonial War of 1904–1908 and Its Aftermath*, ed. Jürgen Zimmerer and Joachim Zeller, 100–112. Trans. E. J. Neather. Monmouth, Wales: Merlin Press, 2008.

Bridgman, Jon, and Leslie J. Worley. "Genocide of the Hereros." In *Century of Genocide: Critical Essays and Eyewitness Accounts*, 3rd ed., ed. Samuel Totten and William S. Parsons, 16–53. New York: Routledge, 2009.

Brown, Lloyd. *Women Writers in Black Africa*. Westport, CT: Greenwood Press, 1981.

Browning, Christopher, et al. *Holocaust Scholarship: Personal Trajectories and Professional Interpretations*. New York: Palgrave Macmillan, 2015.

Brückenhaus, Daniel. "Ralph's Compassion." In Ute Frevert et al., *Learning How to Feel: Children's Literature and Emotional Socialization, 1870–1970*, 74–93. London: Oxford University Press, 2014.

Cameron, Dan. *William Kentridge*. London: Phaidon Press Limited, 1999.

Caminero-Santangelo, Byron. *African Fiction and Joseph Conrad: Reading Postcolonial Intertextuality*. Albany: SUNY Press, 2005.

Chetin, Sara. "Reading from a Distance: Ama Ata Aidoo's *Our Sister Killjoy*." In *Black Women's Writing*, ed. Gina Wisker, 146–59. New York: St. Martin's Press, 1993.

Cheyette, Bryan. *Diasporas of the Mind: Jewish and Postcolonial Writing and the Nightmare of History*. New Haven: Yale University Press, 2013.

Christov-Bakargiev, Carolyn. *William Kentridge*. Brussels: Société des Expositions du Palais Des Beaux-Arts de Bruxelles, 1998.

Clark, Nancy, and William Worger. *South Africa: The Rise and Fall of Apartheid*. Harlan, England: Pearson, 2011.

Conrad, Sebastian. *German Colonialism: A Short History*. Trans. Sorcha O'Hagan. Cambridge: Cambridge University Press, 2012.

Convents, Guido. "Film and German Colonial Propaganda for the Black African Territories to 1918." In *Before Caligari: German Cinema, 1895–1920*, 9th ed., ed. Paolo Cherchi Usai and Lorenzo Codelli. Pordenone, Italy: Edizioni Biblioteca dell'Immagine, 1990.

Cornell, Lieut. Fred C. *The Glamour of Prospecting*. New York: Frederick A. Stokes Company, 1920.

Curson, Peter. *Border Conflicts in a German African Colony: Jacob Morenga and the Untold Tragedy of Edward Presgrave*. Bury St Edmunds: Arena Books, 2012.

Dedering, Tilman. "The Prophet's 'War against Whites': Shepherd Stuurman in Namibia and South Africa, 1904–1907." *Journal of African History* 40:1 (1999): 1–19.

Drechsler, Horst. *"Let Us Die Fighting": The Struggle of the Herero and Nama against German Imperialism (1884–1915)*, trans. Bernd Zöllner. London: Zed Press, 1980. Original German edition, 1966.

Drury, Jackie Sibblies. *We Are Proud to Present a Presentation about the Herero of Namibia, Formerly Known as Southwest Africa, from the German Sudwestafrika, between the Years 1884–1915*. London: Bloomsbury, 2014.

Dubin, Steven C. "Theater of History: William Kentridge's *Black Box/Chambre Noire*." *Art in America* (April 2007): 128–31, 157.

Dubow, Jessica, and Ruth Rosengarten. "History as the Main Complaint: William Kentridge and the Making of Post-Apartheid South Africa." *Art History* 27:4 (September 2004): 671–90.

Eaglestone, Robert. "Reading *Heart of Darkness* after the Holocaust." In *After Representation? The Holocaust, Literature, and Culture*, ed. R. Clifton Spargo and Robert Ehrenreich, 190–209. New Brunswick, NJ: Rutgers University Press, 2010.

Eigler, Frederike, and Jens Kugele, eds. *Heimat: At the Intersection of Memory and Space*. Berlin: De Gruyter, 2012.

Eisenstein, Segei. *Eisenstein on Disney*. Ed. Jay Leyda. Trans. Alan Upchurch. Introduction by Naum Kleiman. London: Methuen, 1988.

Encyclopaedia Britannica Online. academic.ed.com/EBchecked/topic219550/Gustav-Frenssen.

Enwezor, Okwui. "(Un)Civil Engineering: William Kentridge's Allegorical Landscapes." In *William Kentridge: Tapestries*, ed. Carlos Basualdo. New Haven: Yale University Press, 2008.

Erichsen, Casper W. *"The Angel of Death Has Descended Violently among Them": Concentration Camps and Prisoners of War in Namibia, 1904–1908*. Leiden: African Studies Centre, 2005.

———. "Namibia's Island of Death." *New African* 421(August/September 2003): 46–49.

Fanon, Frantz. *Black Skin, White Masks*. New York: Grove Press, 1967.

Findlay, Frank. "Jackboots and Jeans: The Private and the Political in Uwe Timm's *Am Beispiel meines Bruders*." In *Germans as Victims in the Literary Fiction of the Berlin Republic*, ed. Stuart Tabener and Karina Berger. Rochester, NY: Camden House, 2009.

Flaig, Paul. "Life Driven by Death: Animation Aesthetics and the Comic Uncanny." *Screen* 54:1 (Spring 2013): 1–19.

Florer, Warren W. "Gustav Frenssen: A Study." *Pädagogische Monatshefte* 5:3 (February 1904): 71–78.

———. "Gustav Frenssen: A Study (Concluded)." *Pädagogische Monatshefte* 5:4 (March 1904): 97–102.

———. "Note on Gustav Frenssen." *Modern Language Notes* 28:5 (May 1913): 145–47.

Foucault, Michel. *Discipline and Punish: The Birth of the Prison*. Trans. Alan Sheridan. London: Penguin, 1991.

Frenssen, Gustav. *Peter Moors Fahrt nach Südwest*. Ed. Herman Babson. New York: Henry Holt, 1914.

———. *Peter Moors Fahrt nach Südwest: Ein Feldzugsbericht*. Berlin: Grotsche Verlagbuchhandlung, 1944.

———. *Peter Moors Fahrt nach Südwest: Ein Feldzugsbericht*. Windhoek, Namibia: Druck and Verlag, 1998.

———. *Peter Moor's Journey to Southwest Africa*. Trans. Margaret May Ward. Boston: Houghton Mifflin, 1908.

Frevert, Ute, et al. *Learning How to Feel: Children's Literature and Emotional Socialization, 1870–1970*. London: Oxford University Press, 2014.

Friedrichsmeyer, Sara, Sara Lennox, and Susanne Zantop, eds. *The Imperialist Imagination: German Colonialism and Its Legacy*. Ann Arbor: University of Michigan Press, 1998.

Fuchs, Anne. *Phantoms of War in Contemporary German Literature, Films, and Discourse: The Politics of Memory*. New York: Palgrave Macmillan, 2008.

Furlong, Patrick. *Between Crown and Swastika: The Impact of the Radical Right on the Afrikaner National Movement in the Fascist Era*. Hanover, NH: Wesleyan University Press, 1991.

Gann, L. H., and Peter Duignan. *The Rulers of German Africa, 1884–1914*. Stanford: Stanford University Press, 1997.

George, Rosemary, and Helen Scott. "'A New Tail to an Old Tale': An Interview with Ama Ata Aidoo." *Novel* 26:3 (1993): 297–308.

Gewald, Jan-Bart. *Herero Heroes: A Socio-Political History of the Herero in Namibia, 1890–1923*. Oxford: James Currey, 1999.

Ghosh, Bishnupria, and Brinda Bose, eds. *Interventions: Feminist Dialogues on Third World Women's Literature*. New York: Garland, 1997.

Gilbert, Helen, ed. *Postcolonial Plays: An Anthology*. New York: Routledge, 2001.

Gilbert, Sandra, and Susan Gubar. *Madwoman in the Attic: The Woman Writer and the Nineteenth-Century Literary Imagination*. New Haven: Yale University Press, 1979.

Gilman, Sander. "The Image of the Black in the German Colonial Novel." *Journal of European Studies* 8 (1978): 1–11.

Gordon, Robert J. "Hiding in Full View: The Forgotten Bushman Genocides of Namibia." *Genocide Studies and Prevention* 4:1 (Spring 2009): 29–57.

Goyal, Yogita. *Romance, Diaspora, and Black Atlantic Literature*. Cambridge: Cambridge University Press, 2010.

Göttsche, Dirk. *Remembering Africa: The Rediscovery of Colonialism in Contemporary German Literature*. New York: Camden House, 2013.

Gourdine, Angeletta. *The Difference Place Makes: Gender, Sexuality, and Diaspora Identity*. Columbus: Ohio University Press, 2002.

Green, Charles. "The Memory Effect: Anachronism, Time and Motion." *Third Text* 22:6 (2008): 681–97.

Griese, Volker. *Die drei Leben des Gustav Frenssen: Eine Frenssen Chronik*. Münster: Verlagshaus Monsenstein und Vannerdat, 2011.

Guerin, Frances. "The Placement of Shadows: What's Inside William Kentridge's *Black Box/Chambre Noire*?" In *Taking Place: Location and the Moving Image*, ed. John David Rhodes and Elena Gorfinkel. Minneapolis: University of Minnesota Press, 2011.

Gugelberger, Georg M., ed. *Nama/Namibia: Diary and Letters of Nama Chief Hendrik Witbooi, 1884–1894*. Boston: Boston University, African Studies Center, 1984.

Gussow, Mel. "W. G. Sebald, Elegiac German Novelist, Is Dead at 57." *New York Times*, 15 December 2001, C16.

Gyimah, Miriam. "Dangerous Encounters with the West: Gender, Sexuality and Power in Ama Ata Aidoo's *Our Sister Killjoy*." In *Gender and Sexuality in African Literature and Film*, ed. Ada Azodo and Maureen Eke. Lawrenceville, NJ: Africa World Press, 2007.

Hartmann, Wolfram, ed. *Hues between Black and White: Historical Photography from Colonial Namibia, 1860s to 1915*. Windhoek: Out of Africa Publishers, 2004.

Hartmann, Wolfram, et al., eds. *The Colonising Camera: Photographs in the Making of Namibian History*. Cape Town: University of Cape Town Press, 1998.

Hawthorn, Jeremy. "Theories of the Gaze." In *Literary Theory and Criticism*, ed. Patricia Waugh, 508–18. Oxford: Oxford University Press, 2006.

Hell, Julia, and George Steinmetz. "The Visual Archive of Colonialism: Germany and Namibia." *Public Culture* 18:1 (2008): 147–84.

Hennlich, Andrew. "The Shadows of History: Photography and Colonialism in William Kentridge's *Black Box/Chambre Noire*." In *German Colonialism Revisited: African, Asian, and Oceanic Experiences*, ed. Nina Berman, Klaus Mühlhahn, and Patrice Nganang. Ann Arbor: University of Michigan Press, 2014.

Heywood, Anna, Brigitte Lau, and Raimund Ohly, eds. *Warriors, Leaders, Sages and Outcasts in the Namibian Past*. Windhoek: Michael Scott Oral Records Project, 1992.

Hilberg, Raul. *The Destruction of the European Jews*. Chicago: Quadrangle Books, 1961.

Hillebrecht, Werner. "Hendrik Witbooi and Samuel Maharero: The Ambiguity of Heroes." In *Re-Viewing Resistance in Namibian History*, ed. Jeremy Silvester. Windhoek: University of Namibia Press, 2015.

Hochschild, Adam. *King Leopold's Ghost: A Story of Greed, Terror, and Heroism in Colonial Africa*. New York: Houghton Mifflin, 1999.

Hoeller, Hildegard. "Ama Ata Aidoo's *Heart of Darkness*." *Research in African Literatures* 35:1 (2004): 130–47.

Hornstein, Shelley, and Florence Jacobowitz, eds., *Image and Remembrance: Representation and the Holocaust*. Bloomington: Indiana University Press, 2003.

Hunt, Tamara, and Micheline Lessard. *Women and the Colonial Gaze*. New York: New York University Press, 2002.

Hutcheon, Linda. "Historiographic Metafiction: Parody and the Intertextuality of History." In *Intertextuality and Contemporary American Fiction*, ed. Patrick O'Donnell and Robert Con Davis. Baltimore: Johns Hopkins University Press, 1989.

Irwin, Robert. *Dangerous Knowledge: Orientalism and Its Discontents*. Woodstock, NY: Overlook Press, 2006.

James, Adeola, ed. *In Their Own Voices: African Women Writers Talk*. Portsmouth, NH: Heinemann, 1990.

Jana, Reena, ed. *Vitamin D: New Perspectives in Drawing*. London: Phaidon Press, 2005.

Janku, Laura Richard. "Black Box: An Interview with William Kentridge." *artUS* (July–September 2006): 8–11.

Kaplan, Cheryl. "The Time Image: William Kentridge Interviewed." *Performing Arts Journal* 27:80 (2005): 28–44.

Kaplan, E. Ann. *Looking for the Other: Feminism, Film, and the Imperial Gaze*. New York: Routledge, 1997.

Katjavivi, Peter. *A History of Resistance in Namibia*. Trenton, NJ: Africa World Press, 1990.

Kenosian, David. "The Colonial Body Politic: Desire and Violence in the Works of Gustav Frenssen and Hans Grimm." *Monatshefte* 89:2 (1997): 182–95.

Kentridge, William. *Six Drawing Lessons*. Cambridge, MA: Harvard University Press, 2014.

———. "William Kentridge: Automatic Writing" with interview by Dan Cameron. New York: New Museum of Contemporary Art, 2003. DVD.

Kentridge, William, and Rosalind C. Morris. *That Which Is Not Drawn: Conversations.* Calcutta: Seagull Books, 2014.

Klotz, Marcia. "White Women and the Dark Continent: Gender and Sexuality in German Colonial Discourse from the Sentimental Novel to the Fascist Film." PhD diss., Stanford University, 1994.

Knoll, Arthur J., and Hermann J. Hiery, eds. *The German Colonial Experience: Select Documents on German Rule in Africa, China, and the Pacific, 1884–1914.* Lanham, MD: University Press of America, 2010.

Korang, Kwaku Larbi. "Ama Ata Aidoo's Voyage Out: Mapping the Co-ordinates of Modernity and African Selfhood in *Our Sister Killjoy*." *Kunapipi* 14:3 (1992): 50–61.

Kristeva, Julia. "Intertextuality: An Interview with Julia Kristeva." Conducted by Margaret Smallen. www.msu.edu/user/chrenkal/1980/INTEXINT.HTM.

Kropotkin, Petr. *Mutual Aid: A Factor of Evolution.* New York: Garland, 1972.

Langbehn, Volker, and Mohammed Salama, eds. *German Colonialism: Race, the Holocaust, and Postwar Germany.* New York: Columbia University Press, 2011.

Lau, Brigitte, ed. *The Hendrik Witbooi Papers.* 2nd ed. Trans. Annemarie Heywood and Eben Maasdorp. Windhoek: National Archives of Namibia, 1996.

Lemarchand, Rene, ed. *Forgotten Genocides: Oblivion, Denial, and Memory.* Philadelphia: University of Pennsylvania Press, 2011.

Levy, Elizabeth, ed. *William Kentridge: Black Box/Chambre Noire.* Berlin: Deutsche Guggenheim, 2005.

Liss, Andrea. *Trespassing through Shadows: Memory, Photography and the Holocaust.* Minneapolis: University of Minnesota Press, 1998.

Loewenberg, Ernst L. "Gustav Frenssen, 1863–1946." *Monatschefte* 39:4 (1947): 248–54.

Lowe, Lisa. *Critical Terrains: French and British Orientalisms.* Ithaca: Cornell University Press, 1991.

Madley, Benjamin. "From Africa to Auschwitz: How German South West Africa Incubated Ideas and Methods Adopted by the Nazis in Eastern Europe." *European History Quarterly* 35:3 (2005): 429–64.

Mamdani, Mahmood. *When Victims Become Killers: Colonialism, Nativism, and the Genocide in Rwanda.* Princeton: Princeton University Press, 2001.

Marx, Christoph. "Hendrik Verwoerd's Long March to Apartheid: Nationalism and Racism in South Africa." In *Racism in the Modern World: Historical Perspectives on Cultural Transfer and Adaptation*, ed. Manfred Berg and Simon Wendt. New York: Berghahn Books, 2011.

Maybury-Lewis, David. "Colonial Genocide." In *Genocide: A Reader*, ed. Jens Meierhenrich. Oxford: Oxford University Press, 2014.

McGlothlin, Erin. *Second-Generation Holocaust Literature: Legacies of Survival and Perpetration.* Rochester, NY: Camden House, 2006.

McLean, Ian. "Postcolonial Traffic: William Kentridge and Aboriginal Desert Painters." *Third Text* 17:3 (2003): 227–40.

Melber, Henning. *Understanding Namibia: The Trials of Independence*. London: Hurst and Company, 2014.

Mennel, Barbara. "'Germany Is Full of Germans Now': Germanness in Ama Ata Aidoo's *Our Sister Killjoy* and Chantal Akerman's *Meetings of Anna*." In *Gender and Germanness: Cultural Productions of Nation*, ed. Patricia Herminghouse and Magda Mueller. Providence, RI: Berghahn Books, 1997.

Michael, Wolfgang F. "Kulturelle Ziele im Werk Gustav Frenssens by Frank X. Braun." *German Quarterly* 21:2 (March 1948): 136–38.

Mieke, Bal. "Heterochronotopia." *Thamyris/Intersecting*, no. 19 (2008): 35–56.

Moodie, T. Dunbar. *The Rise of Afrikanerdom: Power, Apartheid, and the Afrikaner Civil Religion*. Berkeley: University of California Press, 1975.

Moses, A. Dirk, ed. *Genocide and Settler Society: Frontier Violence and Stolen Indigenous Children in Australian History*. New York: Berghahn, 2004.

Moses, A. Dirk, and Dan Stone, eds. *Colonialism and Genocide*. New York: Routledge, 2007.

Mulvey, Laura. "Afterthoughts on 'Visual Pleasure and Narrative Cinema' Inspired by King Vidor's *Duel in the Sun* (1946)." In *Feminist Film Theory*, ed. Sue Thornham, 31–40. New York: New York University Press, 1999.

———. "Visual Pleasure and Narrative Cinema." 1975. Reprinted in *Visual and Other Pleasures*. New York: Palgrave Macmillan, 2009.

Naranch, Bradley, and Geoff Eley, eds. *German Colonialism in a Global Age*. Durham: Duke University Press, 2014.

Needham, Anuradha. "An Interview with Ama Ata Aidoo." *Massachusetts Review* 36:1 (1995): 123–34.

———. *Using the Master's Tools: Resistance and the Literature of the African and South-Asian Diasporas*. New York: St. Martin's Press, 2000.

Newell, Stephanie, ed. *Writing African Women: Gender, Popular Culture, and Literature in West Africa*. London: Zed Books, 1997.

Noyes, John K. *Colonial Space: Spatiality in the Discourse of German South West Africa, 1884–1915*. Chur, Switzerland: Harwood Academic Publishers, 1992.

———. "National Identity, Nomadism, and Narration in Gustav Frenssen's *Peter Moor's Journey to Southwest Africa*." In *The Imperialist Imagination: German Colonialism and Its Legacy*, ed. Sara Friedrichsmeyer, Sara Lennox, and Susanne Zantop, 87–105. Ann Arbor: University of Michigan Press, 1998.

Nutall, Sarah, and Achille Mbembe. "Afropolis: From Johannesburg." *PMLA* 122:1 (January 2007): 281–88.

Nwankwo, Chimalum. "The Feminist Impulse and Social Realism in Ama Ata Aidoo's *No Sweetness Here* and *Our Sister Killjoy*." In *Ngambika: Studies of Women in African Literature*, ed. Carole Boyce Davies and Anne Adams Graves. Lawrenceville, NJ: Africa World Press, 1986.

Odamtten, Vincent O. *The Art of Ama Ata Aidoo: Polylectics and Reading against Neocolonialism*. Gainesville: University Press of Florida, 1994.

Olusoga, David, and Casper E. Erichsen. *The Kaiser's Holocaust: Germany's Forgotten Genocide and the Colonial Roots of Nazism*. London: Faber and Faber, 2010.

Opara, Chioma. "Narrative Technique and the Politics of Gender: Ama Ata Aidoo's *Our Sister Killjoy* and *No Sweetness Here*." In *Writing African Women: Gender, Popular Culture and Literature in West Africa*, ed. Stephanie Newell. Atlantic Highlands, NJ: Zed Books, 1997.

Osei-Nyame, Kwadwo. "Toward the Decolonization of African Postcolonial Theory." *Matatu* 35 (2007): 71–92.

Owusu, Kofi. "Canons under Siege: Blackness, Femaleness, and Ama Ata Aidoo's *Our Sister Killjoy*." *Callaloo* 13:2 (1990): 341–63.

Pakendorf, Gunther. "The Subversive Nature of the Gospel: Reflections on Uwe Timm's Novel *Morenga*." *Etudes Germano-Africaines* 11 (1993): 128–36.

Pallua, Ulrich. *Eurocentrism, Racism, Colonialism in the Victorian and Edwardian Age*. Heidelberg: Universitätsverlag, Winter, 2006.

Parekh, Pushpa, and Siga Jagne. *Postcolonial African Writers: A Bio-Bibliographic Critical Sourcebook*. Westport, CT: Greenwood Press, 1998.

Patmore, Chris. *The Complete Animation Course*. Hauppauge, NY: Barron's, 2003.

Peary, Danny, and Gerald Peary, eds. *The American Animated Cartoon: A Critical Anthology*. New York: E. P. Dutton, 1980.

Peires, Juliette. *The Holocaust and Apartheid: A Comparison of Human Rights Abuses*. Sea Point, South Africa: Union of Jewish Women, 2006.

Peitsch, Helmut. "Enlightenment and Entertainment—Still? Uwe Timm's Narrative Model and His Reception in the USA and in Great Britain." In *German-Language Literature Today: International and Popular?* ed. Arthur Williams et al. Oxford: Peter Lang, 2000.

"Peter Moors Fahrt nach Südwest." *Journal of the Royal African Society* 6:23 (April 1907): 322.

"Peter Moor's Journey: Present Political Significance of the Latest Work of Fiction by Gustav Frenssen." *New York Times*, 2 March 1907.

"Peter Moor's Journey to Southwest Africa." *Advocate of Peace* 70:10 (November 1908): 248.

Pilling, Jayne, ed. *A Reader in Animation Studies*. Sydney: John Libbey and Company, 1997.

Poewe, Karla. *The Namibian Herero: A History of Their Psychosocial Disintegration and Survival*. Lewiston, NY: Edwin Mellen Press, 1985.

Power, Samantha. *A Problem from Hell: America and the Age of Genocide*. New York: Basic Books, 2002.

Pratt, Effie Louise. *A Comparative Study of the Literary Technique of Theodor Storm and Gustav Frenssen*. Chicago: University of Chicago Press, 1925.

Pratt, Mary Louise. *Imperial Eyes: Travel Writing and Transculturation*. London: Routledge, 1992.

Probst, Lothar. "'Normalization' through Europeanization: The Role of the Holocaust." In *German Culture, Politics, and Literature in the Twenty-First Century: Beyond Normalization*, ed. Stuart Taberner and Paul Cooke. Rochester, NY: Camden House, 2006.

Rooney, Caroline. *African Literature, Animism, and Politics*. London: Routledge, 2000.

Rothberg, Michael. "Progress, Progression, Procession: William Kentridge and the Narratology of Transitional Justice." *Narrative* 20:1 (January 2012): 1–24.

Said, Edward. *Orientalism*. New York: Vintage, 1979.

Samantrai, Ranu. "Caught at the Confluence of History: Ama Ata Aidoo's Necessary Nationalism." *Research in African Literatures* 26:2 (1995): 140–57.

Sarid, A. *There Once Was a Home: Memories of the Lithuanian Shtetls Published in the Afrikaner Idishe Tsaytung—African Jewish Newspaper, 1952–54*. Cape Town: Jewish Publications, South Africa, 2015.

Sartre, Jean-Paul. *Black Orpheus*. Trans S. W. Allen. Paris: Présence Africaine, 1951.

Schaller, Dominik. "'Every Herero Will Be Shot': Genocide, Concentration Camps, and Slave Labor in German South-West Africa." In *Forgotten Genocides: Oblivion, Denial, and Memory*, ed. Rene Lemarchand. Philadelphia: University of Pennsylvania Press, 2011.

Schmitz, Helmut, ed. *A Nation of Victims? Representation of German Wartime Suffering from 1945 to the Present*. Amsterdam: Rodopi, 2007.

Schulte, Rainer. "Interview with Breon Mitchell and Uwe Timm: Collaboration between Translator and Author." *Translation Review* 66:1 (2003): 1–7.

Serfontein, J. H. P. *Brotherhood of Power: An Exposé of the Secret Afrikaner Broederbond*. Bloomington: Indiana University Press, 1978.

Seyfried, Gerhard. *Herero*. Frankfurt am Main: Eichborn Verlag, 2003.

Shohat, Ella. "Imaging Terra Incognito: The Disciplinary Gaze of Empire." *Public Culture* 3:2 (1991): 41–70.

Silverman, Max. *Palimpsestic Memory: The Holocaust and Colonialism in French and Francophone Fiction and Film*. New York: Berghahn, 2013.

Silvester, Jeremy, ed. *Re-Viewing Resistance in Namibian History*. Windhoek: University of Namibia Press, 2015.

Silvester, Jeremy, and Jan-Bart Gewald, eds. *Words Cannot Be Found: German Colonial Rule in Namibia: An Annotated Reprint of the 1918 Blue Book*. Leiden: Brill, 2003.

Smith, Woodruff. *The Ideological Origins of Nazi Imperialism*. New York: Oxford University Press, 1986.

Solomon, Charles, and Ron Stark. *The Complete Kodak Animation Book*. Rochester, NY: Eastman Kodak Company, 1983.

Stam, Robert, and Louise Spence. "Colonialism, Racism, and Representation." *Screen* 24:2 (1983): 2–20.

Steinmetz, George. *The Devil's Handwriting: Precoloniality and the German Colonial State in Qingdao, Samoa, and Southwest Africa*. Chicago: University of Chicago Press, 2007.

———. "The First Genocide of the 20th Century and Its Postcolonial Afterlives: Germany and the Namibian Ovaherero." hdl.handle.net/2027/spo.4750978.0012.201.

———. "Return to Empire: The New US Imperialism in Comparative Historical Perspective." *Sociological Theory* 23:4 (December 2005): 339–67.

Sterling, Cheryl. "Can You Really See through a Squint? Underpinnings in Ama Ata Aidoo's *Our Sister Killjoy.*" *Journal of Commonwealth Literature* 45:1 (2010): 132–50.

Stevenson, Sara. "The Empire Looks Back: Subverting the Imperial Gaze." *History of Photography* 35:2 (2011): 142–56.

Stoler, Ann Laura. *Carnal Knowledge and Imperial Power: Race and the Intimate in Colonial Rule.* Berkeley: University of California Press, 2002.

———. "Colonial Aphasia: Race and Disabled Histories in France." *Public Culture* 23:1 (2011): 121–56.

Tabener, Stuart, and Karina Berger. *Germans as Victims in the Literary Fiction of the Berlin Republic.* Rochester, NY: Camden House, 2009.

Tabener, Stuart, and Paul Cooke, eds. *German Culture, Politics, and Literature in the Twenty-First Century: Beyond Normalization.* Rochester, NY: Camden House, 2006.

Thomas, Frank, and Ollie Johnston. *Disney Animation: The Illusion of Life.* New York: Abbeville Press, 1981.

Timm, Uwe. *Deutsche Kolonien.* Köln: Verlag Kiepenheuer and Witisch, 1986.

———. *Morenga.* Trans. Breon Mitchell. New York: New Directions, 2003.

———. *In My Brother's Shadow: A Life and Death in the SS.* Trans. Anthea Bell. New York: Farrar, Straus and Giroux, 2005.

Tomkins, Calvin. "Lines of Resistance." *New Yorker* 85:45 (2010): 52–59.

Tone, Lilian. "William Kentridge: *Stereoscope*" (an interview). artarchives.net/artarchives/liliantone/tonekentridge.html.

Totten, Samuel, and William S. Parsons. *Century of Genocide: Critical Essays and Eyewitness Accounts.* 3rd ed. New York: Routledge, 2009.

Usai, Paolo Cherchi, and Lorenzo Codelli, eds. *Before Caligari: German Cinema, 1895–1920,* 9th ed. Pordenone, Italy: Edizioni Biblioteca dell'Immagine, 1990.

Vice, Sue. *Holocaust Fiction.* New York: Routledge, 2000.

Von Eckenbrecher, Margarethe. *Africa: What It Gave Me, What It Took from Me. Remembrances from My Life as a German Settler in South West Africa.* Trans. and ed. David Crandall, Hans-Wilhelm Kelling, and Paul Kerry. Bethlehem, PA: Lehigh University Press, 2015.

Von Trotha, Trutz. "'The Fellows Can Just Starve': On Wars of 'Pacification' in the African Colonies of Imperial Germany and the Concept of 'Total War.'" In *Anticipating Total War: The German and American Experiences, 1871–1914,* ed. Manfred Boemeke, Roger Chickering, and Stig Forster, 415–35. Cambridge: Cambridge University Press, 1999.

Warmbold, Joachim. *Germania in Africa: Germany's Colonial Literature.* New York: Peter Lang, 1989.

Waugh, Patricia, ed. *Literary Theory and Criticism.* Oxford: Oxford University Press, 2006.

Wilentz, Gay. *Binding Cultures: Black Women Writers in Africa and the Diaspora.* Bloomington: Indiana University Press, 1992.

———. "Demarcating Political Space: African Women's Domain in the Writings of Flora Nwapa and Ama Ata Aidoo." *Southeast Regional Seminar in African Studies.* 2001.

---. "The Politics of Exile: Ama Ata Aidoo's *Our Sister Killjoy*." In *Arms Akimbo: Africana Women in Contemporary Literature*, ed. Janice Liddell and Yakini Kemp. Gainesville: University Press of Florida, 1999.

Willey, Elizabeth. "National Identities, Tradition, and Feminism: The Novels of Ama Ata Aidoo in the Context of the Work of Kwame Nkrumah." In *Interventions: Feminist Dialogues on Third World Women's Literature and Film*, ed. Bishnupriya Ghosh and Brinda Bose, 3–30. New York: Garland, 1997.

"William Kentridge: Art from the Ashes." From the series *Video Artists, Video Art: Film at the Fringes of Experience*. Princeton, NJ: Films for the Humanities and Sciences, 2005.

Williams, Rhys. "'A Perfectly Ordinary Childhood': Uwe Timm's *Am beispiel meines Bruders*." In *Uwe Timm (Volume II)*, ed. David Basker, 71–84. Cardiff: University of Wales Press, 2007.

Williams, Richard. *The Animator's Survival Kit*. London: Faber and Faber, 2001.

Wilson-Tagoe, Nana. Interview with Ama Ata Aidoo. In *Writing across Worlds: Contemporary Writers Talk*, ed. Susheila Nasta. London: Routledge, 2004.

Wisker, Gina. *Post-Colonial and African American Women's Writing: A Critical Introduction*. New York: St. Martin's Press, 2000.

Zantop, Susanne. *Colonial Fantasies: Conquest, Family, and Nation in Precolonial Germany, 1770–1870*. Durham: Duke University Press, 1997.

Zelizer, Barbie. "Gender and Atrocity: Women in Holocaust Photographs." In *Visual Culture and the Holocaust*, ed. Barbie Zelizer. New Brunswick, NJ: Rutgers University Press, 2001.

---, ed. *Visual Culture and the Holocaust*. New Brunswick, NJ: Rutgers University Press, 2001.

Zimmerer, Jürgen. "Colonialism and the Holocaust: Towards an Archaeology of Genocide." In *Genocide and Settler Society: Frontier Violence and Stolen Indigenous Children in Australian History*, ed. A. Dirk Moses. New York: Berghahn, 2004.

---. "War, Concentration Camps and Genocide in South-West Africa: The First German Genocide." In *Genocide in German South-West Africa: The Colonial War of 1904–1908 and Its Aftermath*, ed. Jürgen Zimmerer and Joachim Zeller, trans. E. J. Neather, 41–63. Monmouth, Wales: Merlin Press, 2008.

Zimmerer, Jürgen, and Joachim Zeller, eds. *Genocide in German South-West Africa: The Colonial War of 1904–1908 and Its Aftermath*. Trans. E. J. Neather. Monmouth, Wales: Merlin Press, 2008.

Index

Page references in italics refer to illustrations

Achebe, Chinua: on *Heart of Darkness*, 115, 117, 151n1; *Things Fall Apart*, 121
Adorno, Theodor: on post-Holocaust poetry, 84
Advocate of Peace (1908), on *Peter Moor's Journey*, 48–49
Africa, natural resources of, 122, 125. *See also* German Southwest Africa (GSWA); names of individual countries
Africa, West: corruption in, 123–34; fiction from, 128. *See also* Aidoo, Ama Ata
Afrikaner, Jan Jonker, 24; correspondence with Witbooi, 23
Aidoo, Ama Ata, 8; accusations of racism against, 119; feminism of, 118; feminist approaches to, 117–18, 152n12; nationalist approaches to, 118, 152n12; postcolonialist approaches to, 119, 152n12; on racial hierarchies, 119; use of intertextuality, 119; women characters of, 118
—"The African Woman Today," 117–18
—*Our Sister Killjoy:* African women in, 118–19; Bluebeard in, 124; British Empire in, 127–28; colonial aphasia in, 128; colonialism in, 126–27, 128; critical readings of, 117–20; European academic system in, 127–28; fairy tale tropes of, 119, 126; format of, 116, 117, 124; genocidal gaze in, 16, 115, 123, 125; genocide in, 120–30; German gaze in, 122; Germany in, 121–23, 126–27; and *Heart of Darkness*, 116–17, 119, 124, 129; heart transplant in, 128; Holocaust in, 122, 126, 151n5; intertextuality of, 116; *Jane Eyre* and, 116, 124; Jewish mother in, 127; lesbian encounter in, 124; loneliness in, 125; missionaries in, 126; narrative voice of, 120, 123; Nazi war widows in, 122–23; optimism of, 129; other in, 117, 123; pastiche in, 116; plum symbolism of, 123; postcolonial themes of, 123, 127–28; sexual objectification in, 124; systems of oppression in, 125
Alberts, Wilhelm, 46
amnesia: concerning genocide, 128, 133; concerning German colonialism, 64–65. *See also* aphasia, colonial; *Vergangenheitsbewältigung*
Andersch, Alfred: *Weltreise auf deutsche Art*, 145n10
animation: in *Black Box/Chambre Noire*, 103–8, 110–12, 114; gesture toward death, 113, 150n32; as transformation, 110–12, 113

Apartheid: in *Black Box/Chambre Noire*, 100, 103; Göring's influence on, 149n11; Herero genocide and, 109, 113; Holocaust and, 149n13; influence of European nationalism on, 148n10; Nazism and, 15, 103, 148n11; pass laws of, 148n7; transition to democracy, 103

aphasia, colonial, 128; German, 41, 64–65, 69, 76, 85, 142n24. *See also* amnesia; *Vergangenheitsbewältigung*

archives: of *Black Box/Chambre Noire*, 100–102; Nazi, 65; Witbooi's, 13, 19, 20–32, 140nn9–10. *See also* German Colonial Archive

Arendt, Hannah: continuity thesis of, 4

Art and Press exhibit (Martin-Gropius Bau, 2012), *Black Box/Chambre Noire* in, 99, 100, 101, 108

Aryanism, 103; in *Black Box/Chambre Noire*, 104; in *In My Brother's Shadow*, 96, 97

Asante, Yaw, 124

Attie, Shimon: *The Writing on the Wall*, 111 12

Aus den Geheimakten des Welt-Detektiv (magazine), 106

authoritarianism, Nazi: transfer to postwar family, 91, 92

Babson, Herman: contact with Frenssen, 143n7; edition of *Peter Moor's Journey*, 19, 47, 61; on Nama, 52

bambuses, 72; as Schutztruppe servants, 146n12

Barnard, Christiaan: heart transplant by, 128–29

Bartels, Adolf, 58

Battle of Waterberg (1904), 10, 11, 30; atrocities at, 32–33; in *Black Box/Chambre Noire*, 106; genocide at, 64; memorial to, 109; in *Morenga*, 68; in *Peter Moor's Journey*, 55; site of, 109; skirmishes preceding, 54. *See also* rebellion, GSWA

Bechuanaland Protectorate (British territory), 34

Berlin Conference (1884-85), 117, 147n1

Bhabha, Homi, 59

Bismarck, Otto von, 134; and colonization, 9, 10

Bittel, Kurt, 62

"Bluebeard" (fairy tale): in *In My Brother's Shadow*, 94; in *Our Sister Killjoy*, 124

Blue Book, British, 2, 133; German objections to, 141n17; Shark Island in, 34; suppression of, 33; witnesses to genocide in, 17

Blue-Book on Native Affairs (Cape Colony), Witbooi in, 18–19

Boa, Elizabeth, 58

Boers: antipathy toward Germans, 36, 51; in *Peter Moor's Journey to Southwest Africa*, 36–37, 50, 51; racial attitudes of, 40

Bondels, 89, 90

Bondelswart rebellion, 69, 87

Bower, Alan: on *Peter Moor's Journey*, 59

Bowman, Peter, 78

Braun, Frank: on *Peter Moor's Journey*, 58–59

Brehl, Medardus, 142n

Broederband (Apartheid organization), Nazism of, 103

Brontë, Charlotte: *Jane Eyre*, 116, 124

Brückenhaus, Daniel, 59; "Ralph's Compassions," 144n21

Bundestag, German: rejection of genocide apology, 134

camels, 73, 75, 87; on patrol, *fig. 14*

camera: in *Black Box/Chambre Noire*, 103, 104, 105; in surveillance, 103. *See also*

German Southwest Africa (GSWA), photographs of
Cape Colony, 34
childhood, traumatic photographs in, 102–3, 148n8
children, German: beating of, 98
children, Herero: German indoctrination of, 43–44
Cholodenko, Alan, 113
Cleverly, John: correspondence with Witbooi, 25–26
Coetzee, J. M., 133
colonialism: diaspora of, 127, 128; loneliness in, 153n23
colonialism, British, 12, 34, 127–28; racial/racist hierarchies of, 129
colonialism, German: African perspective on, 21; amnesia concerning, 64–65; as civilizing, 70–71, 107–8, 117; in cultural memory, 68; ethics of, 51; exterminationist, 27; film clips of, 99, 107; financial gain in, 90; Holocaust and, 3–4, 14–15, 124, 126; interdisciplinary studies of, 12; justifications for, 49, 50; legacy of, 68; literature of, 11, 13, 44, 45; and Nazism, 3, 59, 85; racial hierarchies in, 3, 5, 10, 36, 57; romanticism concerning, 81; of Third Reich, 5; *Vergangenheitsbewältigung* concerning, 135. *See also* imperialism, German
colonials, German: antipathy toward Boers, 36, 51; antipathy toward British, 141n18
Colonial School for Women (Germany), 135
colonization, German: Bismarck and, 9, 10; motives for, 82, 83
concentration camps: British, 12; Nazi, 34, 53–54, 96, 117
concentration camps, GSWA, 12, 69, 139n28; destruction of evidence for, 40–41; disease in, 42; eyewitness accounts of, 38–43; forced labor in, 106; in *Morenga*, 71; mortality rates at, 41, 43, 133, 146n11; Witbooi at, 27, 31. *See also* Shark Island
Congo Free State, genocide in, 9
Conrad, Joseph: as racist, 151n1
—*Heart of Darkness*, 16; Achebe on, 115, 117, 151n1; intertexts of, 116; and *Our Sister Killjoy*, 116–17, 119, 124, 129; in postcolonial literature, 115
continuity thesis (Holocaust), 3–5, 14, 18, 132, 133; advocates of, 134; Arendt's, 4
Cornell, Fred C.: antipathy toward Germans, 35
—*The Glamour of Prospecting*, 44; genocidal gaze in, 36; indigenous peoples in, 35, 38; on Nama rebellion, 37; photographs in, 141n20; purpose of, 141n20; Shark Island in, 35, 38–40, 142n22; World War I in, 35
Cramer, Hildegard, 2
Cramer, Ludwig, 137n3; floggings by, 2
Crimea, massacres in, 97

Dachau concentration camp: creation of, 53; photographs of, 96
Deimling, Colonel, 83, 88
Deutscher Kolonialismus: Fragmente seiner Geschichte und Gegenwart exhibit (Deutsches Historisches Museum, Berlin), 134–35
Drechsler, Horst, 4, 79; on land treaties, 145n6; *Südwestafrika unter deutscher Kolonialherrschaft*, 65
Dürer, Albrecht: bestiary of, 150n22

Eaglestone, Robert: "Reading *Heart of Darkness* after the Holocaust," 120
Einsatzgruppen D (Nazi killing squad), 97

Erichsen, Casper, 44, 88, 132, 139n28; *The Angel of Death Has Descended Violently among Them*, 40, 42, 43, 146n11
essentialism, Sartre's, 137n
ethnic cleansing, Nazi, 58. *See also* genocide, Nazi
ethnographic discourse, precolonial/postcolonial, 100
eugenics: in *Black Box/Chambre Noir*, 104; genocide and, 126; in GSWA, 12

Fanon, Franz, 59; *Black Skin, White Masks*, 121
Fischer, Eugen, 131
Flaig, Paul, 150n31
flogging: of Herero, 1–2, 105, 137n2; of Herero women, 2, 132; toys depicting, 134
Fontane, Theodor: *Die Stechlin*, 78
Foucault, Michel: on gaze, 6; Western institutionalism of, 138n13
Fredericks, Edward, 34
Fredericks, Joseph, 34
Frenssen, Anna Walter, 47
Frenssen, Gustav, *fig. 6*; early life of, 46–47; education of, 47; ethics of, 50; history of Hitler, 59; marriage of, 47; Nazi cult of, 61; Nazism of, 14, 59; Nobel Prize nomination, 48
—*Jörn Uhl*, 47
—*Peter Moor's Journey to Southwest Africa*, 11, 19; African landscape in, 52–53; Battle of Waterberg in, 55; bestial imagery of, 52, 54; Boers in, 36–37, 50, 51; brotherhood in, 51, 57; colonial attitudes in, 45; cover design (1943 ed.), *fig. 7*; critical reception of, 48–50, 57–60; editions of, 60–61, *fig. 7–8*; English translations of, 45, 49; exterminationist racism in, 60; genocidal gaze in, 13–14, 52, 57, 61, 63, 138n17; German imperialism in, 60; German soldiers in, 48, 50, 53; as *Heimatkunst*, 58; Herero genocide in, 54–57; impact on children, 62; imperial gaze in, 51; indigenous stereotypes in, 51; influence of, 48; missionaries in, 51, 57; *Morenga* and, 76–77; motive for writing, 47–48; narrator of, 58, 60; nomadism in, 58; paratextual material of, 49–50; peace motif of, 48–49, 50; racial hierarchies in, 51, 52; rebellion in, 50–51; Schutztruppe images in, 61; semiotics of clothing in, 59; sexual abuse in, 55; sources for, 45, 48; success of, 47; use in classrooms, 60, 61; von Trotha in, 56; Wehrmacht edition of, 60–61, *fig. 8*; as Young Adult literature, 59–60, 144n21
Freud, Sigmund: on *Trauerarbeit*, 99

Gâbemab, !Nanseb. *See* Witbooi, Hendrik
gaze: in postcolonialist theory, 6; power dynamics of, 8; upon *genocidaires*, 16; on Western imperialists, 115
gaze, colonized peoples', 7–8; on colonizers, 12–13, 17; on white subjectivities, 22. *See also* resistance, gaze of
gaze, colonizers', 6; appropriating, 8; on colonized peoples, 12–13; the subhuman in, 11
gaze, genocidal, 6–8; among Western observers, 19; animal imagery in, 85–87; in *Black Box/Chambre Noire*, 99, 102–3, 104, 106–7, 110–12; children's toys reflecting, 62; in colonial memorabilia, 15; enabling, 7; evidence for, 41; as final solution, 14; in German colonial texts, 89; German discussion of, 98; German guilt and, 15; in German

mores, 98; in *In My Brother's Shadow*, 91–98; intergenerational transmission of, 92, 112; Kubas's witness to, 32–34; in medical experiments, 43; in *Morenga*, 64, 72, 79, 80, 81; Nama resistance to, 20; nationalist aspects of, 58; normalized, 8, 21; in *Our Sister Killjoy*, 16, 115, 123, 125; in *Peter Moor's Journey*, 13–14, 52, 57, 61, 63, 138n17; racial/racist hierarchies of, 3, 7, 83, 92, 120, 131–32; of Schutztruppe, 84, 86; Timm's critique of, 66–69; transition from imperial gaze, 4–5, 27, 37, 52, 55, 71, 132; von Trotha's, 29–30

gaze, imperial: degrading, 135; effect on identity, 6; ethnographic discourse of, 100; gaze of resistance to, 128; on GSWA people, 5; in *Morenga*, 70, 87; Nama resistance to, 20; in *Peter Moor's Journey*, 51; racist hierarchy of, 51; transition to genocidal gaze, 4–5, 27, 37, 52, 55, 71, 132; Witbooi on, 26, 28

gaze, male: on women actors, 138n11

gaze, resisting, 8, 24, 46, 138n11; to imperial gaze, 128; in *Morenga*, 74; Nama's, 20

gender difference, in Holocaust studies, 3

genocidaires, 34; accountability for, 8; gaze upon, 16

genocide: American Indian, 129; amnesia concerning, 128, 133; at Babi Yar, 94, 96; in Congo Free State, 9; "other" in, 5; in *Our Sister Killjoy*, 120–30

genocide, African: in Congo Free State, 9; imperialism and, 117

genocide, German: African perspectives on, 34; eugenics and, 126; forgotten victims of, 107; German imperialism and, 13–14, 43, 64, 131; silence about, 100; of twentieth century, 3–6. *See also* Holocaust

genocide, GSWA, 1, 3; cleansing of land, 7, 14, 46; failure to mourn, 113; Holocaust and, 3–5, 7, 46, 67–69, 102, 113; justification for, 57; in *Morenga*, 64, 69–76; rationale for, 6; scholarship on, 101–2; silence over, 101–2; witnesses to, 17

genocide, Herero, 1, 5; amnesia concerning, 133; Apartheid and, 109, 113; at Battle of Waterberg, 64; in *Black Box/Chambre Noire*, 15, 104; centenary of, 33, 67–68, 101; erasure from memory, 111; exhibits concerning, 132; following rebellion, 11, 55–56; Holocaust and, 5, 102, 103, 109, 131, 133; Nazism and, 12; in *Peter Moor's Journey*, 54–57; as racial war, 74; suppression of memory, 33; under von Trotha, 30. *See also* Herero

genocide, Nama, 1, 5, 31–32; amnesia concerning, 133; Apartheid and, 113; erasure from memory, 111; exhibits concerning, 132; Holocaust and, 5, 102, 131; oral histories of, 18; as racial war, 74. *See also* Nama

genocide, Nazi, 97, 117; colonialism and, 129; Einsatzgruppen in, 124; means of, 5. *See also* Holocaust

Genocide Studies, 3; Postcolonial Studies and, 116, 117, 132; transnational approach to, 6

German Colonial Archive, 92, 145n5; closure of, 64–65; Morenga in, 88; reopening of, 65; Timm's use of, 83, 84. *See also* archives

Germans: othering of, 26; as victims, 119, 128, 152n15. *See also* colonials, German

German Southwest Africa (GSWA): administrators of, 20; anti-Semitism in, 38; colonial grotesque of, 9–11; eugenics in, 12; forced labor in, 1, 2, 13, 42–43, 46, 68; genocidal rhetoric of, 11; German loss of control over,

German Southwest Africa (*continued*) 33, 46, 149n19; German victories in, 147n28; history of, 8–11; influence on Third Reich, 4, 11–12; judicial system of, 2; land grab in, 10, 19–20, 35, 51, 71, 147n1; leadership of, 26, 29; map, *fig. 1*; military presence in, 27, 29; pass laws of, 148n7; photographs of, 14, 39, 88, 132, 135, 147n28, *fig. 11–13*; railway of, 144n15; state institutions of, 9. *See also* concentration camps, GSWA; genocide, GSWA; indigenous peoples, GSWA; Protection Treaties

Germany: Africans in, 135; Colonial School for Women, 135; as Heart of Darkness, 117; Namibian negotiations with, 134; in *Our Sister Killjoy*, 121–22, 126–27. *See also* colonialism, German; genocide, German; imperialism, German; Third Reich

Gewald, Jan-Bart, 132; *Words Cannot Be Found*, 33–34, 141n17

Ghana: British colonization of, 127; literature of, 116, 151n4

"Gibeon Pass" (metal tag), for indigenous people, 133

Gilbert, Helen, 151n4

Gilbert, Sandra: *Madwoman in the Attic*, 118

Gilman, Sander, 45, 143n13

Gordimer, Nadine: *July's People*, 116, 149n12

Gordon, Robert, 40

Göring, Heinrich: GSWA administration of, 10, 12, 20; in *Morenga*, 90; Witbooi's correspondence with, 22–23, 24

Göring, Hermann, 10, 12; influence on Apartheid, 149n11

Goyal, Yogita, 152n18

Great Britain: concentration camps of, 12; control of Southwest Africa, 33,

149n19; Mandate in South Africa, 149n18; in *Our Sister Killjoy*, 127–28. *See also* colonialism, British

Grimm, Hans, 59

Grimm Brothers, "Bluebeard," 94

Griqua people, 32

GSWA. *See* German Southwest Africa

Gubar, Susan: *Madwoman in the Attic*, 118

guilt, German, 15; in *Black Box/Chambre Noire*, 99; in *Deutscher Kolonialismus* exhibit, 134. See also *Vergangenheitsbewältigung* (coming to terms with past)

Hamburg, contact with GSWA, 65

Heart of Darkness (video game), 116

heart transplants, black/white, 128–29

Hegel, Georg Wilhelm Friedrich: master/slave dialectic of, 59

Heimatkunst (regional literature), 47, 143n6; nationalism in, 62; and Nazi literature, 58–59; *Peter Moor's Journey* as, 58. *See also* literature, German

Herero: animal imagery for, 85–86; cattle economy of, 10, 20, 73; confiscation of guns from, 44; as expendable, 56; expulsion to Omaheke Desert, 30, 32, 55–56, 68, 109, 135, *fig. 3*; eyewitness narratives of, 148n5; flogging of, 1–2, 105, 137n2; German perceptions of, 46; humanity of, 17; loss of land, 10; medical experimentation on, 131; military prowess of, 29; in *Peter Moor's Journey*, 46, 54–57; Schutztruppe gaze on, 84; warfare with Witbooi, 20, 23–25, 30. *See also* genocide, Herero; indigenous peoples, GSWA

Heroes Acre (memorial, Namibia), 145n4, 150n32

Hilberg, Raul: *The Destruction of the European Jews*, 3

Hillebrecht, Werner, 140n7
Himmler, Heinrich: on racial hierarchy, 97
history, as progress, 116. See also *Vergangenheitsbewältigung* (coming to terms with past)
Hitler, Adolf, 5; Final Solution of, 54
Hochschild, Adam: *King Leopold's Ghost*, 139n19
Hoeller, Hildegard: "Ama Ata Aidoo's *Heart of Darkness*," 119
Holocaust: Apartheid and, 149n13; in *Black Box/Chambre Noire*, 99, 105; causes of, 138n10; continuity thesis of, 3–5, 14, 18, 132, 133, 134; denial of, 96; fiction of, 76; German colonialism and, 3–4, 14–15, 124, 126; German imperialism and, 62; and GSWA genocide, 3–5, 7, 46, 67–69, 102, 113; Herero genocide and, 5, 102, 103, 109, 131, 133; measurement of skulls in, 109; in *Our Sister Killjoy*, 122, 126, 151n5; photographs of, 39, 96, 142n25; physical traces of, 117; poetry following, 84, 112; smoke from, 124; visualization of, 112; witnesses to, 112. See also genocide, Nazi
Holocaust art: *Black Box/Chambre Noire* in, 100; ethics of, 112; memorialization in, 111–12
Holocaust literature, 112; fiction, 76; hybridity in, 84; intertextuality in, 146n17
Holocaust Studies, 16; gender difference in, 3; interdisciplinary, 5–6; and Postcolonial Studies, 132; transnational approach to, 6
homosexuality, African perceptions of, 124
Hoornkrans, German raid on, 26–27
Hottentots: connotations of, 140n3; etymology of, 144n16. See also Nama
Huizinga, J.: *Homo Ludens*, 75

imperialism, German: beginnings of, 9; in *Black Box/Chambre Noire*, 99; genocide following, 13–14, 43, 64, 131; and Holocaust, 62; in *In My Brother's Shadow*, 91; in *Morenga*, 69, 82; in *Peter Moor's Journey*, 60; Third Reich and, 4, 11–12; violence in, 4; Witbooi on, 26. See also colonialism, German
Indians, American: genocide of, 129
indigenous peoples: emotional connections with, 60; European representations of, 45; mutual aid among, 78; nomadism of, 58
indigenous peoples, GSWA, 9–10; animal imagery for, 52, 54, 143n13; destabilized identities of, 18; ethnographic discourse concerning, 143n14; flogging of, 1–2, 26, 137n2, 140n11; forced labor by, 1, 2, 13, 42–43, 46, 68, 79; imperial gaze on, 5; intertribal warfare among, 20, 23–25, 140n7; Jews and, 18, 38; land treaties with, 145n6; as *Lebensunwerten Lebens*, 7; loss of land, 10, 19–20, 35, 51, 71, 147n1; precolonial conceptions of, 140n4; sexual violence against, 1, 34, 41–42, 54; stereotypes of, 51; as subhuman, 46, 109; unity among, 25, 26; unrevisable subalternity of, 19–20; voices of, 8, 13. See also Herero; Nama; Witbooi
intertextuality: as critique, 76, 77; disruptive, 116; of *Heart of Darkness*, 116; in Holocaust literature, 76, 146n17; Kristeva on, 76; in *Morenga*, 69, 76–83; of *Our Sister Killjoy*, 116; in postcolonial fiction, 116; and textual stability, 116
Isaac, Fritz, 34
Isaac, Samuel, 34

Jews: and GSWA indigenous peoples, 18, 38; in Night of Broken Glass, 112;

Jews (*continued*) of South Africa, 148n6; as subhuman, 109
Johnston, Ollie, 110

Kafka, Franz: "The Penal Colony," 105
Kamaherero: death of, 24; under Protection Treaty, 23, 24; Witbooi's correspondence with, 22
Kaplan, Cheryl, 109
Kaplan, E. Ann, 6
Kenosian, David, 59
Kentridge, Sydney, 102
Kentridge, William: animation process of, 110–11; creative process of, 110; early life of, 102; on German colonial violence, 101; interest in Enlightenment, 111, 150n29; Lithuanian Jewish descent of, 102; postcolonial art of, 113; as stage designer, 101; visit to Namibia, 105, 109
—*Black Box/Chambre Noire*, 99, *fig. 17–19*; animation in, 103–8, 110–12, 114; Apartheid in, 100, 102, 104; archive of, 100–102; in *Art and Press* exhibit (2012), 99, 100, 101, 108; Aryanism in, 104; Battle of Waterberg in, 106; black box camera in, 103; calipers man in, 104, 107; camera in, 103, 104, 105; catalog of, 100; colonial film clips in, 107; description of, 100–102; in Deutsche Bank exhibit (2005), 100–101; eugenics in, 104; filmic versions of, 147n2; genocidal gaze in, 99, 102–3, 104, 106–7, 110–12; German imperialism in, 99; Herero women of, 105, 107, 108; Holocaust in, 104, 105; indigenous genocide in, 15, 104, 105; Kentridge's essay in, 108–10; Megaphone man in, 105, 107, 108, 113; memento mori in, 103–8; mourning in, 113; music in, 105, 108; as palimpsest, 100, 104, 111, 113, 114; performative nature of, 99; postcolonial ethnographic discourse of, 100; puppets in, 103, 104–7, 113; research for, 105; rhinos in, 103, 104, 107, 150n22; running man of, 105, 106, 107; skulls in, 103, 106–7, 108; subject matter of, 99; surveillance in, 104; swastika in, 106; texts of, 106, 108; and Timm's works, 112; on totalitarianism, 103; *Trauerarbeit* in, 107, 108; typewriter in, 104; use of charcoal, 111, 112–13; von Trotha in, 134
Kiefer, Anselm: *Breaking of the Vessels*, 112
Kincaid, Jamaica, 153n23
Kolbe, Paul: *Unsere Helden in Sudwestafrika*, 147n28
Kristeva, Julia: on intertextuality, 76
Kropotkin, Peter: *Mutual Aid*, 75, 78–81
Kubas, Jan: Griqua ethnicity of, 32; service with German troops, 32; testimony to British, 13; witness to genocidal gaze, 32–34; witness to German genocide, 17
Kundrus, Birthe, 4

Lacan, Jacques, 59
Langer, Lawrence: "Art from the Ashes," 150n28
Lanzmann, Claude: *Shoah*, 142n26
Lau, Brigitte, 33
Lebensraum, *Heimat* ideology and, 59
Leopold II (king of Belgium), Congo colony of, 9, 139n19
Leutwein, Theodor, 2, *fig. 9*; communication with Herero, 29; correspondence with Witbooi, 28; *Elf jahre Gouverneur in DSWA*, 44; military force under, 20; on Protection Treaty, 28; treaties of, 20, 32, 68; Witbooi and, 32, 140n13
literature, colonial Namibian: racist, 11

literature, German: GSWA victories in, 147n28; racial discourse in, 59. *See also* *Heimatkunst*
literature, Ghanian: narrative techniques of, 116, 151n4
literature, postcolonial: intertextuality in, 116. *See also* Holocaust literature
Longhi, Pietro: bestiary of, 150n22
Lüderitz, Adolf, 9; deception of indigenous people, 145n6
Lüderitzbucht, detention-camp at, 39, 142n22

"Die Macht der Gewohnheit" (German cartoon), 132
Maherero, Samuel, 10, 65, 109, *fig. 5*; communication with Leutwein, 29; correspondence with Witbooi, 24, 140n12
Mamdani, Mahmood: *When Victims Become Killers*, 131, 135
Mandela, Nelson, 103
medical experimentation: on Herero, 131; at Shark Island, 43
Memory of the World objects (UNESCO), Witbooi's archive in, 20
Mengele, Josef, 131
Miller, Lee: Dachau photographs of, 96
Millet, Kitty, 4–5
missionaries, German, 9, 35; in *Our Sister Killjoy*, 126; in *Peter Moor's Journey*, 51, 57; racism of, 18; von Trotha on, 131
Mitchell, Breon, 67, 85, 89, 146n23
Mohrenköpfe (candy), *fig. 20*
Moodie, T. Dunbar, 148n10
Morenga of the Nama, *fig. 16*; death of, 74; diary of, 14, 67, 69, 85, 88–89; in German Colonial Archive, 84, 88; in *The Glamour of Prospecting*, 37; leadership of, 10; name of, 141n21, 146n26; as soldier, 88; in Timm's *Morenga*, 69, 73–74, 87–90; wounding of, 88
Mulvey, Laura: "Visual Pleasure and Narrative Cinema," 138n11
Munich Agreement (September, 1938), 127
museums, relationship to colonial power, 135
mutual aid, human, 78–79
Muuondjo, Kasisanda, 43

Nama: animal imagery for, 85–86; cattle economy of, 73; German cannon use against, 28; German perceptions of, 46; as Hottentots, 18; humanity of, 17; language of, 73, 74; peace treaty with Germans, 32; in *Peter Moor's Journey*, 46; resistance to imperial gaze, 20; Schutztruppe gaze on, 84; at Shark Island, 31; as subalterns, 55. *See also* genocide, Nama; indigenous peoples, GSWA; Witbooi (Nama people)
Namibia: editions of *Peter Moor's Journey* in, 61; Heroes Acre (memorial), 145n4, 150n32; independence of, 14, 135, 145n7; negotiations with Germany, 134; repatriation of skulls to, 150n24; South Africans' relocation into, 140n7. *See also* German Southwest Africa
Namibia-Deutschland: Eine geteilte Geschichte exhibition (German Historical Museum, 2004-2005), 101
natural resources, African, 125; exploitation of, 122
Nazis, in Southwest Africa, 133, 149n18
Nazism: Apartheid and, 15, 103, 148n11; *Blut und Boden* in, 58, 62; and German colonialism, 3, 59, 85; Munich and, 126–27; racist hierarchies of, 7; on the subhuman, 54. *See also* genocide, Nazi; Holocaust; Third Reich

Negritude, Sartre on, 137n
Nels, Louis, 23
neo-Fichtean philosophy, 148n10
Night of Broken Glass (attack on Jews), 112
Njanekua, Willy, 43
Nkrumah, Kwame, 118
Noyes, John, 8; on *Peter Moor's Journey*, 58
Numsen, Numme, 46
Nuremberg laws (Germany, 1935), 54
Nussbaum, Felix, 111

Ohlendorf, Otto, 97
Olpp, Johannes, 20
Omaheke Desert, Herero expulsion to, 30, 32, 55–56, 68, 109, 135, *fig. 3*
Other: gaze of, 22; gaze upon, 6; in genocide, 5; in *Morenga*, 90; Nazi attitudes toward, 53; in *Our Sister Killjoy*, 117
Ovaherero/OvaMbandero, German massacre of, 11, 133
Owusu, Kofi: "Canons under Siege," 118
Ozick, Cynthia: on post-Holocaust literature, 84–85, 146n25

Patchett, Anne: *State of Wonder*, 116
Pathfinder groups (German boy scouts), 60
poetry, post-Holocaust, 84, 112
postcards, GSWA: semi-pornographic, 42
postcolonialism: governmental corruption of, 123–24; in *Our Sister Killjoy*, 123–24, 127–28
Postcolonial Studies, 3, 16; Genocide Studies and, 116, 117, 132; Holocaust Studies and, 132; white, 121
Postcolonial Theory, universality in, 120
Pratt, Effie Louise, 47
Pratt, Mary Louise: *Imperial Eyes*, 5
Le Premier Génocide du XXe Siècle exhibit (Mémorial de la Shoah, Paris, 2017), 132

Protection Treaties (GSWA), 10, 139n23; Göring and, 22–23; Kamaherero under, 23, 24; under Leutwein, 20; Witbooi and, 25, 28, 54–55, 141n16; Witbooi people under, 29
Pyncheon, Thomas: *Gravity's Rainbow*, 146n18

race branding, 131, 135
racial/racist hierarchies: Aidoo on, 119; of colonization, 129; of genocidal gaze, 3, 7, 83, 92, 120, 131–32; in German colonialism, 3, 5, 10, 36, 57; of imperial gaze, 51; Nazi, 7, 97; in *Peter Moor's Journey*, 51, 52
Rassenschande (racial shame), in interracial marriage, 11
readers, resisting, 138n11
rebellion, GSWA (1904-7), 37; end of, 32; enslaved Herero in, *fig. 4*; forced labor following, 79; genocide following, 11, 41, 55–56; guerilla warfare in, 57; killing of noncombatants in, 41; leaders of, 10; in literature, 13–15; in *Morenga*, 68, 72–76; in *Peter Moor's Journey*, 50–51; Schutztruppe in, 29; soldiers' life during, *fig. 15*; white fear of, 2; Witbooi in, 30. See also Battle of Waterberg
resistance: African voices of, 15–16; gaze of, 8, 24, 30, 74, 128, 138n11; Jewish, 74; readers', 138n11
resistance, Nama: leaders of, 17–18
Rhenish Missionary Society, 35
rhinos: in *Black Box/Chambre Noire*, 103, 104, 107, 150n22; endangerment of, 149n22

Said, Edward, 6
Salomon, Charlotte, 111
Samantrai, Ranu, 118
Sartre, Jean-Paul: *Black Orpheus*, 137n

Schlink, Bernhard: *The Reader*, 85, 92
Schnee, Heinrich, 135
Schulte, Rainer, 67
Schutztruppe, German, 29; genocidal gaze of, 19, 84, 86; land grab of, 19–20; in *Morenga*, 79; photographs of women's breasts, 42, 132, *fig. 12*; sexual abuse by, 42; tin soldier toys of, 62, 134. *See also* soldiers, German
Schwabe, R.: *Der Krieg*, 147n28
Sebald, W. G., 39
Seitz, Theodor, 2–3
self, as geological formation, 75
Serfontein, J. H. P., 149n11
Shark Island (concentration camp), 12, 13, 139n28; as Auschwitz prototype, 34; closure of, 142n22; in exhibitions, 133; eyewitnesses to, 18, 34, 35, 38–40, 142n22; forced labor at, 42–43; German photographs of, 39, *fig. 11–13*; medical experiments at, 43; in *Morenga*, 69, 75; Nama at, 31; scholarly accounts of, 40–43; Witbooi people at, 27. *See also* concentration camps
Sharpeville Massacre (1960), 102, 148n7
Silvester, Jeremy, 40; *Words Cannot Be Found*, 33–34, 141n17

sjambok (whip), flogging with, 1
Social Darwinism, 79, 131
soldiers, German: atrocities by, 32–33, 39; *Heimat* of, 53; in *Peter Moor's Journey*, 48, 50, 53; sexual abuse by, 41–42, 54, 86. *See also* Schutztruppe, German
Solomon R. Guggenheim Foundation, 100
South Africa, British Mandate in, 149n18
Spiegelman, Art: *Maus* books, 112, 147n32
Steinmetz, George: *The Devil's Handwriting*, 9, 18, 19, 140n4; on ethnographic discourse, 100, 143n14; on Nama genocide, 31–32; on Shark Island, 43
Sterling, Cheryl, 124
Stoler, Ann Laura, 64, 142n24
Stülpnagel, Conrad: *Heisse Tage*, 147n28
Styron, William: *Sophie's Choice*, 85
Swakopmund, detention-camp at, 39
swastikas, in *Premier Génocide* exhibition, 133

Third Reich: attitudes toward other, 53; colonialism of, 5; and German imperialism, 11–12; GSWA imperialism and, 4, 11–12
Thomas, Frank, 110
Timm, Karl-Heinz: Aryanism of, 97; death of, 66, 91, 95, 97; diary of, 91, 92–93, 97, 98; father's pride in, 95; photographs of, 96; in SS Death's Head Division, 92, 95. *See also* Timm, Uwe: *In My Brother's Shadow*
Timm, Uwe: Allied bombing of home, 97; death of brother, 66, 91, 95, 97; early life of, 65–66; father of, 66, 93, 95, 96, 147n32; father's beating of, 98; perceptions of German colonialism, 146n26; travel to Namibia, 92
— *Deutsche Kolonien*, 88
—*In My Brother's Shadow*, 63, 66; Aryanism in, 96, 97; "Bluebeard" in, 94; critical reception of, 93; diary in, 94; dreams in, 92, 95–96; encryption in, 94; genocidal gaze in, 91–98; German imperialism in, 91; the hidden in, 94, 96; hybridity in, 93; indictment of German beliefs, 96–97, 98; kinds of texts in, 93–94; Nazi ideology in, 96; relationship to *Morenga*, 77, 92, 94; research for, 92, 97; socio-political history in, 91; as *Väterliteratur*, 15, 92, 93, 96, 98

—*Morenga*, 8, 141n21; alienation in, 79–80; animal imagery in, 69, 85–87, 122; anticolonialism of, 69; Battle of Waterberg in, 68; coexistence of discourses in, 78; colonialism in, 64, 70–71; concentration camps in, 71; diary device of, 70, 73, 74–75, 76, 80–82, 86; discourses of, 93; dreams in, 80–82, 86, 95; English translation of, 89; Eurocentrism in, 71; fantastic elements of, 84; forced labor in, 79; format of, 82, 146n23; genocidal gaze in, 64, 66–69, 71, 72, 79, 80, 81; genocide in, 64, 69–76; German Colonial Archives in, 83; German imperialism in, 69, 82; German past in, 90; German purity in, 90; German violence in, 63; and *Gravity's Rainbow*, 146n18; Heinrich Göring in, 90; hero/antihero of, 14; historical accuracy of, 85; historical characters in, 68; hybridity of, 82, 83–85; imperial gaze in, 70, 87; intertextuality in, 69, 76–83; Morenga in, 69, 73–74, 87–90; *Mutual Aid* in, 75, 78–81; Nama in, 72, 73; narrator of, 75; Nazi foreshadowing in, 90; Other in, 90; pacifism in, 80; *Peter Moor* references in, 76–77; post-Holocaust hybridity in, 84; as postmodern novel, 84; preparation for, 65–66, 67; purpose of, 67, 79; rebellion of 1904-7 in, 14, 68, 72–76; rediscovery of, 90; relationship to *In My Brother's Shadow*, 77, 92, 94; research for, 77, 85, 88, 89; Schutztruppe in, 79; Shark Island in, 69, 75; sources for, 67, 68; Vietnam in, 90; von Trotha in, 83; Witbooi in, 70

—"The Problem of Absurdity in Albert Camus," 66

Toll, Nelly, 111

toys, German: dissemination of stereotypes, 134–35; of Schutztruppe, 62, 134

Trauerarbeit (working through grief), 99, 102; in *Black Box/Chambre Noire*, 107, 108

Treaty of Berlin (1885), 9, 35, 134; Witbooi on, 26

Treaty of Versailles, sense of victimization following, 152n15

Ukraine, massacres in, 97

United Nations Convention on Genocide, 3, 43

van Wyk, Hermanus: correspondence with Witbooi, 30–31

Väterliche Züchtigung ("paternal chastisement"), 2, 11, 132

Vergangenheitsbewältigung (coming to terms with past), 66, 113; concerning colonialism, 135; failure of, 110. See also guilt, German

Vernichtungskrieg (war of annihilation), 11–12

Verwoerd, Hendrik, 103, 149n11

Vice, Sue, 76

victims: forced complicity of, 1, 137n2, 142n26; Germans as, 119, 128, 152n15

victims, genocide: as aspect of environment, 4–5; forgotten, 107; as subhuman, 5, 6–7, 44, 131

Visser, Paul: Witbooi's correspondence with, 23–24

Volkstum (national heritage), in *Heimatkunst* movement, 62

von Caprivi, Leo, 26

von Dincklage-Camp, Friederich: *Deutsche Reiter im Südwest*, 89

von Eckenbrecher, Margarethe: *Africa: What It Gave Me, What It Took from Me*, 77–78, 141n18

von François, Curt: attack on Witbooi people, 26–27; Witbooi and, 20, 25

von Heydebreck, Tennen: *Black Box/ Chambre Noire* description, 100–101
von Salzmann (Oberleutnant), *Im Kampf*, 147n28
von Trotha, Lothar, 3, 5, 109, *fig. 10*; colonial warfare under, 29; genocidal gaze of, 29–30; on missionaries, 131; strategy at Waterberg, 55, 56; triumph over Leutwein, 83; *Vernichtungsbefehl* (annihilation order) of, 11, 30, 33, 41, 64, 105, 132, 134; *Worte an das Volk der Herero*, 104, 149n15

Wainaina, Binyavanga: "How to Write about Africa," 121
Ward, Andrew Henshaw, 49, 143n12
Ward, Margaret May, 49
Warmbad, siege of, 88
Warmbold, Joachim, 62
Warriors, Leaders, Sages, and Outcasts in the Namibian Past (1992), 43
West: Africans residing in, 128; African women in, 118
White Book, German, 141n18
Willey, Elizabeth, 118
Williams, William Carlos, 76
Windhoek (Namibia), *Reiterdenkmal* bronze at, 113–14, 151n32
Witbooi (Nama people): annihilation of, 31–32; in German military, 29, 55; in *Morenga*, 70; Namaland Commando Group of, 23; in Naukluft Mountains, 28; under Protection Treaty, 29; at Shark Island, 27; von François's attack on, 26–27; warfare with Herero, 20, 23–25, 30. *See also* Nama
Witbooi, Hendrik, 8, 10, 19–26, 72, *fig. 2*; appeals for ammunition, 23; archive of, 13, 19, 20–32, 140nn9–10; chiefdom of, 19; Christianity of, 21, 23, 24, 30–31; correspondence of, 20, 22–26, 27–28, 30, 133, 140nn10,12; death of, 13, 17, 31, 74, 140n15, 146n13; diaries of, 22; early life of, 20; European view of, 18–19; family of, 20, 27; followers of, 23; gaze on Germans, 13, 24, 25, 46, 115; on genocidal gaze, 19; on German genocide, 31; on German imperialism, 26, 27; marriage of, 20; Nama name of, 20; othering of Germans, 26; Pan-Africanism of, 20, 25; poetic language of, 22; in *Premier Génocide* exhibition, 132–33; and Protection Treaties, 25, 28, 54–55, 141n16; resisting gaze of, 24, 46; stature of, 141n16; use of guerilla warfare, 57; use of scribes, 21, 22; and von François, 20
Witbooi, !Nanses, 20; capture by Germans, 27
women, African: in colonial fiction, 124; oppression of, 118; as site of cultural authenticity, 118; travel in West, 118
women, Herero: flogging of, 2, 132; murder of, 44; preparation of skulls, 150n24; sexual abuse of, 1, 41–42, 54, 86, 132
women, indigenous: colonial attitudes toward, 144n17
women, Nama: animal stereotypes for, 85; sexual abuse of, 86, 132

Zantop, Susanne: *Colonial Fantasies*, 139n22
Zeller, Joachim, 132; *Genocide in German South-West Africa*, 3
Zeraua, Zacharias: correspondence with Witbooi, 27
Zimmerer, Jürgen, 132, 134; *Genocide in German South-West Africa*, 3

www.ingramcontent.com/pod-product-compliance
Lightning Source LLC
Chambersburg PA
CBHW071957240426
43669CB00049B/2684